COLOR PLATE 1.
The demon in *Dōjōji* menacingly lifts her mallet. She stands on the *hashigakari*, left hand on the *shite* pillar, glaring at the stage. The actor is Kongō Iwao.

 The Classical Theatre
of Japan

text by
DONALD KEENE

photographs by
KANEKO HIROSHI

with an introduction by
ISHIKAWA JUN

Kodansha International Ltd.,
Tokyo, New York and San Francisco.

Distributors:
United States: Harper & Row, Publishers, Inc., 10 East 53rd Street, New York, New York 10022. South America; Harper & Row, International Department. Canada: Fitzhenry & Whiteside Limited, 150 Lesmill Road, Don Mills, Ontario. Mexico and Central America: HARLA S. A. de C. V., Apartado 30-546, Mexico 4, D.F. United Kingdom: TABS, 7 Maiden Lane, London W.C.2. Europe: Boxerbooks Inc., Limmatstrasse 111, 8031 Zurich. Australia and New Zealand: Book Wise (Australia) Pty. Ltd., 104-8 Sussex Street, Sydney 2000. Thailand: Central Department Store Ltd., 306 Silom Road, Bangkok. Hong Kong and Singapore: Books for Asia Ltd., 30 Tat Chee Avenue, Kowloon; 65 Crescent Road, Singapore 15. The Far East: Japan Publications Trading Company, P.O. Box 5030, Tokyo International, Tokyo.

Published by Kodansha International Ltd., 2-12-21 Otowa, Bunkyo-ku, Tokyo 112 and Kodansha International/USA Ltd., 10 East 53rd Street, New York, New York 10022 and 44 Montgomery Street, San Francisco, California 94104. Copyright in Japan 1966 by Kodansha International Ltd. All rights reserved. Printed in Japan.

LCC 66-25756
ISBN 87011-034-9
JBC 3074-780331-2361

First edition, 1966
Third printing, 1975

The text
is dedicated to
NARU *and* ALAN HOVHANESS

TABLE OF CONTENTS

Following page 312 is a translation of the lyrics heard on the
phono-sheet found inside the back cover.

LIST OF PLATES

INTRODUCTION

THE word *nō* means talent and, by extension, the display of talent in a performance. In its earliest forms Nō, an art that today enjoys enormous prestige, may have been little more than a display of acrobatics and circus stunts, but in the course of time the original Nō developed into an aristocratic, almost ritual, art. The remoteness of its style and content from the typical dramatic forms of our own day has often led prophets to declare that Nō could not long survive, that a younger generation accustomed to the pace of films and television could never tolerate the extreme deliberation of Nō. Prophets of doom always sound more authoritative than optimists, but fortunately, they are as often mistaken. Contrary to all the predictions made to me in 1953, when I first saw Nō performed, Nō thrives today as never before, and the audiences consist increasingly of young people, perhaps driven to Nō by dissatisfaction with entertainments supposedly devised for their pleasure.

Nō has often been compared to the Greek drama. The use in both of masks, a chorus, song and stately dances, and poetry of an elevated nature provides some basis for comparison. But there are important differences too. Dramas intended for the huge audiences that filled the Grecian amphitheatres could not help but differ from those intended for a small group of aristocrats at the Japanese court. More important, the conception of drama differed basically. The Greeks, in Aristotle's words, believed that a play must have a beginning, a middle and an end; but the Nō plays tend to be all end, though divided into sections of different musical tempi. The Greek dramas often conclude with the warning that we must not call a man happy until he is dead, even though at the outset of the play the hero seemed to be enjoying great good fortune; but the protagonist of a Nō play has usually died before the play begins, and the end, instead of a warning, is likely to be a promise of deliverance from the tortures he is suffering when he first appears. The Greeks built plays around characters who, though larger than ourselves and confronted by problems far more terrible than any we are likely to face, are recognizably like us; the characters in the Nō plays are hardly more than beautiful shadows, the momentary embodiments of great emotions.

The Greek and Nō dramas, then, are essentially different despite surface resemblances. They are most alike, perhaps, in retaining their appeal to audiences separated by many centuries and infinite numbers of social changes from the periods when the plays were created. Though both dramas were products of particular societies and drew from their myths, their grandeur and lofty disregard of the quotidian enables them to soar eternally. That is why they move audiences today as much as when first performed.

A person equipped with nothing more than a general sensitivity to different forms of art may be deeply moved upon his first visit to a Nō theatre. Yet I believe it is also true that the more one knows about a theatre with traditions as deep-rooted as those of Nō, the greater one's pleasure.

11

I have written this book in the hope of passing on to others the information I have found helpful in the enjoyment of Nō.

Photographs, it hardly needs saying, are indispensable in any study of a theatrical art, particularly one as unfamiliar in the West as Nō. I have been exceptionally fortunate in my collaborator, Mr. Kaneko Hiroshi. The patience and energy—and skill, of course—demanded by his photographs were never begrudged. Nō is perhaps the most difficult form of theatre to photograph. Long intervals pass virtually without motion onstage, to be succeeded by brief and violent action. The photographer seldom has a second chance if he misses the first time. A Nō play is performed in the season with which it is associated, and often but a single time. If the photographer misses, for example, the moment in *Tsuchigumo* when the monstrous spider throws out his web, he may have to wait a whole year before it is staged again, and it may not be staged by the same group of actors for many years. Again, the photographer who is asked for a picture of Nō being performed at the Itsukushima Shrine at a time when the stage is surrounded by water has a total of about one hour in the course of an entire year. The photographing of the masks, however, poses the greatest problems. They are prized for their ability to shift expression, and the photographer therefore bears the responsibility, through his choice of lighting and angle, for the face that each mask presents to the world.

Another indispensable element in a book which is concerned with a lyric drama is the music. I have been fortunate in that a group of performers including Nishikawa Michio, an outstanding artist of the Komparu school, has recorded passages from *Funa Benkei* on the phono-sheet found in the pocket of the back cover.

A problem encountered by anyone preparing an illustrated book on Nō arises from the difficulty of obtaining permission to examine the masks and costumes of the different schools. Mr. Maruoka Akira made it possible to obtain the cooperation of the leading actors; I owe him especial thanks. My thanks also to the Tsubouchi Memorial Theatre Museum for the use of certain photographs which appear in the Pictorial History section of this book.

I have failed thus far to mention the Kyōgen farces which are equally the subject of this book. This does not reflect any lack of esteem. Indeed, I believe my happiest experiences in Japan were studying and performing in Kyōgen for several years. But Kyōgen is altogether a more genial and outgoing art than Nō and requires little introduction here. I wish, however, to express my thanks to the artists of both Ōkura and Izumi schools for their kind cooperation.

Finally, I must thank the staff of Kodansha International Ltd. for having contrived to satisfy my every request for this book, however unreasonable. Requests for photographs that most publishers in other countries would have refused even to consider—for the costumes of the Kongō school in Kyoto, displayed only at the height of the sweltering summer, or for the rustic versions of Nō performed at Kurokawa in the depths of the bitter northern winter—were cheerfully met and the generosity shown me a source of real inspiration.

DONALD KEENE

THE FLOWERS OF NŌ

by ISHIKAWA JUN

When I was a boy I studied the singing of the Nō texts. These lessons, I need hardly say, never came to anything, but I still remember my teacher at the beginning of each session sitting himself in a perfectly erect posture and singing out in his resonant voice some passage from the text. His youthful pupils would imitate him exactly. Or, it would be more exact to say, they strained desperately to mimic him, but their clumsy efforts to match the roar of a tiger never even managed to sound like a cat's meow. Their posture wasn't too bad—the voices were the hitch. The teacher's voice rang out imperiously, and though his pupils sang at the top of their lungs in imitation, their breath soon gave out, and the concluding phrases would trail off pitifully. If, in desperation, they resorted to shouting, their voices at once cracked, ruining the melodic line, and they would end up by emitting something which was a cross between a shriek and a howl, pathetic figures, the butts of ridicule.

Perhaps it was the considerable streak of vanity I was born with that made me feel self-conscious, though a child, and instead of forcing my voice like the others, I concentrated exclusively on following the melodic line in my uncertain little voice, only for the thunderbolt to fall on me immediately. I was severely scolded by the teacher: "Stop showing off. Don't be self-conscious. At this stage you'd do best not to try to be clever with your singing. Give it your whole voice. Sing out with everything you've got." These were his first admonitions.

These admonitions were probably not his invention. The training of beginners, whether future professionals or amateurs, seems in its essentials to have remained unchanged over the centuries. In Zeami's work Fūshi Kaden ("The Transmission of the Flower of the Art") occurs the following passage concerning the actor's training as a youth of seventeen or eighteen: "At this stage in his training he should pay no attention even if people point at him with scorn. When practicing at home he should use his full vocal powers within the range appropriate to his nighttime and early morning voice. In his heart he must summon up his willpower and vow at this decisive moment in his career that he will never abandon Nō, staking his future on this resolve. There is no other way to train for this career."

Zeami's advice is, of course, of the utmost importance to the professional actor. The amateur is not faced with anything so serious as a "decisive moment in his career." Nevertheless, the teacher's reprimands, even when directed at his most hapless disciples, obviously have their roots in the distant past, in the perceptive judgments of the Fūshi Kaden. Even the child who has just begun his parroting of the Nō melodies has only to step by chance into a room where Nō is being rehearsed to be brought quite unexpectedly into direct contact with the presence of Zeami, the great teacher of long ago. This curious mechanism has not been achieved by any recent, hasty efforts; obviously it is the product of a carefully maintained tradition.

The path of training followed by the professional is too arduous for the amateur to pursue or even to comprehend. Yet most of those in the audience seated before the stage on which the professional actor stands are amateurs of the art, and it is as true for Nō as for other forms of theatre that without the element

13

provided by the spectators the world of the stage cannot come completely into being. One might go further: an awareness of this implicit relationship has led to a splendid artistic discovery on the part of the Nō actors. When the actor stands on the stage the limitations of his own vision do not permit him to see his own back. The Nō actor must free himself from this egoistic vision. The spectators' eyes can see the actor's back though his own eyes cannot. Only when the actor looks at himself with the eyes of the spectators is spiritual communication effected between the stage and the audience. In Zeami's words this is "seeing together with the audience."

Other people's eyes. The Nō actor uses their eyes to open a channel of communication to other people's hearts. The stage is the place where this channel manifests itself. It is when something is made to reverberate in the spectators' minds that they see flowers on the stage. "Flower" was a favorite word of Zeami's. For the Nō actors it designates the mystery they seek to apprehend in their pliant, endlessly varied art. It need hardly be said that if an actor's training in techniques is detached from the heart it will produce no effect. That is why Zeami said, "The flower's blossoming comes from the heart; the seeds are the performance." This flower, unlike the kata *(forms) devised by Kabuki centuries later, is not the fixing of forms. The flower is not confined to any single place. Zeami described it in these terms:*

"Which flower lasts forever without falling? It is because a flower falls that we prize it when it is in blossom. In Nō too you should realize that the flower has no fixed abode. It is precisely because it is not fixed but shifts to other forms of expression that it is prized."

Should we credit to Zeami's philosophic insight his discovery that the falling is the essence of the flower and his use of this discovery as a metaphor for art? A man's heart, like the blossoming and falling of the flowers, is constantly shifting. The world of the stage in essence would seem to reproduce the flickering shadows of human emotions. It is by no means impossible to agree with those who consider that the heart of Nō is found in the plays of the third category which give form to the emotions of women. Sometimes they seem to be saying that even fallen blossoms are beautiful.

In fact, however, this was not a discovery of Zeami's; using the flowers of the four seasons as metaphors to describe other things has been common in every age. In the case of the Muromachi period it is probably safe to say that by "flower" was meant a flower arrangement. The styles of flower arrangement then prevalent have long since ceased to exist, and nothing of them survives today. The earlier styles were displaced during the Edo period by the rise of the nageire *style—what we generally call* ikebana. *Probably the refined conception of "giving life" to a few flowers did not exist in the Muromachi period. Instead, people arranged in vases a generous profusion of blossoms. Both* rikka, *the Muromachi style, and* nageire, *the Edo style, were arts of decorating a house with flowers, but* nageire *belongs to the austere room for the tea ceremony, and* rikka *to the reception room of some great mansion. The core of* rikka *assuredly was in its largeness of scale and boldness of design. One can imagine flowers in full glory filling a room; the plants and flowers were disposed there according to preconceived notions of how flowers were meant to be seen and what flowers should look like. It was the function of the beholder's mind to absorb without effort the underlying intent. I wonder if people in the Muromachi period, having the concrete example of* rikka *to guide them, did not find it easy to grasp the metaphors referring to flowers in* Fūshi Kaden. *Responsive to the suggestions, they interpreted the subtle meanings in terms of the* rikka *arrangements.*

Spiritual communication between the stage and the audience, based on a similar understanding of artist and beholder, makes unnecessary, for example, scenery depicting landscapes or buildings. The use of minute gestures to express the perturbations of the emotions also becomes unnecessary. A few steps taken on the level boards of the stage may at times take the actor a hundred leagues to distant mountains and shores. A man's and a woman's sleeves brushing each other lightly as petals will at once signify to the audience that their love has been accomplished. Sorrows and joys, the emotions stirred by the blossoming or falling of the flowers, all are evoked on the bleak expanse of the stage; the acting techniques make the bareness itself seem to speak across the centuries to the spirit of the contemporary theatre. One need not take into account complicated procedures in one's appreciation of Nō. The view that Nō is a forbidding, classic art probably stems from a confusion in the minds of men of later generations who, being accustomed to dealing with complicated matters, were lost when faced with something simple.

National frontiers never divide a Nō audience, and distinctions of East and West cannot exist in the hearts of those witnessing the art. It is natural that a foreigner and a Japanese should appreciate and understand Nō in the same manner. A small amount of preparation, a small amount of effort, and sometimes a small amount of boredom—these are required no less of Japanese than of foreigners. The achievements of foreigners in the field of Nō go back to Noël Peri's superb translations of a program of five Nō plays. It would be impossible to deny that the re-evaluation of Aya no Tsuzumi ("The Damask Drum") in Japan owes much to his translation. Now we have Donald Keene's excellent study. I know of no one else who has Mr. Keene's familiarity not only with Nō but with the Japanese arts in general. We Japanese must look to the future to see what the effects of his studies will be.

Nō

The conventional way of describing Japanese pronunciation, as rendered in roman letters, is to say that the consonants are as in English, the vowels as in Italian or Spanish. This formula is inexact, but at least it suggests the original pronunciations. All vowels are sounded; thus, the word *kakegoe* is pronounced something like *kah-keh-go-eh*, each syllable being given equal stress.

I have used the transcription Nō to designate the art, though Noh is also familiar.

Throughout the book, Japanese names retain their original order, with family name first and given or adopted name last.

I. THE PLEASURES OF NŌ

Nō BEGINS with a mask, and within the mask the presence of a god. Before a performance of *Okina*, the mask to be worn is displayed in the dressing room and honored with ritual salutations. When the actors have filed onto the stage and taken their places, one called the Mask Bearer offers the mask of *Okina* to another, who prostrates himself in reverence before accepting it. The *Okina* mask is unlike that for any other role; though its features are those of a benevolent old man and not a fearsome being, they are nonetheless a god's, and performing this role, devoid though it is of emotion or special displays of technique, is considered so arduous as to shorten the life of the actor.

Okina, the oldest Nō play, is accorded unusual reverence, but even plays not about the gods partake of the mystery of divinity. Before the actor makes his entrance he gazes at his masked face in the mirror, and though until that moment an ordinary man—whether an outcaste or a nobleman—he himself becomes as he stares at the mask a reflection. Other theatres are often said to be a mirror of life, but Nō is an image in the mirror which life approximates.

The wall at the back of the Nō stage (the *kagami-ita*, or "mirror boards") is decorated with the painting of a huge pine, the Yōgō Pine at the Kasuga Shrine in Nara. Old accounts tell how once an old man was seen performing a dance beneath this pine; he proved to be the god of the shrine. Every year, at the festival of the shrine, the head of the Komparu school of Nō stands beneath the Yōgō Pine so that the god may descend into the actor and make him his reflection. Originally, perhaps, the play merely allowed the god to assume visible form. *Okina* opens with the meaningless but portentous syllables of the god's utterance: the actor, like a medium, pronounces a language he himself cannot comprehend. *Okina* is not in the least tragic. It is a joyous celebration of abundance and long life, but the presence of the god exhausts the actor. Of all Nō plays, *Okina* is probably the most widely performed. At the beginning of the year, on important occasions, at village festivals, *Okina* normally opens the program. It has no plot, is largely unintelligible to the audience, and has little in common with popular stage entertainments, but no one would dream of omitting it; *Okina* is an initiation into the world of Nō.

The solemnity of Nō distinguishes it most conspicuously from other theatres. The Japanese are by no means incapable of comedy. Indeed, interspersed between the Nō tragedies during a complete program are farces called Kyōgen which are filled with humor. The mask of *Okina* itself, a cheerful face, has suggested to some Japanese critics that originally it was a festive work, rather than the stately ceremonial of today. For that matter, the origin of all varieties of Japanese theatre is sometimes traced to the lewd and comic dance performed by the goddess Uzume to lure the sun goddess from the cave where she sulked. But whatever the ancient manner of presentation may have been, a felicitous Nō is today performed with the deliberation and gravity reserved in most parts of the world for sacred rites. The plays are almost all tragic, but even on the rare occasion

19

when the actor says, "How happy I am!" (*Ureshi ya!*) he sounds to the uninitiated spectator like a tortured soul.

The plays were certainly not always acted before spectators wrapped in the hushed awe of a present-day Tokyo audience. Nō performances in rural districts are sometimes as informal as the theatre in China or Southeast Asia. People chatter, eat or doze through the performance, and no one takes it amiss if a well-wisher, sympathizing with the actors on a cold night, steps onto the stage to offer them hot saké. This may have been the normal reception of the Nō plays before court patronage in the fourteenth century gave them an aristocratic dignity. The ritualization of Nō in the seventeenth century imparted to the theatre its present solemnity.

But even if Nō was once lighter entertainment, the plays were performed in a building belonging to a shrine, and the actors, then as today, were participants in a rite. The religion served by the performers is Shinto, the Way of the Gods. This native religion of Japan has its sacred book and a body of theological writings, but most Japanese believe in Shinto not in terms of its formal mythology and the scholars' elucidations, but in terms of gods and demons inhabiting the mountains and waters of Japan. These supernatural beings are innumerable, and include emperors, the ghosts of famous men, animals, trees, and even inanimate objects. The good spirits bring happiness and plenty, but there are also malevolent ghosts. One way to appease the dead, who might otherwise return to afflict the living, was to recite or re-enact their deeds on earth, assuring them that they had not been forgotten. The sacred dances at the Shinto shrine, Kagura, originated in this manner, it appears, and Nō may also have been intended to calm the troubled dead. The dead return to life on the Nō stage to tell again their hours of glory and grief.

We cannot be sure how Nō came to assume its present form or what its relation was to religious rituals. Often we must guess from a survival in some remote village, an older form of Nō than the more polished art in the cities. Sometimes too we can obtain hints by examining the theatre elsewhere. In Thailand, for example, plays are performed today on a row of tiny stages before the great stupa at Nakorn Pathom—not for an audience (though a few old people and children may be present), but for the gods. The family of a recently deceased person offers the plays, which are staged with the utmost intensity, even without an audience. Perhaps this was true in Japan in ancient times. Nō stages have three steps leading down from the front. These have no function in performances (though, one may be wryly informed, an actor who fell from the stage could use them to climb back). In the past the actors were rewarded after a performance with gifts from the daimyo they served, presented by an official who used the steps for the purpose. But originally, perhaps, the steps were added so that the actors, priests at a Shinto shrine, might pass from the shrine to the stage where they performed not for an audience of mortals but for the gods.

Today, a performance of Nō, like any other theatrical representation, demands not only a stage and actors but an audience, and its purpose is to provide "entertainment." However, the stage, actors, and audience differ so markedly from those in theatres elsewhere that we are apt to be less conscious of what Nō shares with drama in other countries (or with other forms of drama within Japan itself) than of its uniqueness. The entertainment it provides is unlikely to afford a casual visitor much distraction, but it possesses immediately recognizable beauty: the masks, superb examples of the carver's art; the magnificent costumes; the hypnotically eloquent singing of the chorus; the stately movements of the actors. Yet as soon as one enters a Nō theatre one realizes from the austere stage, the respectful hush of the audience, that it is the scene not merely of drama but of ritual. An appreciation of the ritual of Nō may come intuitively and instantly, as Western visitors sometimes discover, or it may be the product of years of study. Nō gives pleasure in proportion to what the spectators bring to their appreciation, whether a sensitivity to any form of beauty, or a specific knowledge of the texts, movement and music. Because Nō makes no concessions, the slowness of pace and unrelieved gravity may weary, but this risk is taken deliberately.

The purpose of Nō is not to divert on the surface but to move profoundly and ultimately, to transcend the particular and touch the very springs of human emotions.

Of all theatres probably Nō makes the greatest demands on the audience. The texts are in medieval language, studded with quotations from even older classics, and would be difficult to follow even if pronounced with the utmost clarity. The actors scorn as mere "theatricality" any suggestion of realism in representation, and the audience is prepared to accept in the role of a beautiful girl a tottering old man with a quavering voice and heavy jowls visible around the mask. A child may perform as a warrior capable of inspiring terror in demons, and no one in the audience laughs at his high-pitched little voice when he reassures his frightened followers that they have nothing to fear. The masks make it possible to believe that an actor with an unattractive face is a god or a beautiful woman; in this sense they provide a realistic touch, but the unvarying expression on Shizuka's face, whether angry, weeping, or resigned to her fate, must be given shades of meaning by the eye of the connoisseur. The appeal of Nō is by no means entirely intellectual or aesthetic; it moves many in the audience to tears, and leaves haunting and poignant remembrances.

A recent critic, reviewing the performance of a sixty-four-year-old actor in the part of Lady Rokujō in *Nonomiya* ("The Shrine in the Fields"), a play based on *The Tale of Genji* and describing the beautiful, elegant princess who desperately loved Genji, wrote, "I have never seen such a deeply-felt performance of *Nonomiya*. . . . The actor succeeded in leaving so profound and penetrating an impression that for awhile afterwards I was quite overcome, and even now I feel something like a lump in the pit of my stomach. It goes without saying that the play produced a different effect than a reading of *The Tale of Genji*, but even in terms of Nō the impression I received was at times different from any other representation I have witnessed. On this occasion Rokujō of course was beautiful, but one was made to think less of the aristocratic dignity of the woman than of her fate. Above all, I was impressed by the strength in Nō itself and in the actor's art to move men's hearts."

This performance of *Nonomiya*, by an actor whose normal appearance and voice in no way suggested a beautiful court lady, was more deeply affecting than a more realistic representation could have been. The text of *Nonomiya* is a masterpiece, but no one by reading the text alone could sense the shattering loneliness of the moment on the stage when Rokujō, standing before the *torii* of the Shrine in the Fields, lifts her foot to step through, a gesture of symbolic renunciation of the world and Prince Genji, only to return her foot to its place, yielding to a final burst of longing. The performance of the actor as Rokujō must reach its climax at this moment, and he is abetted by the harsh, desolate beat of the hand drum *(ōkawa)*. The actor must not only transcend his physical limitations but convert them into the elements of a supreme artistic experience. The particular qualities of an actress in the part of Rokujō might obscure the eternal, absolute nature of the princess and her tragic love, but an old man's voice, his movements perfected during half a century on the stage, the stylized beauty of his mask, costume and fan, can emphasize the eternal lines of the story. Additional realism would be as foolish as coloring in the lines of Euclid's propositions, or in as bad taste as the rubies and emeralds with which the barbarous sultans adorned their Chinese porcelains.

It has taken some six hundred years for Nō to achieve its present refinement. We have no way of telling whether actors of former days were more or less capable than those today, but the natural human tendency to glorify the past has induced critics at all times to assert that the performers of their day were no match for those of the past. Zeami (1363–1443), the greatest figure in the history of Nō, was sure that no contemporary actor could remotely touch the abilities of his father, and a writer describing performances he had seen in 1658 declared, "Nō in the old days used to encourage virtue by representing the good and chastise vice by representing the bad, and the movements of the actor's feet and head were never at variance with decorum, but modern performances, in complete violation of the old traditions, have reduced the art to vulgarity."

Each age had brought changes to the performing techniques, generally as a reflection of changing times and tastes rather than of a decline in the actors' skill. Today, at a time when other Japanese traditional arts have lost their popular following, new stages have been built for Nō, and hundreds of thousands of amateurs are learning the singing and dancing. Numbers alone do not prove that Nō is now enjoying its period of greatest distinction, but the size of the audiences means that Nō does not survive merely in a fossilized form, revived rarely and piously on special occasions like the European miracle plays. Though confined to a repertory largely established four hundred years ago, and staged in exact conformance to the traditions of the different schools of performers, Nō is a living art, changing subtly but surely with the times, as interpreted by its outstanding performers.

The Nō repertory comprises a great variety of works, ranging from virtually static celebrations of the glories of a particular shrine to pieces of violent movement in which devils assert their terrible powers. It includes works which are almost purely poetic and symbolic, suggesting the loveliness of plum blossoms or the snow, and others which treat betrayal and vengeance. Usually when critics make generalizations about Nō they are thinking of the poetic dramas associated with the name of Zeami; these plays indeed are closest to the essence of Nō. Many earlier or later pieces show a more pronounced dramatic quality and realism. They form an essential part of the repertory and, on the whole, enjoy even greater popularity than Zeami's masterpieces, but it is not for their sake that the audience goes to the Nō theatre. Though the members of the audience may prefer the stirring *Funa Benkei* ("Benkei in the Boat") to the remote loveliness of *Kakitsubata* ("The Iris"), the slow-moving, poetic works give Nō its meaning and ultimate appeal. Modern audiences, no less than their predecessors, are present to witness a special form of drama, and respect its demands. Modern audiences are less inclined than those of fifty or more years ago to sit through a full program of plays, but no less than their predecessors they are present to witness the moment when Rokujō hesitates before the *torii*, or when the ghost of Matsukaze, the fisher girl deserted by a nobleman, disappears for the last time, "leaving only the wind in the pines." The Nō plays are admired because they capture in words, music and dance the tragic climaxes of profound emotions.

Actors today may interpret the parts with greater psychological subtlety than their predecessors, but this is not a violation of the texts, which contain poetic truth of eternal and universal validity, leaving them open to interpretation and appreciation by men of different ages and societies. Every gesture in Nō has centuries of tradition behind it, but the actor has greater leeway in interpreting the roles than in works of more specific content tied to this time or that place. Nō is realistic in its evocations of what a woman experiences when deserted by her lover or what the taste of defeat is to a hitherto unvanquished warrior. This realism, as contrasted with the fantasies of other forms of Japanese theatre, is the glory of Nō. It is found at its intensest in the slow-moving masterpieces of Zeami.

The audience at a Nō performance today consists mainly of connoisseurs. Many have learned the parts as amateurs or have seen performances so frequently they can detect the seemingly slight differences that distinguish a great actor from a merely competent one. Some carry texts of the plays to the theatre and consult them, not in the casual manner of the operagoer skimming through a libretto during the intermissions, but with minute care, noting variations in the performance from the musical notations in the printed text. Some are so engrossed by the musical aspects of the plays that they hardly lift their eyes to the stage, as if the acting were only incidental to their enjoyment. Others watch each gesture raptly, and study the shifting light and shadows on the masks or the details of the costumes. The printed texts are necessary for those who have not studied them in advance, because the deliberately muffled delivery, accentuated by the masks, makes it virtually impossible to understand the lines spoken or sung. Some in the audience, including connoisseurs, doze through whole sections of the plays, awakening instinctively for the climactic moments. The manner of enjoying the performance may differ, but each spectator has shared in the beauty of an art evolved by many men's efforts over the centuries.

Nō, created in the fourteenth century, reached its full growth by the middle of the fifteenth century. It shares much with other forms of expression during the period: it is bare, yet evocative, like the monochrome landscapes; beautiful, yet austere, like the temple gardens; preoccupied with death and the ultimate means of deliverance from life like the literary works inspired by the Buddhism of the time. The movements of the actors owe much to the martial arts that thrived in an age of warfare and to the decorum expected of the Zen priest. The actors' distinctive walk, a bare lifting of the feet from the floor, occurs also in the tea ceremony, another art perfected in the fifteenth century. These arts are all marked by an economy of means used to achieve a maximum effect, a preference for suggestion rather than representation. The Nō plays are staged before the unvarying backdrop of the Yōgō Pine, and in place of the realistic props found in some Western theatres (fountains with real water, doors that slam with a convincing bang), the props for Nō are seldom more than outlines of the objects suggested—a boat, a hut or a carriage. The gestures of the actors are highly stylized: either simplified, as when a hand lifted before the slightly lowered mask denotes weeping, or developed into the pattern of a dance, as when the simple action of noticing something is depicted by the actor's bringing together his opened fan in his right hand to his left hand, slowly lifting the fan diagonally upwards, then lowering his left hand diagonally to the left as his gaze falls on an object. Above all, the masks, by eliminating not only particularities of features but any readily apparent change in emotions, evoke more in the connoisseur than the most expressive actor's face.

Suggestion, achieved through the most restrained means, is not an end in itself; like every aspect of Nō it is intended to achieve beauty. Nō is a supremely aesthetic theatre. Critics and commentators from the time of Zeami have devoted their greatest attention to beauty of effects rather than, say, how an audience can be moved to tears. A Nō play must move the audience, but never by ugliness or violence. The humblest character—a fisher girl or a peasant—wears magnificent robes and speaks great poetry. But even beauty is not the final object. Nō reaches out towards eternity through beauty and the elimination of the temporal and accidental.

The Nō plays are set in the distant past and no attempt is made to give them immediacy. The characters are sometimes historical, sometimes drawn from the fiction of the tenth and eleventh centuries, sometimes the gods of legends, but the subjects and their treatment are so absolute that it is irrelevant to ask whether or not the plays are faithful to the times they portray. The performances too are absolute. The actor's vocal delivery and walk are identical whether he is taking the part of a man or a woman; gestures which might indicate the age or sex of the character are avoided in most plays, and the choice of masks and costumes is governed largely by tradition. Above all, the actor refrains from admixing anything of his own personality in the roles and from allowing any variation to creep into successive performances. Hōshō Kurō (1837–1917), the creator of modern Nō, said that the difference between an amateur and a professional Nō actor was that the professional always played a part in exactly the same manner. The characters depicted in the plays, however vividly they may emerge through the poetry and the movements, exist only as part of the play; it would be absurd to wonder what they were like when younger or in happier circumstances. Their absoluteness makes the plays as valid today as when written; it may be that performances are now closer to the authors' intent than was possible when the whims of courtiers might disrupt a program. In any case, despite their heavy reliance on classical poetry and unfamiliar Buddhist thought, they are immediately affecting both to Japanese and Western spectators, and can be accepted unconditionally by readers capable of enjoying poetry and myth. The powerful effect produced on Yeats and Pound, though they never saw a play performed, suggests the universality of the appeal of the Nō plays as literature.

THE PLEASURES OF NŌ 23

The plays, indeed, are among the supreme masterpieces of Japanese literature, combining a richness of language and an integrity of emotion. They are so filled with ambiguities, allusions and wordplays that it seems hardly possible their first audiences could catch more than the general drift of many passages, yet they definitely were not armchair dramas. For Zeami the plays were chiefly vehicles for the display of the singing and dancing of the actors. In Europe the great plays, whether or not performed, have been read and esteemed as literature, but in Japan the evaluation of the plays has been intimately connected with performance; unstaged plays have aroused no interest. Paradoxically, the Nō is absolutely dependent on the beauty of its texts, for the deliberate manner of delivering the lines tends to exaggerate their qualities. Of the thousands of Nō plays written during the last six centuries (many, of course, intended for performance on a single occasion only), only some 230 survive in the repertory. Some have retained their popularity despite weaknesses in the text, thanks to the beauty of the music or the dances, but the vast majority are works of literary distinction.

If we attempt to examine the Nō plays in terms of some traditional definitions of drama in the West, we become immediately aware of how unsuited these criteria are. Drama begins with conflict, we are often told, but scholars of Nō have insisted that the Nō plays totally lack conflict because there is only one true personage, the *shite*, or protagonist; the other persons are merely observers of the action and not antagonists. The point is overstated, but it contains truth; most Nō plays lack the confrontation of characters typical of drama elsewhere, and some are virtually devoid of action. *Yōrō* ("Nurturing the Aged") tells of the discovery of a mineral spring with miraculous curative powers, a happy augury for the emperor's reign. The story is felicitous, but hardly dramatic. *Unrin-in*, as currently performed, is concerned mainly with explaining the meaning of certain obscure poetical terms in the tenth-century novel *Ise Monogatari*. Numerous other plays are mainly retellings of the history of a shrine or some other auspicious site, described with no suggestion of conflict.

Another Western view of drama, which stresses the importance of the creation of characters, reached its absurd heights with such nineteenth-century studies as *The Girlhoods of Shakespeare's Heroines*. But even though the *shite* is the only personage in a Nō play, he possesses few individual qualities. More often he is the incarnation of some powerful emotion, whether unforgiving enmity, possessive jealousy, or remorse for some unspeakable deed. In the early plays, before Zeami imprinted Nō with his view of the art, and in the late plays written as the form was disintegrating, more distinctive personalities are depicted, and sometimes there is conflict between the *shite* and another character. Normally, however, the *waki* ("person at the side") is little more than a representative of the audience who asks the questions it might ask, not possessing a personality or even a name of his own. The *shite* may have one or more *tsure* ("companion"), but the *tsure* is usually no more than a shadow. The *shite*, then, is generally the only person in a play, but even the *shite* belongs to another world, not our own, and creation of character, in the sense that the term is used in other forms of drama, is meaningless in Nō.

Some students of Nō, calling attention to the prominence of the final dance *(shimai)* performed by the *shite*, which may occupy a third of the total time of the play, have considered Nō as a form of spectacle and the texts as the means of creating the circumstances and atmosphere necessary for the dance. Certainly Zeami devoted enormous care to the choreography of the plays, and our most lasting impression of such a work as *Hagoromo* ("The Feather Cloak") is of the unearthly final dance of the angel. But some Nō plays are without dancing or are provided with only the suggestion of a final dance. Many are virtually without movement. Indeed, the less movement in a play, the higher its "rank" *(kurai)*. *Sekidera Komachi*, a work of so lofty a rank that in the past century only half-a-dozen actors, all acclaimed masters at the close of their careers, have ventured to perform the role, lasts about two hours; during the first hour and a half the *shite* sits motionless inside the prop, a frame representing a thatch-covered hut. A critic who saw the performance in

1955 reported that the interest of the play was mainly in the motionless hour and a half. Zeami himself wrote that the moments without action were especially appreciated by the audience; the actor, unable to rely on movement or words to distract the audience, had somehow to communicate his underlying spiritual strength. The final dance is extremely important to Nō, and may make reading the plays seem only a shell of the whole work, but the dance itself is not so much a display of agility or brilliance of movement as a continuation in different idiom of the mood created by the motionlessness.

It might be imagined, finally, that Nō resembled opera in being a drama which exists primarily for the sake of music. The music is unquestionably a vital part of Nō. The music and words have always been inseparable, the texts being transmitted orally, each syllable sung or declaimed in accordance with the musical traditions of a school of Nō. But no one ever sang the music without the words, as often happens with opera. Nor do the dances exist apart from the words in which they are framed. The music, played by drums and a flute, or sung, and the dances at the end or elsewhere, spring from the words and are in essence one with them.

A Nō play, then, fits badly into any category established by conventional Western theories of drama. To attempt a definition: it is a dramatic poem concerned with remote or supernatural events, performed by a dancer, often masked, who shares with lesser personages and a chorus the singing and declamation of the poetry. The texts of Nō are most properly discussed as literature, as in Chapter III.

Nō can be performed on any kind of stage, whether a hastily revamped modern auditorium stage or the crude platform built for a village festival, but to be appreciated fully it should be seen in a theatre built for its special use. Some old stages survive, such as the one at the shrine at Miyajima on the Inland Sea, where at certain times of day the tide flows between the audience and the stage, heightening the sense of mysterious distance. At the Nishi Honganji in Kyoto one can sit in splendor like the barons of former days, surrounded by sliding screens covered in gold leaf, and watch from a separate building the performance on the old stage. Between the seats of the nobles and the stage is a gravel-covered area where in former days the "groundlings" sat. In all Nō theatres today the tradition of having the stage in a building separate from the audience is vestigially retained by a massive wooden roof over the stage, even in modern concrete theatres. Though the gravelled area has shrunk to a symbolic foot or so, it too continues to divide the world of the audience from that of the actors.

The audience sits on two sides of the stage, to the center and to stage-right. Most Nō theatres today have seats like those in a Western theatre, but the ground floor of the older ones is divided into boxes where four or five people can sit in Japanese style, warming their hands over a *hibachi* in winter, or perhaps eating lunch from tiered lacquer boxes. The stage itself, some eighteen feet square, is built of polished but unpainted *hinoki* wood. At each of its four corners are pillars supporting the heavy curved roof. Behind the stage proper is an addition about nine feet deep (*atoza*) where the musicians and stage assistants sit; it is distinguished from the main stage by the horizontal direction of the floor boards. To stage-left is another extension, a mere three feet wide, where the chorus sits in two rows. The boards here run parallel to those of the stage. A passageway called the *hashigakari*, of the same width as the *atoza*, leads to the stage from the backstage. The *hashigakari* ranges in length from eighteen to forty-five feet, depending on the size of the theatre. On the side closer to the audience three small living pines are planted at regular intervals. At the far end is a brocade curtain with vertical stripes of contrasting colors which is lifted to permit actors to make their entrance. Two other architectural features are a low door (*kirido*) to the left of the *atoza* and the three steps leading from the stage to the gravel. Underneath the stage, invisible to the audience, are large jars placed to increase the resonance of the actors' voices and the musical instruments.

The beginning of a play is signalled from offstage by a flute. The Nō flute has not the softly melodic quality of the European flute, but sounds shrill and sometimes harsh. Its notes at the start of a performance seem to come from another world, not the Elysian Fields of the celebrated flute solo from Gluck's *Orfeo ed Eurydice* but a world infinitely distant from ours filled with a suffering we cannot comprehend. After the flute has sounded, the brocade curtain is lifted by men holding bamboo poles inserted in the hems, and the musicians enter, gravely walking in single file along the edge of the *hashigakari*, as if unwilling to tread the same boards in the center over which the actors presently will appear. The members of the chorus, eight or ten men, enter at the same time from the *kirido* at stage-left and take their places, sitting in formal Japanese style, their fans on the floor before them. The musicians sit in a prescribed order: the flutist, on the floor, farthest to stage-left; next, the player of the small drum (*kotsuzumi*) on a folding stool; the *ōkawa* drummer, also on a stool; and finally, (in many but not all plays) the bass drum (*taiko*) player, kneeling on the stage a little to the rear of the others. Stage understudies (*kōken*), attired in formal black kimonos, sit at the rear of the stage, rising occasionally during the course of performance to straighten an actor's robe. The *kōken* is normally a distinguished performer capable of taking over from the *shite* if he becomes indisposed or to prompt if an actor forgets his lines.

When the musicians are seated, the flutist again plays, this time joined by the percussion instruments—the hollow thud of the *kotsuzumi* and the sharp crack of the *ōkawa*. These sounds are augmented by the inarticulate, portentous cries of the drummers, suggesting again the immense distance separating the audience from the persons in the play. The brocade curtain, lowered after the musicians had all appeared, is again lifted, this time to permit the entrance of an actor and the beginning of the play.

The roles in a Nō play are known not by the names of the characters, as in a Western drama, but by the category of the role. In addition to the *shite*, *waki*, and *tsure* mentioned above, there are *kokata* (child parts, a variety of *tsure*) and *kyōgen*, generally rustics or menials. In the late Nō plays these distinctions often seem arbitrary. In some, the *waki* is more important than the *shite*, and in a few it is not even clear which part is *shite* and which *waki*. But in the plays of the great period, the first half of the fifteenth century, the *shite* is of predominant importance. The distinction between *shite* and *waki* is heightened in performance by the marked difference in costume (the *shite* wears brocades, the *waki* usually the black robes of a priest); in the use of masks for the *shite*, but never for the *waki*; in the different quality of the singing and recitation; and in the dances, which give the role of the *shite* its authority even if the part has less dialogue than the *waki*'s.

Many plays open with the entrance of the *waki*, often an itinerant monk, who tells us he intends to visit a certain shrine. His walk is deliberate, and his facial expression grave. He may describe his journey, but it is suggested in performance merely by a few steps. Eventually, he goes to the pillar at front stage-left, known as the *waki* pillar, and there awaits the appearance of the *shite*.

Nō plays are in either one scene or two. The difference is not merely in setting or length, but depends also on the nature of the play—whether about a ghost or a more realistic work. Most plays in one scene are about persons who belong to this world. The *shite*, if taking the part of a male character of his own age, may appear without a mask. In plays in two scenes, however, the *shite*'s appearance changes in the second part, and he may even be an entirely different person. In *Atsumori* we see the *shite* in the first scene as a humble reaper, but after the interlude he reappears in the second scene wearing the splendid armor of a general, his "true" appearance; this time, if not before, he wears a mask. In *Funa Benkei*, the *shite* in the first part is the unhappy Shizuka, a beautiful woman whose lover, Yoshitsune, must leave her behind as he sets out on a dangerous journey; in the second scene the *shite* is the terrible, vengeful spirit of Tomomori, a warrior vanquished by Yoshitsune, who rises from the sea to menace his ship. In this case, naturally, every detail of the *shite*'s appearance will be different in the second scene. The *tsure* accompanying the *shite* may also change appearance, but the *waki*, who belongs to this world, remains the same throughout whether in plays of one or two scenes.

The *kokata* performers appear not only in the roles of children, but also as fully-grown emperors, perhaps to avoid any suggestion of disrespect, and in most plays where an inappropriate romantic element might be created if fully grown actors appeared as man and woman in the *shite* and *tsure* parts. Yoshitsune in *Funa Benkei* is played by a boy, but in *Shōzon* a boy takes Shizuka's part. *Kokata*, whether they appear as males or females, are never masked.

The chorus, eight or ten men dressed in matching formal kimonos, sits at the side of the stage throughout the play, taking no part in the action. The function of the chorus is to recite for the actors, particularly when they are dancing. Unlike the chorus in a Greek play, it makes no comment on the action, and is never identified as townsmen, warriors or demons; the chorus, in fact, has no identity, but exists solely as another voice for the actors. Any *shite* actor, from the head of the school down, may appear in the chorus, remaining anonymous in the ranks.

The *kyōgen* parts are taken by actors attired in conspicuously humbler costumes than even the *waki*'s sombre robes. In the two-scene plays they appear during the interlude *(ai)*, generally as a rustic or "a man of the place," who explains to the *waki* the history of some remarkable occurrence. The interval *kyōgen* recitations possess slight interest for modern day spectators, who often go out for a smoke when the performer appears, but originally, when the texts were not yet printed nor so carefully studied, the *ai-kyōgen* actor was probably welcomed by the audience because he explained in a more colloquial, though eloquent, language the story so cryptically related elsewhere in the play. Perhaps also *ai-kyōgen* satisfied a craving for rhetoric, for occasions did not exist for oratory in the days when Nō was created. Today, the *ai-kyōgen*'s chief importance is that it fills the stage while the *shite* is changing costume, though a few are display pieces of narration or have an intrinsic dramatic interest.

In contrast to the *ai-kyōgen*, which rarely are humorous and are considered of such slight literary interest that they are usually omitted from texts of the plays, the independent Kyōgen, presented in alternation with the Nō plays as part of the program, are enjoyed as comedies, the best Japanese literature provides. Kyōgen farces seem to have supplied the necessary compensating humor to the unrelieved tragedy of the Nō plays from the inception of this form of theatre. Kyōgen may even be older than Nō; Kyōgen actors figure prominently in performances of *Okina*. An account of 1464 indicates that Nō and Kyōgen regularly alternated by that time if not much earlier. Although denied the prestige of Nō, Kyōgen has long shared its stage and some of its glory.

A single Nō play now takes from one to two hours to perform, depending chiefly on the length of the dances; even the most extended texts rarely run to ten pages of print. In the past the plays were performed much more quickly than today, perhaps at twice the speed, as we can judge from the number of plays presented as part of a single day's program. One play, however perfect, was never considered sufficient entertainment, and it was the practice instead to perform a series of plays in a prescribed order of categories. *Okina* was set apart, no doubt because it clearly belonged to an older tradition than the rest, and was invariably performed at the start of a program. The other plays of the repertory were divided into five categories: (1) plays about the gods *(waki Nō)*; (2) plays about martial heroes *(shuramono)*; (3) plays about women *(kazuramono)*; (4) plays of a miscellaneous or contemporary character *(genzaimono)*; and (5) plays about demons *(kiri Nō)*. The order of these five categories was determined primarily by their prevailing tempo. Each play was considered to consist of three main sections: *jo*, the introduction; *ha*, the development; and *kyū*, the climax. The pace of the play gradually increases in tempo from the deliberate introduction to the strenuous and sometimes agitated movements of the final dance. A program of Nō plays followed the same pattern. Plays of the first category, though possessing *jo*, *ha* and *kyū* sections, on the whole are slow-moving; their fastest sections are only relatively fast, and can by no means by compared to the *kyū* episodes of plays in the fourth or fifth categories. Plays of the second, third and fourth categories were considered to correspond to the *ha* section, increasing within this category from the generally slower tempo of the plays about warriors to some plays in the fourth category which depict demons in a manner almost indistinguishable from the fifth category, the *kyū* section of the program. The progression of plays was intended to provide the audience with a complete theatrical experience, starting with the stately movements of a religiously-inspired piece about the gods, a suitably elevated opening of the program, gradually increasing in human interest through the warrior play until the "woman" play, the most lyrical part of the program, was reached. The intensity of the woman's love portrayed in these plays might be pushed to the extreme of madness, as in some fourth-category works, or the human interest might become so dominant as to eliminate the supernatural or lyrical elements, as in the "contemporary" plays. Finally, the demon plays produced an exciting and satisfying effect at the end of a program similar to that of the presto finale of a symphony. The Kyōgen farces staged between the plays did not break the mood so much as they gave the audience a temporary and welcome respite from the overpowering emotions of the tragedies.

Audiences today are not often prepared to spend the eight or more hours at the theatre that a complete program of Nō and Kyōgen would require. Often a program consists of three Nō and a single Kyōgen. The sedate god plays are performed relatively seldom, and even the woman plays, long termed the "rice bowl" of the actors, figure less frequently on the programs than plays of the fourth and fifth categories. But an over-emphasis given to the more exciting Nō plays tends always to weaken the effect and even defeat the purpose of the art. If the audience is not prepared spiritually by slower, more symbolic works before it sees a play like *Ataka*, the experience will hardly differ from seeing *Kanjinchō*, the Kabuki play derived from *Ataka*. It is not only forgivable but perhaps even necessary that the spectators be bored or made drowsy by a program of Nō. The plays are works of such lofty aspirations that a certain magnitude and even tedium is part of the total effect. If the audience has sat through a full program, its reaction to *Ataka* when presented as the fourth work will not be simple enjoyment of the exciting story and interesting characters; the audience will see *Ataka* as part of the world permeated by the atmosphere of Nō. Dramatic excitement is an element in Nō, and the stories have a concentrated intensity which rivals that of any stage, but Nō is prized above all for what it and no other theatre can achieve.

The special vocabulary of Nō makes discussion difficult for the uninitiated. The term *yūgen* is especially important as a criterion of Nō, but its meaning is not easy to define. Originally *yūgen* meant "dark" or "obscure" with overtones of mystery. It was frequently employed in Japanese poetic criticism of the twelfth century to describe beauty which is suggested rather than stated. There is *yūgen* in this famous poem by Fujiwara no Shunzei:

yū sareba	Evening has come;
nobe no akikaze	The autumn wind from the fields
mi ni shimite	Cuts into the flesh
uzura naku naru	And the quails are calling now
Fukakusa no sato	In Fukakusa Village.

The atmosphere evoked in this poem is lonely rather than inviting, monochromatic rather than colorful, but beneath the externals one may glimpse a deeply-felt beauty. Poets of this school felt that the emotions aroused by more conventionally admired sights were real but limited, but there was no limit to what might be evoked through suggestion. A monochrome suggests more than the most brilliantly tinted landscape; the evening in autumn evoked by Shunzei's poem is eternal and universal, not the happy or sad experience described by one man alone.

The ideal of *yūgen* shifted in meaning during the three centuries between Shunzei and Zeami. The word came to mean "charming" or "graceful" and was used, for example, to describe dancing boys at a shrine or even the traditional court football *(kemari)*. When Zeami himself attempted to define *yūgen* by giving examples from the manners, appearance and speech of people he knew, he chose the courtiers, and indicated that *yūgen*, at least at this period of his career, meant "grace" or "elegance." His insistence that Nō be filled with *yūgen* may have meant no more, then, than that it should aim at graceful expression even when representing ugly or frightening characters, unlike harsher and cruder types of theatre. The grace of an old woman or even a demon—let alone a beautiful woman—is certainly apparent in contemporary performances. In part this is due to the use of masks, but in Zeami's day the physical beauty of the actors, especially the boys who performed without masks, must have contributed much to the *yūgen*. Zeami himself, as a boy of eleven, attracted the attention of the young Shogun Yoshimitsu in 1374, and Yoshimitsu's infatuation (as much as his interest in the theatre) occasioned the patronage which the shogunate was to bestow on Nō for almost five hundred years. The plays provide for an unusually large number of children's roles, probably for this reason. Grace and beauty in the appearance of the actors, achieved if necessary by wearing masks, and in the language of the texts made up much of Zeami's *yūgen*.

But it is hard to imagine that Zeami meant nothing more profound by the term. In Zeami's later critical works *yūgen* takes on a darker coloration, and this return to the earlier poetic ideal has remained its prevailing meaning. If a critic says of a woman play that it possesses *yūgen*, he clearly does not mean merely that it is gracefully written or that the actor performed attractively. *Yūgen* in fact tends to reject conventional notions of beauty: if a display of feminine grace on the Nō stage were the highest aim, real women could now take the parts, though they were not permitted on the stage in Zeami's day. But the thought of a woman performing the role of, say, the courtesan Eguchi is repugnant to lovers of Nō who insist that a man in his sixties with a cracked bass voice and large, ugly hands has more *yūgen*. They are right: anyone who saw Kita Roppeita dance the role of the *shite* in *Sagi* ("The White Heron"), a man in his eighties taking the part of a bird, surely sensed the mysterious, indefinable presence of *yūgen*.

It is impossible to tell how Zeami's changing conceptions of *yūgen* may have been reflected in his works; though his criticism is dated, the plays are not. The texts of the plays in any case have been much altered. Zeami himself advocated that plays constantly be modified to suit the tastes of successive audiences. Zeami is now credited with authorship of only some twenty-five of the plays, though formerly he was believed to have written about half the plays in the repertory. Ironically, only one play of the third category, *Izutsu*, is now definitely attributed to Zeami, though the woman plays embody most perfectly his ideal of *yūgen*. Perhaps further research will restore to Zeami some of the masterpieces now labelled "of unknown authorship"; if not, we may become aware of the existence of one or more playwrights no less gifted than Zeami. Even in this unlikely case, Zeami's supreme importance in Nō will remain unshaken, not only because of the place he occupies in the historical development but because of his critical writings.

Zeami says disappointingly little about the composition of his plays even in his critical work devoted specifically to the subject, but his analysis of the art of acting is superb. Zeami's enumeration of the nine levels of actors reveals his philosophical as well as practical grasp of the art:

"*The Art of the Flower of Mystery*. This can be symbolized by the phrase, 'In Silla at midnight the sun is bright.' It is impossible to express in words or even to grasp in the mind the mystery of this art. When one speaks of the sun rising at midnight, the words themselves do not explain anything; thus too, in the art of Nō, the *yūgen* of a supreme actor defies our attempts to praise it. We are so deeply impressed that we do not know what to single out as being of special excellence, and if we attempt to assign it a rank, we discover that it is peerless artistry which transcends any degrees. This kind of artistic expression, which is invisible to ordinary eyes, may be what is termed the Art of the Flower of Mystery.

"*The Art of the Flower of Profundity*. This can be symbolized by the verse, 'Snow has covered the thousand mountains; why does one lonely peak remained unwhitened?' Someone long ago once said, 'Mount Fuji is so high that the snow never melts.' A Chinese, hearing this, criticized the expression as inadequate and insisted that one should say instead, 'Mount Fuji is so deep that the snow never melts.' Anything which is extremely high is also deep. One might also say, perhaps, that there is a limit to how tall a thing can be, but the depth, being limitless, cannot be measured. Perhaps that is why the immeasurable wonder of a landscape in which, though a thousand mountains are buried in snow, one peak alone remains unwhitened can be taken as an equivalent of the Art of the Flower of Profundity.

"*The Art of the Flower of Stillness*. This can be symbolized by the words, 'Snow piled in a silver bowl.' The whiteness and purity of snow piled in a silver bowl is truly a lovely sight: may we not say it represents the Art of the Flower of Stillness?

"*The Art of the Flower of Correctness*. This can be symbolized by the words, 'The mist is bright, and the sun sinks, turning the countless mountains crimson.' The vast panorama of countless mountains sharply defined in bright colors by the light of the sun shining on the world from a perfectly clear sky represents the Art of the Flower of Correctness. The artistic rank of this art is superior to that of Versatility and Precision, and is the rank of an actor who has already mastered a flower of the art of Nō and entered its domain.

"*The Art of Versatility and Precision*. This can be symbolized by the words, 'To tell completely of the clouds on the mountains, the moon on the sea.' The intent to depict completely the vast spectacle of nature is most surely present in the training for the Art of Versatility and Precision. This art is the turning point where the actor either advances to the higher ranks or falls back.

"*The Art of Faint Patterns*. This can be symbolized by the words, 'The Way that can be explained is not the eternal Way.' The actor should first learn to tread the eternal way and then learn of the Way that can be explained. By 'faint patterns' is meant that the actor, still not deeply etched with the art, shows its first beauty. This Art of Faint Patterns is considered the entry into the study of the Nine Levels.

"*The Art of Strength and Delicacy*. This can be symbolized by the words, 'The metal hammer moves, the precious sword glints coldly.' The movement of the metal hammer suggests the strong movements of this art. The coldness of the glint of the precious sword suggests an astringent style of acting, one suited to the discriminating spectator.

"*The Art of Strength and Crudity*. This can be symbolized by the words, 'The tiger, three days after it is born, is ready to devour an ox.' The strength displayed by the tiger in being disposed barely three days after its birth to eat an ox suggests the strength of this art. 'Eating an ox' indicates its roughness.

"*The Art of Crudity and Coarseness*. This can be symbolized by the words, 'The innate faculties of the flying squirrel.' Confucius said, 'The flying squirrel has five talents. It can climb a tree, swim in the water, dig a hole, fly and run. But these five talents are appropriate to the level of the flying squirrel; it performs none of them well.' When art lacks delicacy it can be said to be crude and a distortion of the true qualities."

Zeami's descriptions are elusive but there can be no doubt that he knew exactly what he meant. The highest "flower"—by "flower" Zeami seems to have designated the particular beauty an actor displayed—is that of "mystery." Though not a commonly mentioned aesthetic ideal in Western performing arts (technique, "sincerity," emotional intensity, etc. would be more common standards of excellence), it is not difficult to understand. Perhaps the closest embodiment of this ideal among twentieth-century artists was Greta Garbo, who managed always to remain inviolate, untouched by the vulgarity of the world around her, mysterious and supremely beautiful. The next highest flower is that of the master actor, a superbly accomplished performer, who deliberately admixes an element of imperfection into his art lest audiences become bored with too great, unrelieved perfection: the single unwhitened peak is this coarser element, lending greater allure to the many peaks covered by the flawless snow of *yūgen*. The art of Sarah Bernhardt, to judge from contemporary accounts, had qualities suggesting this "flower." The next flower, that of stillness, may bring to mind the voice of Elizabeth Schumann—absolute purity, lacking the touch of vulgarity that might have made her a supreme artist or destroyed her. "Snow piled within a silver bowl" is perfectly evocative of the stillness and mystery of *yūgen* incarnate.

As one descends further Zeami's nine levels, mystery and purity yield to accuracy and, finally, energy. Zeami insisted that an actor must begin his training not with the crude vigor of the bottom levels but about halfway up the scale, with the "Art of Faint Patterns." He studies the "two arts" (singing and dancing) and the "three roles" (the warrior, the woman and the old person) and improves his acting ability until he can be said to have attained the level of versatility and precision. If he achieves these qualities, he may be able to display the first of the "flowers," that of correctness, the level of the highly competent, professional actor. If he fails to display this flower, he will drop to the lower levels of performers, where he can still be a useful member of a troupe in roles requiring stamina or acrobatic skill. Had he started at the bottom levels, however, without having received the training suited to the higher roles, he would not be qualified to perform even roles of a more superficial nature.

Zeami considered *yūgen* to be the touchstone of his school of acting, but he did not ignore *monomane*, "imitation of things." The actor must perform the three roles convincingly to appear frightening as a demon or pathetic as a beggar. Despite the highly stylized nature of Nō performances, details needed to create a convincing character are not overlooked, as we can tell most easily from adverse comments. Here is how Shūō, the author of the seventeenth-century book of criticism *Bushō Goma*, denounced an actor who had played Shizuka in *Funa Benkei*: " 'I thought I would accompany you wherever you might go, but a feeble comfort, not to be depended on, is the human heart. Alas, there is nothing I can do!' are lines where the character weeps, but this hard-hearted Shizuka showed not the least inclination to weep. The woman does not exist who does not weep when she thinks she may never again see the man she was prepared to accompany to the ends of the earth."

Many similar examples could be found in the criticism written today. The actor playing Shizuka must be sufficiently versed in *monomane* to corroborate every phrase of the text, not with the literalness of the gesture-language of the dances of India, but within recognized, symbolic terms. He must not, on the other hand, forfeit the mysterious beauty of *yūgen* in the interests of convincing realism; an actor who attempted to persuade us he was really Shizuka by imitating a feminine voice, swaying seductively as he walked, or weeping convulsively, would be unspeakably vulgar on the Nō stage. Skill at *monomane* means a mastery of the symbols of the parts. The genius of a particular actor enables him to make these symbols seem exactly appropriate, so that when the blind Yoroboshi appears on the stage the angle of his head at a certain moment (certainly not any gesture of sniffing) exactly suggests that he has caught the scent of plum blossoms, telling him as he wanders in the dark of his blindness that he has reached his destination, the Tennōji Temple. An actor is usually able in the latter part of his career to embody in his performance the combination of *monomane* and the *yūgen* fitting each role; only then can he be called a master actor.

Zeami, like his father Kannami, was at once playwright, actor, and composer, a practical man of the theatre who took into account both his audience and the actors he worked with. His audience consisted chiefly of aristocrats who, he could assume, possessed an expert acquaintance with Nō and a sensitivity to slight variations in performance; they also were familiar with the original literary texts from which the plays derived and with earlier plays on the same subjects. Zeami wrote, "Many of the recent Nō plays have been based on old Nō, and are revised versions set to new music. . . . They stem from seeds which are capable of blossoming brilliantly at any time; it is necessary only to change the words somewhat and add a new flavor to the music so as to accord with the tastes of a different age. The Nō plays of the future should also be written in accordance with their times and prevailing tastes." The plays, then, had to meet the demands of the audience, but this did not mean playing down to their level; Zeami's experience in the theatre convinced him that actors with *yūgen* (rather than those with cruder, more striking talents) enjoyed the most lasting popularity. The author was no less bound by the actors; Zeami declared that "in composing Nō the most important thing is to write parts suited for the available actors." We know little about the actors of Zeami's troupe, but we can infer that *Atsumori* and *Kiyotsune* were written for young actors. An old actor in such parts, as Zeami pointed out, would not convince the audience even if disguised by a mask and youthful attire. But Zeami created his greatest works for older actors. He occasionally used the word *hie* ("chill") to describe the *yūgen* of the old actor. The term, also found in the literary criticism of Zeami's day, seems to have meant an interiorization of *yūgen*, an invisible *yūgen* which is no longer external grace or charm but comes from within. This highest development of *yūgen* has remained the actor's goal, and is still appreciated by audiences more than the most dazzling virtuoso display. Great actors possess this *yūgen*; it is instantly recognized by spectators, even those witnessing Nō for the first time; it never disappears.

Zeami thought that even demons should be represented with *yūgen*, and grudgingly admitted that actors of Kyōgen, which he seems to have held in low esteem, might be said to possess *yūgen* if their comedies amused audiences without descending into vulgarity. Zeami's disapproval of low comedy may account for the remarkably clean humor of Kyōgen, certainly when compared to the European medieval farces. In Zeami's day the plays may have been largely impromptu, with some admixture of obscene or slapstick comedy, but today the texts have considerable literary finish and the lines are delivered with a meticulous attention to clarity of diction which is unique among the Japanese theatrical arts. Kyōgen places little emphasis on singing and dancing, though both are present. The plays are essentially dependent on dialogue and the antithesis of the characters, rather than on the aura given off by a single character as in Nō. The roles are types, rather in the manner of the commedia dell'arte, but the range is severely limited by the conditions which prevailed in Japan at the time. Japan was virtually isolated from the rest of the world, and the occasional Chinese or Korean who made his way to Japan in the fifteenth or sixteenth century was much too uncommon a sight to figure in the farces. This meant that Kyōgen, unlike the European farces, made virtually no use of the comic possibilities of the foreigner—the amorous Frenchman, the reserved Englishman, the uncouth American, and so on. Isolation was not the only reason for the absence of foreigners: the humor of Kyōgen is essentially vertical, depending on the complications in the relations between master and servant rather than on the horizontal relations between two servants, two masters, or two people from different countries. In Kyōgen, moreover, rustics are funny not because of their accents (all persons of the same station tend to talk in exactly the same language) or the use of Japanese equivalents of zounds! or gadzooks! but because they behave inappropriately to their station. (The rustic baron cannot compose poetry decently.) The most frequent comic situation revolves around a foolish master and his clever servant. Invariably, the servant manages to trick the master, who realizes he has been duped only when it is too late. The successes of servants over masters have been cited by some scholars as expressions of protest by the lower classes. A few plays would seem to confirm this thesis, but common sense indicates that a farce would not be funny if it told of a clever master who gets the better of his hapless servant. The shoguns and their courts, the patrons of Nō and Kyōgen, would certainly never have tolerated satire of themselves if they thought it threatened their authority.

Kyōgen, like Nō, have been divided into categories, but they are less rigid. Only plays of the first category, the *waki* Kyōgen, are truly distinct; like the *waki* Nō they deal with gods or with auspicious occasions. The other categories include plays about daimyos, the great lords, and *shōmyō*, the lesser lords; about bridegrooms and sons-in-law; about devils or *yamabushi*, the fierce mountain ascetes; about priests and blind men, and so on.

Some Kyōgen, like *Uri-nusubito* ("The Melon Thief"), are constructed around a single farcical idea, others, like *Tsukimi Zato* ("The Blind Man Looks at the Moon"), rise above the level of farce to that of a warm humanity. The best Kyōgen, as might be said of the best comedies anywhere, approach the borderline between comedy and tragedy, where we recognize the foibles of the characters but do not necessarily laugh at them. A few Kyōgen cross the borderline and are cruel rather than comic, but these are seldom performed.

The humor of Kyōgen stems mainly from the situations but, as we might expect in a theatre which places such emphasis on vertical relationships, it owes much also to the contrasting manner of delivery of characters belonging to different classes. Phrases which would have to be translated almost identically into English sound utterly different when pronounced by a daimyo or by Tarō-kaja, the servant, and some of the pleasure of Kyōgen comes from hearing the same lines pronounced in the strikingly dissimilar rhythmic patterns of master and servant.

The contribution of the actors to a performance is so overpowering that one tends to forget that Kyōgen must have had authors. Unlike Nō, we know virtually nothing about who wrote the Kyōgen plays, though many have been attributed to the learned priest Gen'e (1270–1350) or to Komparu Shirojirō (d. 1473). These attributions, repeated to this day, are no longer seriously believed because so little evidence supports them. Perhaps these men supplied the germs of the plays with which they are credited, but the plots are simple, and have unquestionably been much altered by the actors over the years.

Kyōgen, though performed in close connection with the Nō plays, bear little resemblance in plot, unlike the European interlude farces which often specifically derided the action of the tragedies they followed. Some Kyōgen plays require masks, mainly when the actor performs as a god or a devil, but the actors normally appear without masks or makeup. Performing in Kyōgen seems to impart a remarkably warm and amiable quality to the faces of aged actors. This impression may owe much to the imagination of the beholder, but an aged Kyōgen actor performing one of the major roles may well bring to mind Zeami's remark that even the humblest role should be crowned with flowers. The level of Kyōgen is humble when compared to Nō, but within its chosen domain it has developed into an art at once engaging and heartwarming, the other side of the tragic world depicted in Nō and its necessary complement.

II. THE HISTORY OF NŌ AND KYŌGEN

THE EARLY PERIOD

The Yōgō Pine in Nara provided a passage for the descent of Nō from the world of the gods to the world of men, and the dancer at the annual festival still re-enacts the birth of Nō beneath the tree, moving at the will of a god as his creature, a medium possessed of the divine spirit. It would be meaningless to discuss the dancer's skill or his powers of interpretation; he is supposed merely to allow the god to guide his movements. In former days it was customary for an entire village to participate in its festivals. There were no spectators, and any man might perform as the central figure of the festival, the god. Eventually, however, one villager was deemed to excel as the interpreter of the god, his vehicle, and he was chosen from then on to give corporeal form to the unseen divinity. Other villagers believed he would please the god by the beauty of his actions. The first actor, then, may have only gradually become aware that he was a man playing the part of a god; the first spectator was the god. The dancer performed with the hope that the god, satisfied with the representation of his own actions, would grant long life and prosperity.

In time other spectators were attracted, and the performance of the dances or playlets at the festivals came to be the responsibility of the most talented men. Stages were built within the precincts of Shinto shrines facing the main object of worship, and the actors served as celebrants of a religious rite intended to benefit either a whole village or else a particular donor.

We have yet to uncover documentary evidence revealing when plays recognizable as Nō originated. Certainly by the twelfth century *Okina* was being staged. This play contains both Buddhist and Shinto elements, inseparably intertwined. The two religions, though entirely different in origins and sometimes absolutely contradictory in teachings, had early been woven by the Japanese into a single faith. Far from attempting to resolve the differences between the optimistic, this-worldly Shinto and the prevailingly pessimistic, other-worldly Buddhism, the Japanese took from each religion what suited them best, ignoring the contradictions. A desire for long life makes little sense in terms of the Buddhist tenet that this world is a place of trial and suffering preparatory to the true life after death, but the Japanese prayed for long life anyway, guided by the Shinto love of this world. The plays often describe the Shinto gods, but a strong Buddhist coloring runs through them in the language, the allusions to Buddhist texts, and the underlying acceptance of such Buddhist concepts as the impermanence of life. However, the ghosts who play so prominent a part in the Nō plays, returning from the world of the dead to speak to the living, those fearsome presences who must be exorcised so that the living may escape harm, originate in folk beliefs unsanctioned by either Shinto or Buddhism. An ill-defined, shamanistic religion, sharing much with similar beliefs on the mainland of Asia, provided a core around which formal Shinto and Buddhist tenets accumulated.

The union between the two religions was demonstrated by the close association of Buddhist temples and Shinto shrines. The Kōfukuji Temple, which exercised jurisdiction over the Kasuga Shrine (the site of the Yōgō Pine), was the scene of many early dramatic presentations. Priests of esoteric Buddhism known as *shushi* (or "spell makers") performed songs and dances by way of making their magical rites more intelligible to the onlookers. The *shushi* priests, dressed in splendid robes befitting their ecclesiastical functions, attracted spectators as well as worshipers, and their performances acquired dramatic elements. Probably they were the first to present *Okina*. This baffling conglomeration of songs and dances may originally have been a presentation in entertaining form of a Buddhist text, but the meaning is now buried under the accretions of the centuries.

The performances by the *shushi* priests were accompanied by lighter diversions—acrobatics and the like—in which professional actors known as *sarugaku* appeared. These actors belonged to entirely different, secular traditions, though they were likewise attached to the Kōfukuji and other temples for financial support. Their art can ultimately be traced back to *gigaku*, a kind of dancing imported from China in 612 A.D. This oldest recorded Japanese stage entertainment has almost completely disappeared, but more than 220 *gigaku* masks are preserved. Fragmentary records suggest that a *gigaku* performance began with a procession of actors masked as lions, birds, "strongmen," barbarians, and so on, in all a dozen or more parts. The procession was followed by dances accompanied by flutes and drums: in one an actor masked as a bird executed a dance in which he pretended to be pecking for worms; in another a contest was portrayed between the "strongman" and the barbarian for the favors of a beautiful girl, ending in triumph for the "strongman," who leads off the barbarian by a rope tied to his penis. One *gigaku* entertainment that has survived is the *shishimai* (or "lion dance"), a popular feature of many festivals.

The Japanese court, in a mood of enthusiasm for all things Chinese, initially welcomed *gigaku* and commanded that youths be trained in the art. The high point in *gigaku* history occurred in 752, on the occasion of the ceremonies marking the inauguration of the Great Image of Buddha at the Tōdaiji Temple, when sixty *gigaku* performers appeared. Half a century later only two men were still qualified as *gigaku* artists. The court in the meantime had discovered a more decorous entertainment in *bugaku*, stately court dances. Two varieties of *bugaku* were introduced in the seventh century: "left dances" (*samai*), imported from China, included Indian music; "right dances" (*umai*) were of Korean and Central Asian origin. The names "left" and "right" denoted the direction from which the dancers made their entrances. The *bugaku* dances were in some sense representational, depicting a moment of a longer story, such as the triumphal return of a king from battle, but so highly stylized that the surviving dramatic element is negligible.

The *bugaku* dances, still performed at the Imperial Palace and at certain Shinto shrines, impart a distinctly alien atmosphere, largely because of the exotic masks and costumes. The original Chinese or Korean dances have nevertheless been altered by Japanese influences over the centuries. *Bugaku* in turn influenced Japanese dramatic and musical arts, including Nō. The division of each *bugaku* piece into three musical sections of increasingly rapid tempo—the *jo, ha, kyū* of Nō—was perhaps the greatest influence. *Bugaku* was at its full maturity when first introduced to Japan, and because it continued to retain its alien character it became in time a petrified ritual which could only be repeated, not developed. The changes that occurred in *bugaku* were doubtlessly unintentional and even unnoticed. By the end of the twelfth century *bugaku* had become a palace ceremonial.

The variety of entertainment called *sangaku* had been introduced to Japan from China together with *bugaku*. *Sangaku* included feats of magic, acrobatics, juggling, animal shows, etc. A picture of one stunt survives: a dancing girl wearing high clogs crosses a rope strung between poles balanced on the chins of two recumbent men, the girl juggling as she walks. *Sangaku* playlets were on such themes as "The head clerk of a temple slips on the ice and loses his trousers" and "The nun Myōkō begs for swaddling clothes," probably satirical pieces deriding the distraction or incontinence of the Buddhist clergy. Other playlets, like "The clever repartee of a Kyoto man" or "An easterner's first visit to the capital," seem to have been skits contrasting the sophisticated ways of city-dwellers with the artlessness of rustics. We know little more than these outlines, mentioned in a work written about 1160, but they prove that *sangaku* (or *sarugaku*, as it was known in a corruption of the word) included plays with plots and dialogue as well as dances and acrobatics.

From the grab bag of variety entertainments performed by the *sarugaku* players would eventually develop Nō and Kyōgen. The secular *sarugaku* actors, rather like the mimes of medieval Europe, began as clowns and acrobats but in the end presented works of an exalted, religious nature. Even the name *sarugaku*, though written with characters meaning "monkey music," lost its comic flavor when the performers, ever eager to add to their repertory, borrowed the plays of the *shushi* priests and presented them as entertainment rather than as religious instruction. *Sarugaku* also absorbed influences from two other early theatricals, *dengaku* and *ennen*, which shaped it artistically.

Dengaku (or "field music") was the name originally given to the songs and dances performed by country people, at times as part of the harvest celebrations. *Dengaku* of this nature can still be seen at festivals all over Japan. The court nobles in Kyoto, always on the lookout for new diversions from their usual activities, heard of these country dances and invited the performers to the capital. If *dengaku* in the thirteenth century was no more engrossing than its counterparts today, the nobles must have been stupendously bored before they could derive pleasure from such crude and inartistic caperings. Be that as it may, the original *dengaku* dancers—farmers and priests— soon gave way to professional actors who modified the performances to accord with the tastes of more sophisticated audiences. The simple costumes formerly worn in *dengaku* were replaced by elegant robes, and the songs were embellished with poetic language. By the fourteenth century, when the provincial lords also began to sponsor *dengaku*, the staging had become quite elaborate. The expenses incidental to performances were indeed so enormous that the downfall of Hōjō Takatoki (1303–33), the regent for the shogun, has been attributed to his mania for *dengaku*. By Kannami's day *dengaku* and *sarugaku* had become similar arts, much influence passing between the two. *Dengaku* failed to keep pace with *sarugaku*, perhaps because of the historical accident that it had no outstanding performers during the crucial period when Kannami and Zeami were developing *sarugaku* into a great dramatic art.

Ennen, the name of the other early dramatic form which influenced *sarugaku*, means "prolong years." It originated as ceremonies of prayer for the prolongation of some exalted person's life, but as early as 1100 the *ennen* prayers were followed by dances. The dances developed into plays by the fourteenth century. An account of *ennen* performances in 1429 indicates that the plays, in highly poetic language, were staged with ornate sets. *Ennen* influenced Nō by providing a model of how old songs, quotations from religious and secular literature, and a vocabulary including words of Chinese as well as Japanese origins might impart to the texts a dignity and beauty not found in older forms of drama. Probably each innovation in *sarugaku*, *dengaku* or *ennen* was quickly adopted by the others, making it difficult to distinguish among these arts. On the other hand, slight differences in the manner of recitation or dance were elevated into secrets by performers whose livelihoods might depend on their possessing (or seeming to possess) unique traditions. Already in Kannami's day there were four troupes of *sarugaku* actors in the province of Yamato: Yūsaki (founded by Kannami himself), Tohi, Emai, and Sakato, the ancestors of the present Kanze, Hōshō, Komparu, and Kongō schools respectively. Three other *sarugaku* troupes performed in the province of Ōmi, and there were troupes of *dengaku* and *ennen*. In contrast to the rigidly partisan divisions characteristic of the schools of Nō in later times, relations among the different *sarugaku* and *dengaku* players apparently were friendly, and a member of one troupe often studied the acting techniques of another. But even in the early days each troupe took care not to fall behind the others in techniques or in patrons.

Whatever the form of theatre, the most important factor in its development was the patronage of the upper classes. Without the backing of the nobles, *dengaku* would have remained no more than the prancing and artless singing of the country festival; *sarugaku* acquired its dignity only when enabled to abandon the crude realism demanded by the provincial audiences in favor of the poetic beauty appreciated by the court. Not only did the nobility patronize the drama and the actors, but by 1250 nobles themselves were performing in *sarugaku* for their own amusement. The future of *sarugaku* as the exalted art of Nō was determined in 1374 when Ashikaga Yoshimitsu, the shogun, attended performances at the Imakumano Shrine in Kyoto. On that occasion Kannami, then forty-one, appeared in *Okina* as the old man, and his son, later known as Zeami, in the role of Senzai. Yoshimitsu, entranced, lent his patronage to both father and son. Kannami, who had formerly toured the provinces with his troupe, was assured of court protection and was enabled to write plays not for illiterate farmers but for the most discriminating audiences.

YOSHIMITSU AND NŌ

Ashikaga Yoshimitsu was only seventeen when he witnessed the performances at Imakumano, but he was unquestionably the outstanding man in the entire country, not only by virtue of his office—Barbarian Quelling Great General—but because of his remarkable intelligence and ability. Yoshimitsu, the grandson of the founder of the Muromachi shogunate, did not forsake the martial traditions of his ancestors, as so often happened by the third generation, but he possessed also the literary and cultural talents of the courtier. He was an expert *tanka* poet (a number of his poems were selected for the imperially-sponsored anthologies), accomplished in linked verse (*renga*), Chinese poetry, music, and Zen philosophy. He enjoyed travel, combining the business of consolidating his power over the country with his pleasure in excursions to Mount Fuji, the Inland Sea or the Great Shrine of Ise. As shogun he not only represented the apex of power during the Muromachi period (1336–1568) but ranks among the most powerful men of Japanese history. His success in military affairs was crowned by his reunification of the country in 1392 after sixty-four years of bitter division. Yoshimitsu has nevertheless been treated as a traitor by Japanese historians because his passion for things Chinese induced him to accept the title "King of Japan" bestowed on him by the Chinese court. His treatment of the imperial family, by no means reverent, has also aroused condemnation. Despite his failings, however, Yoshimitsu was a remarkable combination of martial statesman and aesthete.

Yoshimitsu's passion for Nō continued throughout his life. His patronage was extended not only to Zeami but to Dōami, a rival *sarugaku* actor, and to Kyōgen performers. His thorough grasp of poetic tradition and Buddhist language allowed Zeami to enrich his texts with a vocabulary and imagery of startling complexity. Yoshimitsu himself never performed, but he enjoyed theatrical display, as we know from the diary of his visit to Itsukushima, when he embarked wearing a "narrow-sleeved, wide-hemmed costume of a pale blue lozenge pattern tied with a red sash, green leggings and red knee-length breeches." This bizarre attire, the current craze among city dandies, excited comment, but was typical of Yoshimitsu's eccentric taste in dress.

Yoshimitsu abdicated the office of shogun in 1394 and took Buddhist orders the following year, but remained in control of the government. He also maintained his interest in *sarugaku*, an enthusiasm he transmitted to his son, the shogun Yoshinori, creating the tradition that the shogun, whatever his tastes, would protect Nō. Yoshimitsu may have found Nō brick, but he certainly left it marble.

KANNAMI AND ZEAMI

Yoshimitsu had probably already heard of Kannami when he decided for the first time in his life to attend a *sarugaku* performance and commanded that the most accomplished, rather than the senior, actor of the troupe should appear in *Okina*; he wished to see Kannami in the role. Kannami performed with such success that he was elevated to the position of "companion" (*dōhōshū*) to Yoshimitsu, sharing this distinction with other notable artists of the day. Kannami, however, never renounced his earlier audiences; he died in 1384 while on a tour of Suruga, an eastern province. Zeami spoke of his father with the utmost reverence, whether as an actor, composer, choreographer or playwright, but Kannami's greatest single contribution to the development of Nō may have been the incorporation into the plays of *kusemai*, a dance to an irregular, strongly-accented rhythm. *Kusemai* was to figure as the climactic, narrative section of most Nō plays, adding far more complexities of plot than the older dramatic forms permitted. Kannami is credited also with many celebrated works of the repertory, including *Matsukaze, Sotoba Komachi, Kayoi Komachi,* and *Eguchi.* Some critics claim that Kannami's style was simpler and directer than Zeami's, but little evidence supports this. *Jinen Koji,* it is true, startles at times by its realism, but *Matsukaze* and *Eguchi* reach summits of poetry rarely surpassed by later Nō dramatists. Kannami's plays were often adaptations of older works, and were in turn revised and augmented by Zeami and later men, leaving in the end only elements of Kannami's distinctive style; the eight or ten surviving plays believed to have been written by Kannami show few mutual resemblances, and stand apart also from later works. Scholars have argued that in the earliest Nō only one character, the *shite,* was of consequence, but *Kayoi Komachi* develops from the antithesis between the *shite,* Shii no Shōshō, and the *tsure,* Komachi; and *Sotoba Komachi* includes a theological dispute between the *shite,* Komachi, and the *waki,* a priest. The works attributed to Kannami suggest dramatic possibilities which most later dramatists rejected. Kannami's importance is unquestionable, but because he left no critical or autobiographical writings, most of what we know about him derives from his son's lavish but unverifiable praise.

Far more is known about Zeami. He emerges indeed as a distinct historical figure, though the basic biographical data is missing or incomplete. Our only source of information for his birthdate is the statement made in 1432 that he had reached his seventh *chitsu,* a word meaning decade; the words have therefore been interpreted as signifying that Zeami was then seventy years of age by Japanese reckoning, or sixty-nine by ours, fixing his date of birth at 1363. The six hundredth anniversary of his birth was accordingly celebrated in 1963, only for a new theory to be published which claimed that 1364 was correct. If this is correct, other dates must be shifted accordingly, placing the Imakumano performances in 1375 instead of 1374; but whichever the year, Zeami was eleven when he first appeared before Yoshimitsu.

Eleven is now considered too young for an actor to appear in adult roles, but Zeami believed that this was the time to begin mastering the repertory. "His childish appearance will give him *yūgen,* whatever role he may take. At this age too his voice is charming. These two advantages will make people forget his defects and call attention to the development of his qualities." By the time the actor is sixteen or so his voice has changed and he will have lost the "flower" of the boy performer. "Now that he is taller his charm has disappeared; it is no longer so easy for him to escape criticism because of the beauty of his voice and his physical charm." The emphasis Zeami gives to the beauty of the boy actor reflects the contemporary partiality, especially in samurai society, for young boys. Senzai, the role danced by Zeami before Yoshimitsu, is still assigned to the handsomest actor of a company, who dances without a mask. We know how much Zeami attracted Yoshimitsu from the account written by a nobleman in 1378, which describes Yoshimitsu taking Zeami to see the Gion Festival. Special stands had been erected for the Shogun and Zeami to watch the floats passing down Shijō, the main avenue. "The Shogun was accompanied by a boy, a Yamato *sarugaku* player, who watched the festival from the Shogun's box. The Shogun, who has for some time bestowed his affection on this boy, shared the same mat and passed him food from his plate. These *sarugaku* performers are no better than beggars, but because this boy waits on the Shogun and is esteemed by him, everyone favors him. Those who give the boy presents ingratiate themselves with the Shogun. The daimyos and others vie to offer him gifts, at enormous expense. A most distressing state of affairs."

At nineteen Zeami was already an established actor when he succeeded in 1384 as head of the troupe, following his father's death. Zeami seems, however, to have fallen into a slump afterwards; in *Kadensho* ("The Book of the Transmission of the Flower") he describes in terms that suggest autobiography the ridicule which the public often directs against an actor between the ages of seventeen and twenty-four, a period when his youthful charms have disappeared but his powers as a full-fledged actor have not yet emerged. During this critical period the actor must summon up all his resolve to keep from abandoning Nō altogether, in despair.

Zeami apparently recovered from his depression during his middle twenties, when he achieved recognition as an outstanding performer. He wrote, "By this period the actor's voice has settled completely, and his body has assumed its adult proportions. . . . People begin to notice him and to comment on his skill. He may be awarded a prize in a competition, even against actors of considerable ability, the public being delighted by the freshness of the talent he displays on that occasion. The public and the actor himself may then begin to think he is truly accomplished, but this is most detrimental to the actor. His is not a true 'flower'; he is merely in the prime of his youth, and the audience has been momentarily captivated by his charm. The true connoisseur will recognize the difference." The actor, in order to avoid serious harm to his career, must not let himself be deluded by flattery, but study all the harder the techniques of older actors, particularly *monomane*, "the imitation of things."

Zeami, in his middle thirties when he wrote *Kadensho*, described this as the culminating period of the actor's career. If he has still not won public recognition, he clearly has not acquired a genuine "flower," and his abilities will presently deteriorate. Zeami insisted on public recognition as the gauge of an actor's talents; the actor's function is to please the audience, and it alone will ultimately judge his merits. Zeami believed that the actor who had established a solid reputation by his middle thirties might preserve his "flower" even when his physical beauty began to fade in his forties. A truly remarkable performer, like Kannami, who appeared on the stage just a few weeks before his death in his fifty-second year, may still dazzle an audience though his repertory and range of color are now drastically limited by his age. (Zeami would probably have been astonished to see contemporary performances in which an actor in his sixties still takes the parts of beautiful young women.) Zeami likened the talent of the aged actor to flowers still blossoming on an aged tree with few remaining leaves.

In 1399, the year before writing *Kadensho*, Zeami appeared in festive performances of Nō attended for three days by the new shogun, Yoshimochi. The great success he scored on this occasion clearly established him as the leading *sarugaku* actor. It was a logical moment for him to take stock of his art. Most of Zeami's opinions concerning acting techniques were admittedly derived from his father; his purpose in writing *Kadensho* was, in fact, to preserve for his descendants the teachings of Kannami. The emphasis on *monomane* found throughout this work reflects Kannami's experience as an actor who habitually appeared before a public which demanded believable representation. Zeami in this work reveals himself as a practical man of the theatre whose desire to please his audiences took precedence over interpretative or aesthetic matters. He wrote, for example, that if persons of quality happen to arrive early for a performance it is improper not to begin immediately; if, on the other hand, exalted persons arrive towards the close of a performance their presence will so affect the audience that the usual order of plays must be altered.

Zeami contrasted the *sarugaku* styles of Yamato, which emphasized *monomane*, and of Ōmi, which gave priority to *yūgen*, considering elegance to be the basic element of Nō. This statement suggests how much Zeami's own art in his maturity was to be indebted to the Ōmi school; indeed, Zeami acknowledged that he owed much to Inuō (later known as Dōami), the leading Ōmi player. Inuō had first been introduced to Yoshimitsu by Kannami, and never forgot this kindness. His relations with Zeami were close, especially after Kannami's death, and the two men were almost equally respected as artists by Yoshimitsu. During the performances of Nō staged before the Emperor Go-Komatsu in 1408, on the occasion of his visit to Yoshimitsu's mansion at Kitayama, Zeami appeared on the eleventh of April and Inuō a week later. This was the apogee of Zeami's career as an actor. A month later Yoshimitsu fell ill, and on the thirty-first of May he died, in his fifty-first year. This event came as a severe blow to Zeami: Yoshimitsu had not only been a generous patron of Nō but its most discerning critic. Komparu Zenchiku, Zeami's son-in-law, wrote of Yoshimitsu that he had seen all the actors from Yamato and Ōmi, and could distinguish their qualities, "rejecting the crude and vulgar and insisting on *yūgen*." Yoshimitsu, we are told, "searched into the old and understood the new . . . He was scrupulously fair when it came to the arts." *Sarugaku* might have remained a folk entertainment but for Yoshimitsu's financial and artistic support, which enabled Zeami to develop it into a complex and elevated art.

Yoshimitsu's successor, Yoshimochi, bestowed his patronage chiefly on a *dengaku* actor named Zōami. We can gather from Zeami's description that Zōami was unusually accomplished; he wrote that he all but wept with emotion at Zōami's performance, which he likened to the "flower of stillness." Yoshimochi's appreciation of Zōami is easier to understand than his coldness towards Zeami. During the decade from 1413 to 1423 Zōami and *dengaku* reigned supreme in Kyoto. A dozen or more benefit performances of *dengaku* attest its popularity; not a single *sarugaku* benefit occurred during those years. Zeami, in his fifties, wrote some of his finest criticism, including *Shikadōsho* ("The Book of the Way of the Highest Flower," 1420) and *Nōsakusho* ("The Book of Nō Composition," 1423). In these works Zeami seems less interested in the elements of a successful performance—the "flower" of the actor, the intrinsic interest of a play, or the novelty of presentation—than in the unchanging aesthetic values of Nō. He emphasizes the importance of the combination of song, dance and *yūgen*, the latter term having now shifted in meaning from "charm" to "mysterious beauty." Undoubtedly Zeami also composed Nō plays while writing these essays, but we cannot tell which works fall in this period.

In 1422 Zeami, having reached the age of sixty by Japanese reckoning, became a Buddhist priest and withdrew as head of his company, leaving the position to his son Motomasa, about thirty years old at the time. Zeami had one other son, Motoyoshi, for whom he wrote *Nōsakusho* and who in turn recorded Zeami's sayings in *Sarugaku Dangi* ("Conversations on *Sarugaku*," 1430). We can assume that he entertained high hopes for both sons. Motomasa quickly established himself as a superlative actor in Zeami's tradition, and his future seemed assured when a threat unexpectedly arose in the person of Zeami's nephew Motoshige. The latter's spectacular rise to fame began in 1427 when he was selected by Gien, the abbot-prince of the Shōren Temple, to appear in a benefit performance of Nō. On the death of Yoshimochi without heir in 1428, this same Gien, Yoshimochi's brother, returned to the laity to assume the office of shogun under the name Yoshinori. He too was hostile to Zeami and Motomasa and, as Motoshige's protector, was determined to make him first among the *sarugaku* actors. In August, 1428, at Yoshinori's command, Motoshige performed Nō at the Muromachi Palace. Neither Zeami nor Motomasa was invited. In 1429 Motomasa and Motoshige both appeared in plays staged on the riding grounds of the Muromachi Palace, spectacles distinguished by the use of "real horses and real armor," a far cry from the symbolic use of props that distinguishes Nō today. Ten days later Yoshinori issued an order forbidding Zeami and Motomasa from appearing at the palace of the Retired Emperor; from then on Motoshige gave the New Year's performances for the Retired Emperor. In 1430, again by order of Yoshinori, Motomasa was dismissed from his post as Master of Music at the Kiyotaki Shrine and replaced by Motoshige. Motomasa, dismayed by these repeated indications of Yoshinori's hostility, left Kyoto to live in the hinterland of Yamato Province. Towards the end of the same year, 1430, Zeami's second son, Motoyoshi, gave up the stage to become a priest.

These events were terrible blows to Zeami, but the worst was yet to come: in 1432 Motomasa suddenly died. A month later Zeami wrote a final tribute:

"'To the roots the blossoms return, to old nests the birds hurry back; will the spring go the same way too?' This expression of love for the blossoms and envy for the birds must surely have been written by a man of feeling. I have known such inconsolable grief for the beloved son I have lost that I have envied the mindless blossoms and birds; the color of the blossoms and the songs of the birds have brought me only pain and uncertainty. I realize now, however, that the emotion involved must be the same.

"On the first day of the eighth moon my son Zenshun died at Anonotsu in Ise Province. It may seem foolish of me not to have resigned myself long ago to the fact that the young do not necessarily die after the old, but the blow came so unexpectedly that it quite overwhelmed my aged mind and body, and tears of grief rotted away my sleeves. Zenshun, though I say it of my own son, was an incomparable master of acting. Long ago my late father established our family name in this art, and I too, succeeding him, labored selflessly for it. Now I have reached my seventh decade. It seemed to me that Zenshun's talents surpassed even those of his grandfather, and I recorded for him all the secret traditions and mysteries of the art, remembering the text which says you must tell a man the truth while you can, for otherwise you may waste his talents. But all that I wrote down is now the dream of Rosen, and I have no choice but to let these teachings, which nobody will master and which will benefit no one, turn to dust and smoke. If I preserve them for posterity now, whom will they help? The sentiments described in the poem, 'Now that you are not here, to whom shall I show these plum blossoms?' are true indeed. But my grief is unendurable when I think that the destruction of our art is at hand, and that I must witness such a disaster with my own eyes, in the meaninglessness of the lingering last years of my life. Alas! Confucius was heartbroken at the death of his son, and when Po Chü-i was preceded in death by his son, they say he vented his hatred on the medicine still left by the boy's pillow.

"Zenshun came into this phantom world. For a moment we became father and son. Now, in grief over parting, I have scattered words aimlessly as leaves tumbling from a bough, truly a sign my grief is too much to bear. 'Did I ever dream it? That while I, a withered tree, linger in this world, I should see the fall of a flower in full bloom?'

9th moon, 4th year of Eikyō [1432]   Shiō [Zeami]

" 'If I did not think my life had a term, how could I know any end to the tears shed by this aged body?' "

Zeami's despair was eventually mitigated by the achievements of his son-in-law Komparu Zenchiku (1405–1468), his artistic successor and the heir to his teachings, but his despondency over Motomasa's death darkened this whole period of his life. Motomasa was not only a superb actor, as we know from Zeami's testimony, but a gifted dramatist. His surviving works include *Sumidagawa* and *Yoroboshi*, among the most affecting plays of the repertory; the unhappy circumstances at the end of his life may account for their strong element of pathos. After his death the headship of the Kanze school went to Motoshige (now known as Onnami), probably at Yoshinori's insistence. An account of the benefit performances staged in Kyoto in May, 1433, before Yoshinori and members of the imperial court suggests the lavish scale on which Yoshinori supported Onnami's art.

One further disaster awaited Zeami: in 1434 he was banished to the island of Sado. Yoshinori's reasons for exiling Zeami are not known, but his hatred must have been implacable indeed to send a man in his seventies to a distant, lonely island. Zeami probably remained on Sado until 1441 when a general amnesty was declared after the assassination of Yoshinori. Zeami's exile was lightened by the solicitude displayed by Zenchiku. After his return to Kyoto, Zeami apparently lived with Zenchiku until his death in 1444, at the age of eighty. While on Sado, Zeami wrote *Kintōsho*, a series of prose-poems describing his exile. One account reports that seven plays written by Zeami at the time were responsible for his securing pardon. The story is dubious, but it indicates at least that some plays may date from the last years of Zeami's life.

NŌ AFTER ZEAMI

The brutal assassination of Yoshinori while he was watching a performance of *sarugaku* is indicative of the unrest which seriously threatened the government. Yoshimitsu's authority had been absolute, but the strength of the shogunate was constantly eroded during the fifteenth century. Frequent uprisings against authority occurred throughout the country, the climax occurring with the Ōnin Rebellion of 1467 to 1477, when most of Kyoto was destroyed. After the rebellion the rule of the shogunate was largely a fiction.

The Nō theatre was a fitting form of drama for these chaotic times. The presence of ghosts and the world of the dead (as if they had displaced the living not only in importance but in reality) reflects the Buddhist conviction that this world is a place of foulness and corruption, a temporary dwelling before we move on to the more lasting realities of the life after death; it also suggests the agonizing uncertainty of a world where destruction was the rule and the heritage of the past had been reduced to ashes. In the first year of the Ōnin Rebellion, Ichijō Kaneyoshi, the Prime Minister and a great noble, was forced to go begging for food after his house and library, the repository of centuries, were wantonly destroyed. In such times it is not surprising that men turn to comfort promised beyond the grave.

Buddhist thought, though important in the works of Kannami and Zeami, becomes dominant both in the plays and essays of Komparu Zenchiku. Few details are known about Zenchiku's life, partly because he performed mainly in Nara, rather than in the capital, but records bear witness to his friendship with the leading Buddhist priests of the day, including the celebrated Ikkyū (1394–1481). One essay by Zenchiku is purely theological, a criticism of a certain Buddhist sect, and the others make frequent use of Buddhist terminology, explaining in metaphysical terms the nature of Nō. The search for a meaning beyond appearances, rejected as illusory, is found also in the works of Shōtetsu (1381–1459), a Buddhist priest and the best poet of his day. For him *yūgen* was that ultimate reality: "What we call *yūgen* lies within the mind and cannot be expressed in words. Its quality may be suggested by the sight of a gauzy cloud veiling the moon or by the autumnal mists swathing the scarlet leaves on a mountainside. If one is asked where *yūgen* can be found in these sights, one cannot say; a man who cannot understand this truth is quite likely to prefer the sight of the moon shining brightly in a cloudless sky. It is quite impossible to explain wherein lies the interest or wonder of *yūgen*." Clouds and mists, veiling the bare truths of a landscape, lend ambiguity and mystery, and suggest more than a brightly illuminated scene. The poet himself may not be able to explain the ultimate meaning of his words, but the sensitive person will detect and respond to something lying beneath the surface; what each man finds is likely to be different. If the sceptic dismisses the mystery as nothing more than the emperor's new clothes, or prefers crimson leaves radiant in the sunshine to glimpses of them through mist, one obviously cannot convince him that he is wrong.

The need that Zenchiku and Shōtetsu experienced to believe in the existence of some ultimate meaning behind the terrible spectacle of the world induced them to seek beauty which might be sensed if not described. Their preference for suggestion and mystery was shared by the masters of the tea ceremony, and by the landscape architects who created gardens bare of flowers or trees. Zen philosophy gave direction to their aestheticism. Zeami's critical writings showed an increasingly marked Zen coloration; with Zenchiku it became dominant. The aesthetics of Nō may owe more to Zenchiku than to Zeami: the bare stage, the insignificant props, the movements of the actors, recalling at once the Zen priest and the warrior. The overpoweringly sombre tone of the plays certainly brings to mind not Zeami's "flowers" but the gloom of a monochrome, flowerless world.

Zenchiku's successors, however, turned to realistic or dramatic themes with few symbolic overtones. The plays of Miyamasu treat mainly martial subjects; the characteristic works of Nobumitsu (1435–1516), like *Dōjōji* or *Momijigari,* are "demon" plays filled with violence; those of Kanze

Nagatoshi (1488–1541) often have such large casts as to make them resemble Kabuki more than Nō. Zenchiku's grandson, Komparu Zempō (c. 1474–c. 1520) wrote one play, *Hatsuyuki*, in the *yūgen* manner, but his characteristic vein was straightforwardly dramatic. Even at the court of the shogun in Kyoto the dramatists, unable to hope for a patron like Yoshimitsu, were obliged to entertain with works which pleased by their novelty and dramatic excitement. With the collapse of the shogun's power in the sixteenth century, the Nō troupes had no choice but to rely on popular support, and the general public was ever more insistent on dramatic action.

Even in the sixteenth century, however, Nō did not reject altogether its unique qualities in favor of theatrical excitement. It remained prevailingly a repertory theatre, and the different troupes continued to stage the works of Zeami and Zenchiku. Surviving records indicate that the individual plays most often performed were *Yuya*, *Kureha*, *Takasago*, and other relatively static works, though plays of the fourth and fifth categories as a whole were by far the most frequently staged. Evidently the public still appreciated the solemn beauty of some plays, though the bulk of the programs was given over to dramatic pieces.

Kojirō Nobumitsu's background as a *waki* actor probably accounted for the prominence of *waki* roles in his plays; in *Chōryō* and *Rashōmon* the *waki*'s part is more important than the *shite*'s, and in *Shōzon* by Nobumitsu's son Nagatoshi, the last important Nō dramatist, the distinction between *shite* and *waki* has become so arbitrary that the nomenclature varies today according to the school.

During the sixteenth century the schools of Nō emerged as distinct and sometimes hostile groups, each jealously guarding its particular traditions. The Kanze school had virtually monopolized performances given in the shogun's presence, but after the death of the Shogun Yoshinao in 1489 and of the former Shogun Yoshimasa in 1490, the Ashikaga family lost control of the court. A relaxation of the rules of precedence enabled the other three schools of Nō—Hōshō, Komparu and Kongō—to participate in court performances. In 1493, for example, the Kanze and Komparu schools staged rival presentations at the shogun's palace, and in 1497 the Komparu and Kongō schools were pitted against each other. The Kongō and Hōshō schools hardly figure in the earlier history of Nō, but with greater opportunities to perform they now began to gain prominence.

Kongō Ujimasa (1507–1576), a colorful as well as talented performer, was known by the nickname of "Nose Kongō," apparently because of his large nose and nasal voice. The nickname occasioned the legend that he was once so determined to dance with the head of a certain Buddhist statue for his mask that he broke the head from the statue and made its face into a mask. He performed wearing this mask, only for a terrible boil soon to form on his nose; eventually the tip rotted away, giving Ujimasa his sobriquet. Legends aside, Ujimasa was a tempestuous figure, profiting by the new freedom in the world of Nō to assert himself and his school. In 1541 he had a bitter quarrel with the head of the Komparu school over precedence at the Kasuga Festival. He had his way, but two years later an even more violent dispute broke out, which aligned the Komparu, Kanze and Hōshō schools against the Kongō, forcing Kongō Ujimasa to yield. The Komparu and Kongō schools, though enemies on this occasion, generally resembled each other in their conservative style of performance. They were called *shimogakari*, which meant the style of Nara, in contrast to the *kamigakari*, or style of Kyoto, favored in Kyoto and practiced by the Kanze and Hōshō schools.

During the sixteenth century, Nō attained its greatest popularity with the general public, especially as performed by amateur actors. The imperial court, though poverty-stricken, was also devoted to Nō, but its tastes no longer swayed the actors. The scanty remaining evidence concerning Kyōgen in this period indicates that the farces had become established as an integral part of Nō programs, and that the texts, though still unrecorded, were gradually acquiring a fixed form, though improvisation had hitherto been the rule. Performances of Nō and Kyōgen by women were popular; they seem to have been received with equal enthusiasm in tragedy and comedy, suggesting that the audiences made little differentiation between Nō and Kyōgen, treating both with an irreverence which would have dismayed Zeami. New plays continued to be written, in response to a demand for novelty, but they failed to remain in the repertory. Despite its flourishing condition Nō had ceased to be a living dramatic form.

HIDEYOSHI AND NŌ

At the end of the sixteenth century Nō found a new patron in Toyotomi Hideyoshi (1536–1598), the self-made ruler of all Japan. After over a century of civil warfare, Hideyoshi succeeded in re-uniting the country and establishing an effective government. Once secure in his position, he felt he must prove that he was not culturally inferior to the nobles and priests; the best way, he decided, was to study Nō. He chose the Komparu school, probably under the influence of Shima-tsuma Shōshin (1551–1616), a priest and amateur actor who left some invaluable studies of Nō. Hideyoshi became passionately fond of the art, and other daimyos were obliged to study Nō in order to stay in Hideyoshi's good graces. In 1593, while Hideyoshi was in Kyushu waiting for the start of the invasion of Korea, he spent his time learning Nō, memorizing fifteen roles in the course of fifty days; before long he was confidently performing them before the public. On receiving word of the birth of his son, Hideyoshi hastily returned to Kyoto, and as part of the festivities himself performed for three days before the Emperor Go-Yōzei. Hideyoshi appeared in sixteen plays, including *Okina*, *Matsukaze*, and *Eguchi*. Tokugawa Ieyasu performed *Nonomiya*, and on the second day joined with Hideyoshi in a newly composed farce, *Kubihiki*.

Hideyoshi's passion for Nō reached its climax in 1594 when he performed at the imperial palace, not only in various classical works including *Sekidera Komachi*, the most difficult play of the entire repertory, but also in five new dramas written at Hideyoshi's order by his biographer Ōmura Yūko (d. 1596) to celebrate Hideyoshi's accomplishments. *Yoshino-mōde*, a "god" play, describes Hideyoshi's visit to the cherry blossoms of Yoshino. The *waki*, a courtier, explains at the beginning that Hideyoshi has ruled the country as he sees fit for three years and conquered Korea. Lately, moreover, he has won martial glory against the Chinese, desisting from warfare only at their earnest request. He has returned to the capital and built a great castle at Fushimi, and now has come to Yoshino to admire the cherry blossoms. In the second scene of the play the god of Yoshino appears and announces he will protect Hideyoshi on his return to the capital. *Shibata*, a warrior play, relates Hideyoshi's exploits in defeating Shibata Katsuie; the *shite*, the ghost of Shibata, describes how he triumphantly led his forces into Ōmi Province and seemed about to win a great battle when "Hideyoshi himself came riding up against us, and the tens of thousands on my side, slashed down by his sword, fled the field, unable to withstand him." The *shite* of *Kōya-mōde*, a "woman" play, is none other than Hideyoshi's mother. She appears first as a nun, but in the second scene reveals herself as a bodhisattva of song and dance, and informs us that she owes her salvation to the prayers of her filial son. Hideyoshi himself is the *shite* of *Akechi-uchi*, and the play concludes with a paean of praise for his martial prowess. *Hōjō* has virtually an identical plot. *Toyokuni-mōde*, written by another dramatist after Hideyoshi's death, is a fitting conclusion to the series of plays, presenting him as the god Toyokuni Daimyōjin. The *tsure* is Yūgeki, a Chinese general, who comes with tribute offerings for the god, declaring that Toyokuni Daimyōjin is worshiped not only in Japan but in China too.

The Nō plays written for Hideyoshi are typical of the man, but they suggest also the exuberance of the Momoyama period—the end of the sixteenth century—when Japan, after long years of warfare, enjoyed a rebirth of secular learning and pleasures. The military men threw themselves eagerly into cultural pursuits. The study of *The Tale of Genji* in particular developed into a craze, and Nō based on this novel (like *Aoi no Ue*) enjoyed the greatest popularity. The plays about Hideyoshi reflect his enormous pride in his cultural attainments. It would have been extraordinary in any theatre for an actor to perform as himself in a heroic drama, but the Nō theatre especially avoided any taint of contemporary realism; the dramas of Zeami and his successors were set in the past, either a remote, dateless antiquity or else the period of the twelfth-century wars. Hideyoshi's Nō plays describe events that had just occurred, pointing the way to the highly topical Kabuki and Bunraku plays of the seventeenth century.

We know of other startling changes in Nō from the letters of European missionaries in Japan at the time, who mention dramas on Biblical themes, apparently cast in the form of Nō. The addition of contemporary and foreign subjects and the use of dramatic forms which ignored the traditional division of parts into *shite* and *waki* and tended to make the chorus superfluous made it seem that Nō was about to break with the past and develop into a form of drama closer to that of Europe. In fact, however, precisely the opposite occurred.

TOKUGAWA NŌ

At the close of the sixteenth century the great cultural ferment created a demand for more theatrical entertainment. Two new forms of theatre, Kabuki and Bunraku, better suited to the general public than Nō, came into being and usurped the audiences from the older drama. There were hardly any benefit performances of Nō under Hideyoshi, a sure sign that it was fast becoming an upper-class entertainment, normally not open to the general public. After the death of Hideyoshi in 1598 the Nō actors were forced to look for new patrons. They turned not to the public but to Tokugawa Ieyasu. As soon as Ieyasu's castle in Edo (the modern Tokyo) was completed in 1606, the Kanze and Komparu troupes hurried to the scene, eager to perform for the Shogun. The Kongō and Hōshō schools followed the example, and in 1608 all four schools gave performances in the castle.

From this time on, Nō served as the official music of the Tokugawa regime. The shoguns, devoted to Confucian doctrines, considered rites and music to be essential elements of government, and just as *bugaku* had provided the ceremonial music for the emperor's court, the gravity and stately movements of Nō won favor at the shogun's court, which was run according to the decorum imposed by the Confucian code. The performances of Nō, especially at the New Year, were elaborate rituals believed to be capable of affecting the prosperity and welfare of the state. Skillful actors, because they contributed to the stability of the régime, were therefore provided with stipends in rice or money by the government and ranked as samurai. They lived far more luxuriously than most samurai because their incomes were frequently swelled by presents from the daimyos and other pupils. The gifts received after the first performances of the year might be so generous as to provide the leading actors with their living expenses for the entire year. However, the rulers were not only munificent patrons but exacting critics. They tolerated no idleness, let alone mistakes. An actor who committed a lapse during a festive performance was immediately and unsparingly punished; in extreme cases, actors were condemned to commit ritual disembowelment or were sent into exile for faulty performances. The severity of the punishments was not only inspired by aesthetic standards but by the belief that mistakes in the execution of the ritual music might lead to national calamity.

The outstanding actor of the early seventeenth century, Kita Shichidayū (1586–1653), had served Hideyoshi and fought against the Tokugawa at the battle of Osaka. So renowned was he as an actor, however, that his offense against the Tokugawa family was pardoned by the Shogun Hidetada. He was even granted permission to found a school of Nō bearing his name, the first new school since the time of Kannami. The Kita school, though derived from the Kongō, is still distinguished by its martial quality in performance. Shichidayū was by far the most popular actor at the shogun's court: in the year 1629 alone Hidetada requested him to appear in eleven special performances as against only one by another actor. In 1631, when Hidetada was stricken with a mortal illness, all five schools performed Nō by way of prayer for his recovery. The death of Hidetada deprived the Kita school of its protector, and the jealousy of the other schools threatened its existence. In 1634 Shichidayū's performance of *Sekidera Komachi* was denounced as being unorthodox and at variance with tradition, grave charges in a Confucian society. The Shogun Iemitsu, acting on the advice of the heads of the other schools, condemned Shichidayū to six months' imprisonment. He was released after special intercession in his behalf by the powerful daimyo Date Masamune, but seldom performed afterwards.

The shogun's government frequently showed its concern about Nō by directing admonitions to the actors. In 1647, for example, these commands were issued:

"Actors must not neglect the performing techniques handed down in the various schools. They should not indulge in inappropriate arts but devote themselves exclusively to preserving the traditions of their profession. They should in all things obey the directions of the head of the school; in the event of a lawsuit, they should request the head of the school to petition the authorities. Any misdemeanor on the part of the head should be reported at once to the authorities.

"On the occasion of command performances of *sarugaku*, the actors will be informed on the previous day. They should assemble at the residence of the head of the school, rehearse the works to be performed thoroughly, and make sure that there will be no mistakes on the following day.

"As repeatedly directed, actors should refrain from any display of luxury and should practice strict economy at all times. Their houses, clothing, food, etc. must be in keeping with their station and modest. Actors are forbidden to abandon their family careers and to learn the military or other arts unsuited to their station. . . .

"Actors should not accumulate unnecessary possessions beyond the costumes and equipment used in *sarugaku*.

"When invited to appear before nobles and other persons of quality they should not eat with their hosts.

"The Komparu school for generations has enjoyed renown. However, the present head of the school, though adult in years, in still immature as an artist. He should henceforth devote himself energetically to his art. Older actors of his school should help and guide him. Any further negligence on his part will be considered a misdemeanor."

It is hard to imagine any other government issuing an official edict of this nature, but the Tokugawa régime considered that it was just as important to its stability that actors perform the official music properly as for priests to offer prayers in an orthodox, acceptable manner. The necessary atmosphere of decorum and dignity implied a suitable magnificence of accoutrements, and the government, though insistent that actors refrain from luxury in their private lives, never prohibited extravagance in the Nō costumes, which became miracles of weaving and dyeing.

Initially, at least, the shogun's government welcomed the enthusiasm exhibited by the daimyos for Nō, preferring this peaceful avocation to warlike pursuits that might endanger the state. When the daimyos themselves began to perform Nō, however, the government felt obliged to issue admonitions, though appearing in Nō was obviously not as serious an offense as playing the samisen or singing popular songs. The daimyos continued to learn Nō without major interference. At the time of the revival of Nō in the late nineteenth century, several nobles ranking as daimyo appeared prominently in performances. Throughout the Tokugawa period, samurai of lesser rank were also active in Nō. Some performed at the Imperial Palace in Kyoto, where professional *sarugaku* actors were still treated as outcastes.

Nō was open to the general public from time to time in the form of benefit performances (*kanjin* Nō). In the Muromachi period such performances had genuinely been for the benefit of a temple or shrine, but in the Tokugawa period they came to be purely commercial ventures on the part of the actors. Most benefits required only the permission of the local magistrate, but there were also special "once-in-a-lifetime" benefits for outstanding actors, performances staged for the townsmen, who may have felt that attending Nō placed them higher up the social ladder than going to see Kabuki or Bunraku. In most respects these benefits were performed with the same degree of ceremonial as if before the shogun, but the press of the crowd was sometimes so intense that the stiff, formal holiday attire of the spectators was in danger of being ripped to shreds. Elderly people sent substitutes to hold their places, and these men, dressed in nondescript clothes, would cheerfully shout greetings to the shogun and other high officials when they arrived— "There's the chief!" "Best in Japan!" Such informality normally would have been unthinkable in the rigid society of Tokugawa Japan, but the theatre, like the gay quarters, was immune from the usual hierarchical demands, and the guards stationed inside the theatre made no attempt to suppress the rowdy spectators.

Because of the ritual nature of Nō during this period the repertory remained virtually static. Many plays were written, perhaps two thousand, but generally for a particular occasion and never repeated. None of the two hundred or more surviving plays of the period has been deemed worthy of a revival. The Tokugawa Nō plays, bound both in language and plots to the traditions of a departed age, are usually no more than pastiches of the mannerisms of Nō without any emotional involvement. The subjects were remote, the dramatists (unlike those of Hideyoshi's time) too timid to treat contemporary subjects. The best may actually be no inferior to some works in the current repertory, but the latter have at least the advantage of being genuine.

The elevation of Nō to the status of court ceremonial meant also that its dramatic appeal need no longer be considered. The dialogue, originally close to the tempo of speech, came to be pronounced in a deliberate, protracted manner, and the sung parts were delivered in muffled, almost unintelligible tones. The dances too were greatly prolonged, and moments when nothing occurred on the stage, save for an occasional beat of the drum and a strangled cry from the drummer, came to occupy as much as a quarter of the length of the play. The *monomane* elements were largely sacrificed. But, it may be argued, the slow, ritualistic presentation may have accorded better with Zeami's ideals than the livelier performances of his own day.

The extreme solemnity of Nō probably whetted the appetite of the spectators for Kyōgen as comic relief. During the Muromachi period Kyōgen was so unimportant that it was scarcely noticed by the diary writers who supplied detailed accounts of Nō; they treated the Kyōgen plays with the silent disdain of the learned film critic of today discussing a program of avant-garde masterpieces which happens to include a Donald Duck cartoon. During the Tokugawa period the Kyōgen actors ranked lowest among the performers associated with Nō, below the flutists and drummers, but thanks to the general patronage of the art as a ceremonial, Kyōgen acquired a measure of dignity. The texts were established for the first time and, inevitably it would seem, three distinct schools—Ōkura, Izumi and Sagi—insisted on their own versions. The new dignity did not destroy the humor of Kyōgen. On the contrary, a comparison of the oldest surviving texts with the definitive versions compiled later in the seventeenth century reveals that the comic features were sharpened and the satirical elements—the fun poked at pompous but foolish daimyos and the like—made more effective.

It may seem strange that the daimyos should not only have tolerated but enjoyed comedies in which they were the butt of the humor. Probably even in the Muromachi period they felt no class solidarity with the parvenu daimyos depicted so irreverently, finding them as absurd as the court of Louis XIV found the *petit marquis* of a Molière farce. In the Tokugawa period the members of the shogun's court could view with amusement and utter detachment the daimyo in *Kombu-uri* who, after forcing his servant to carry his sword, is compelled by the servant to sing like a peddler hawking his wares. It was inconceivable that any daimyo of the seventeenth century would be on terms of such familiarity with a servant.

The transcribing of the Kyōgen texts in the seventeenth century inhibited the improvisation which had always been part of its humor. It also petrified the humor: though far easier to understand than Nō, the language of Kyōgen had become archaic by the Tokugawa period and no longer could express effectively the amusing experiences of daily life. Most of the two hundred or so surviving Kyōgen plays depict Muromachi life, though revised versions of old works and, more rarely, new plays continued to be staged in the traditional manner.

The Kyōgen actors shared some of the glory surrounding Nō during the Tokugawa period. They had patrons among the daimyos and pupils even in the imperial court, but the comic relief they lent to a program must have been tolerated grudgingly by the sterner Confucianists of the court. The actors took their art extremely seriously, and if given less than due credit when they performed in the forbidding atmosphere of the shogun's presence, they came into their own before the crowds at a benefit performance.

The last and most spectacular of the gala benefits occurred in 1848, the "once-in-a-lifetime" performances given by the head of the Hōshō school. The shoguns, from the days of Yoshimitsu, had favored the Kanze school, but with the eleventh shogun, Ienari (1773–1841), the Hōshō school gained preference, and subsequent shoguns continued this patronage. Permission was granted to Hōshō Yagorō to stage benefit performances on fifteen clear days. The series began on March 6, 1848 but did not reach the fifteenth day until June 13, the rainy spring having interfered with the outdoor performances. An elaborate theatre seating five thousand spectators was constructed in Edo. The audiences consisted of an extraordinarily varied cross-section of Japanese society. The gentry and their wives paid three pieces of silver for the privilege of sitting in upstairs boxes protected from the public gaze by curtains of purple silk dyed with their family crests. The commoners paid two pieces of silver to sit below; but even upstairs, in locations with poor views of the stage, townsmen sat crosslegged in breeches and striped cloaks alongside country bumpkins in cotton kimonos and old women wearing aprons. The audience was at liberty to drink saké, but keeping one's head covered or stripping to one's underwear was strictly prohibited. The crowd downstairs included low-ranking samurai, lady shampooers, Confucian scholars, doctors, fortune-tellers, Shinto priests, poets and many others, all jammed together indiscriminately. Upstairs, the daimyos and their consorts observed the plays "set out in a row, like a display of penny dolls."

The audience was by no means respectful. When Hōshō Yagorō made his entrance, instead of the solemn silence we expect today there were cries of, "Here's the man from Hatago!" (the quarter of Edo where Yagorō lived), and when the actors left the stage at the end of the play they were encouraged by shouts of, "Thanks for your trouble!" The spectators directed comments not only at the actors but at the gentry upstairs. No matter how interesting the Nō or Kyōgen in progress, the arrivals and departures of ladies of quality were greeted with a barrage of wisecracks, sometimes of a decidedly improper nature. A contemporary account relates, "The tumult inside the theatre was indescribable. Everyone was making so much noise all at once that it was impossible to understand what was being said." Clearly, the audience was enjoying not only the plays but the rare opportunity to give vent to their high spirits in the presence of the grandees of the country. The actors no doubt found it a strain to perform before such spectators, but they endured the discomfort, remembering that the purpose of the benefit performances was to make money. In this they succeeded admirably. Enterprising merchants also seized the opportunity to profit by the crowds; concessions were given out for tea, saké, *sushi*, cushions, and even for the disposal of waste matter in the public toilets. Hōshō Yagorō earned twenty thousand *ryō*, and the government itself considered the event of such importance that the reign-name was changed to Kaei ("celebration of eternity") in commemoration.

The benefit performances each day consisted of *Okina*, one Nō from each of the five categories, a final, congratulatory Nō, and five Kyōgen. Hōshō Kurō, who was to emerge as the leading actor of the Meiji period, appeared as the *shite* on each day of the series, though only a boy of eleven in

1848. He succeeded as head of the school in 1853, the year that Commodore Perry's ships arrived off Edo, and performed at New Year both in 1854 for the Shogun Ieshige and in 1858 for his successor Iemochi. These were the last command performances of the shogunate, though Hōshō Kurō continued until 1861 to appear occasionally on the stage inside the castle.

MEIJI NŌ

Nō had been associated with the shogunate ever since the days of Yoshimitsu. With the overthrow of the shogunate in 1868 the actors were forced to decide whether to remain loyal to their old masters, now retired to Shizuoka, or to profess allegiance to the imperial government. Whichever course they might choose, there seemed little chance of ever performing again. Nō, like the Tokugawa régime which had so long supported it, was now in disgrace. Most actors gave up their profession, some to become farmers or shopkeepers, others to work with their hands. A few actors, notably Umewaka Minoru in Tokyo, struggled to preserve Nō. People were suspicious of Minoru, but he persisted, performing on a makeshift stage until he could secure a better one. Minoru with great difficulty persuaded Hōshō Kurō to revoke his decision of 1871 to retire from the stage and become a farmer. Kurō, an exceedingly cautious man who was hypersensitive about his dignity, finally consented in 1875 to appear on Minoru's stage when he realized that even under the new régime, with its passion for novelty and foreign things, there were still people capable of appreciating his art.

The subsequent revival of Nō, at a time when most old traditions were summarily rejected, was paradoxically due to the desire to emulate Western countries in offering suitably dignified entertainments on state occasions. The first performances of Nō after the Restoration were held in 1869 in honor of the visit of the Duke of Edinburgh. The Duke had to be entertained, but Kabuki was judged to be too vulgar for so exalted a guest, and Nō (despite its being in disgrace) was chosen instead. When Iwakura Tomomi, a court noble and high-ranking officer of the new government, visited Europe and America in 1871 he noticed similarities between Nō and opera, the usual entertainment provided state visitors abroad. A member of Iwakura's party commented, "I was never interested in Nō until I saw historical dramas abroad and thought how much they resembled Nō." The turning point in the modern history of Nō occurred on April 4, 1876, when the Emperor Meiji paid a visit to Iwakura Tomomi's residence and witnessed a program of Nō. Iwakura had decided, in the light of his experiences in Europe, that Nō was the appropriate entertainment to offer his sovereign. Performances for the Emperor were followed by another program intended for the Empress and the Empress Dowager, and a further program for the imperial princes and princesses. Umewaka Minoru, who had been entrusted with the performances, was able to find room for Hōshō Kurō in the program, though this had not originally been planned. His determination to draw Kurō back to the stage succeeded, and the collaboration of these two great actors made possible the revival of Nō.

The patronage of the imperial family protected Nō from any criticism of its association with the discredited shogunate. In the past, when the court was still in Kyoto, imperial approval had eagerly been sought by actors though it did not benefit them financially. The Emperor Kōmei, Meiji's father, had been especially fond of Nō and Kyōgen, but the actors who performed for him were rewarded not with robes or gifts of money, but with tastefully costumed little dolls. The Emperor Meiji's mother, the Empress Dowager Eishō (1833–1897), became after the Restoration the chief patron of Nō. In 1878 Meiji built for her pleasure a stage in the Aoyama Palace. Hōshō Kurō in later years described his experience at the inaugural performance: "I was to perform by command the difficult role of *Dōjōji*. The date for the opening had already been set when Ōkubo, the Minister of the Interior, was assassinated, and the inauguration of the stage was consequently delayed several times, finally being set for the fifth of July. I was in a state of extreme agitation for the weather was naturally very hot at that time of year and the role was demanding . . . When

I appeared on the stage I could see the Emperor's seat, but the heat and the demands of the role made me forget everything else. By the time I reached the *rambyōshi* section I had forgotten even the heat. At last came the interval, when I entered the bell. Once inside, I breathed a sigh of relief, only to begin feeling dizzy in the oppressive sultriness. I started to change my costume, wiping with a towel the waterfall of sweat pouring from me, when I discovered that someone had thoughtfully left a fan inside the bell. I used it to stir up a little breeze, put on my robes, turned myself into a serpent, and appeared once again on the stage." The performance, which lasted for nine hours, was judged an eminent success.

The visit of General Grant, the former President of the United States, in the summer of 1879 again provided an occasion for the presentation of Nō to a foreign visitor. Grant was the first head (or former head) of a foreign country ever to visit Japan, and the Japanese were understandably worried about how to entertain him. Grant, in the end, was treated to both Nō and Kabuki. At the conclusion of the Nō he witnessed at Iwakura's residence Grant is reported to have said, "So noble and beautiful an art is easily cheapened and destroyed by the changing tastes of the times. You must make efforts to preserve it." It is difficult to imagine the grizzled old soldier Grant being so powerfully impressed by the remote beauty of Nō, even with the assistance of the translation hastily prepared for the occasion, but his words were taken to heart by Iwakura, who decided that an organization was needed for the preservation of Nō. The Nō Society (*Nōgakusha*) which he founded built the first permanent Nō stage for the general public. In April, 1881, in the presence of the Empress Dowager and two hundred of the highest ranking nobles, the stage in Shiba Park was officially opened. On the third day, when the general public was admitted, over seven hundred persons attended. Umewaka Minoru's son (later known also as Umewaka Minoru) recollected his first stage appearance at the time, when he was four years old. "I was only a child and had no impressions worth mentioning, but I can still remember how beautiful everything seemed. On one side sat the Empress Dowager Eishō, her long hair hanging over her kimono, wearing a scarlet *hakama*, and with her were more than twenty court ladies, all in the same costume, sitting in a row. On the other side was the Empress Shōken. She and her attendants were all in Western costume, looking so beautiful they almost blinded me."

Public performances of Nō became frequent. The five schools, which had gladly appeared on the same stage in Shiba Park when their fortunes were low, before long found the financial support to build theatres for their exclusive use, and the differences between the various schools, which had not been so great as to prevent Umewaka Minoru of the Kanze school from appearing with Hōshō Kurō of the Hōshō school or Sakurama Bamba of the Komparu school, the third great actor of the period, from appearing on the Hōshō stage, were exaggerated. Rivalry over pupils, essential now that the government gave no direct support, further accentuated the differences. The Kanze school, the richest and most important, attracted a disproportionate number of students, perhaps sixty percent of the total, followed by Hōshō with another twenty percent or so; the remaining ten percent was divided among Komparu, Kongō and Kita, small schools whose existence at times has been threatened by the preference for more fashionable styles of Nō. Even the small schools, however, have produced outstanding performers such as Sakurama Kintarō (Komparu), Kongō Iwao (Kongō), and Kita Roppeita (Kita).

NŌ IN RECENT TIMES

The popularity of Nō continued to grow after the death or retirement of the great actors of the Meiji era, confounding the many prophets who had predicted that the younger generation would not respond to so outdated an art as Nō. Like other forms of traditional drama, Nō was favored by the wartime governments, anxious to foster belief in the importance of "pure" Japanese culture uncontaminated by foreign influences. New plays of a patriotic nature, like *Miikusabune* ("Imperial Warship") were composed and widely performed between 1942 and 1945, but quickly forgotten. Almost all the Nō stages in Tokyo were destroyed in 1945 by bombing, and for a time immediately afterwards all schools shared the one remaining stage, under conditions reminiscent of the early Meiji period. Renewed prosperity enabled most schools to build their own stages again.

Nō is today supported chiefly by people living in all parts of the country who study the singing, but not the performance, of the texts. The tuition fees they pay make it possible for Nō to be presented in the theatres, and when they visit Tokyo they naturally wish to see the plays they have learned by heart. We can judge how much they influence the programs from the fact that between 1949 and 1960 the Kanze school performed *Funa Benkei* 208 times and *Hagoromo* 193 times, though some masterpieces were seldom staged. *Teika* was performed only twenty-seven times, *Koi no Omoni* and *Eguchi* thirty-five times.

Performances by amateurs who have mastered the roles are also common and include some by women. Although no formal prohibition was placed on women appearing in Nō in the seventeenth century, when Kabuki was deprived of its actresses, they disappeared from the stage, and today people generally consider their voices and figures totally inadequate for even the most feminine roles. Nevertheless, women persist in their studies, and some day they may achieve recognition.

The study of Nō as a literary and theatrical art dates mainly from the Meiji period when such scholars as Yoshida Tōgo (1864–1918) discovered the texts of Zeami's criticism and other essential documents. Only since the 1930's, however, have truly scientific studies taken the place of the aimless compilation of facts or recollections which previously passed for criticism. The secrecy with which texts are still surrounded by some Nō masters has impeded basic research into the evolution of the texts, but this situation cannot long persist.

Performances today are at a high level. It is true that in some details the standards of the past cannot be equalled; for example, it has become prohibitively expensive to replace the covering of the drums for each performance, the practice in former days. Again, the actors' preference for the Western haircut means that sometimes in roles without masks they look incongruously modern. But these are minor flaws when compared to the devotion and scholarly attention which the roles receive. The reverent hush in the Nō theatre, as we have seen, is a relatively recent phenomenon. Certainly the manner of enjoying Nō must have been different when people brought food and drink to their boxes and divided their attention between the stage and their stomachs. Some today regret the changes, recalling wistfully easier-going days, but artistically they would seem to be in the right direction, pointing to a return to the ideals of Zeami and, indeed, to the solemn beginnings of Nō.

III. NŌ AND KYŌGEN AS LITERATURE

THE TEXTS of the Nō plays have often been likened to brocade woven of brilliant bits of silk to form a magnificent fabric, a simile which suggests how liberally the texts were embellished with scraps from the literature of the past. The *tanka*, the classic verse form, in particular gave the poetry of Nō its distinctive tone. Ever since the tenth century, when the anthology *Kokinshū* ("Collection of Ancient and Modern Poetry") was compiled, the *tanka* had been revered as the noblest form of Japanese poetry, and a thorough knowledge of the *tanka* in the dozen imperial anthologies was assumed of educated men. Zeami urged aspiring Nō actors not to dissipate their talents on other arts, but he made an exception for the *tanka*, the source of so much beauty in the Nō.

The *tanka* had even been credited with supernatural powers. The preface to the *Kokinshū* asserts that the *tanka* can move the gods and demons. We find echoes of this belief in the plays. The central theme of *Shiga* is that the *tanka* promotes the security and happiness of the people because it enjoys the protection of the gods and Buddhas. In *Utaura* a knowledge of the *tanka* is declared to be a means of knowing the future, for poetry reflects the minds of the gods. Zeami often quoted famous *tanka*, sometimes a whole poem, sometimes only a verse or two, confident that his audience would catch the allusions. Quotation of the old *tanka* not only confirmed the mood of a scene by its reference to similar feelings described in the past, but enhanced the text with the magical aura of divinely-favored words.

The bits of silk making up the brocade of the texts did not consist entirely of *tanka*. The play *Atsumori*, for example, quotes not only four *tanka* but phrases from the preface to *Kokinshū*, poems in Chinese by Po Chü-i and others, Buddhist works, *The Tale of Genji* and, above all, *The Tale of the Heike*, the thirteenth-century novel which inspired the play. The number of quotations should not suggest that *Atsumori* is a mere tissue of allusions, a pastiche composed of famous tags from the old classics. Only a small part of the text can be traced to earlier literature, and even these borrowings usually consist of a few key words rather than extended passages. The texts are original works given added depth and complexity by the use of quotations and allusions.

Zeami in his critical writings was concerned mainly with analysis of the art of acting, but he also mentioned on occasion his conviction that the texts themselves were of paramount importance. Unquestionably he took enormous pains with the literary effects of his plays. Zeami's style is marked not only by his reliance on quotations from literary works but by extraordinary complexity in the expression, far beyond the requirements of the theatre. Zeami's use of wordplays, especially the *kakekotoba* or "pivot word," which shifts in meaning depending on the words preceding and following, was another aspect of his constant attempt to supply additional layers of meaning to his words. Zeami did not invent the *kakekotoba*, but he used it with greater effect than any of his predecessors. This passage from *Hanjo* by Zeami contains four *kakekotoba*:

> YOSHIDA: *konata ni mo*   I too have a keepsake
>
> *wasuregatami no*   Impossible to forget:

	koto no ha wo	The words we spoke.
	Iwade *no mori no*	But if, like azaleas hidden
	shita tsutsuji	In the silent wood of Iwade,
	iro ni idezu wa	You do not speak,
	sore zo to mo	You show nothing in your face,
	mite koso shirame	How am I to understand?
	kono ōgi	Seeing it, I shall know:
		Your fan.
HANJO:	*mite wa sate*	Seeing it?
	nani no tame zo to	What use would that be?
	yūgure *no*	What good can it do
	tsuki wo idaseru	Importuning me so
	ōgi no e no	For a fan with a picture
	kaku *bakari*	Painted to reveal
	nani no tame naruran	The twilight moon?

In this passage Yoshida asks the courtesan Hanjo for the fan he gave her as a pledge of his love, a fan showing the moon at twilight. The translation resorts to double meanings for the *kakekotoba*, but it is unfortunately impossible to suggest in English the force of the Japanese puns. *Wasuregata* means "difficult to forget" with the preceding phrase, but the added syllable *mi* yields another word *katami* ("keepsake") when used with the next phrase. Similarly, *iwade* with the preceding phrase means "not speaking," but with the following phrase is the proper noun Iwade, the name of a forest. *Yū* means "to say," but the suffix *gure* forms the word *yūgure* (twilight). *Kaku* means "to paint" but also "so." Each wordplay enriches the texture with relevant meanings, and affords a compression parallel to the economy of the Nō theatre itself; it is like a magnificently attired actor moving in intricate patterns against the starkly austere setting.

Another feature of Zeami's style is his use of *engo*, or "related words." *Engo* are words chosen from among possible synonyms for their overtones, with the intent of creating a unity of echoes even when the surface meanings are seemingly unrelated. A similar use of language can be found, say, in the thirtieth sonnet of Shakespeare:

> When to the *sessions* of sweet silent thought
> I *summon* up remembrance of things past . . .

Although the main theme is grief over the passage of time, the pervading echoes are those of the courtroom. In Nō the underlying imagery may give a unity to the text: in *Hachinoki* the dominant images are related to snow and purity; in *Obasute* to the moon; in *Eguchi* to a river. The use of this unifying imagery makes it far easier for the Nō actor, with the limited means of representation at his disposal, to project the essential mood of a play.

The most impressive feature of Zeami's style is the power of the imagery. The art of Nō demands a transformation of violent and jagged emotions into a prescribed, unruffled form. In this respect it may remind us of the tragedies of Racine; the surface elegance is broken only occasionally, but those moments stand out with electrifying intensity. Zeami's most powerful work, *Kinuta*, is dominated by the hollow sound of clothes being beaten on a fulling block, evoking the loneliness of long autumn nights. The woman in the play, incensed at her husband's failure to return to her, calls for a fulling block on which to pound out her grief:

inga no mōshū	Tears of remembrance
omoi no namida	For sins committed
kinuta ni kakareba	Fall on the fulling block;
namida wa kaette	The tears turn to flames,
kaen to natte	And choked by the smoke

mune no kemuri no	Of the fire in my breast,
honō ni musebeba	I shriek, but my voice
sakedo koe ga	Does not escape my lips.
ideba koso	The fulling block is soundless,
kinuta mo koe naku	The pine wind too, unheard . . .
matsukaze mo kikoezu	Only the shouts of hell's tormentors,
kashaku no koe no mi	Horrible their cries!
osoroshiya	

In this passage Zeami used with superb effect the Buddhist terms *inga* ("cause and effect"), *mōshū* ("deep-rooted delusion"), *kaen* ("flames"), and *kashaku* ("tormentors"), words that not only possess powerful religious overtones but by their very sounds, unlike the softer syllables of pure Japanese, give sharp contours to the lines. The intensity of the imagery—tears that turn into flames, mute shrieks of anguish, the cries of the fiends of hell—imprints the passage with the controlled violence of Nō at its most dramatic.

A whole play could not, of course, be maintained at this level. Sections are in prose, declaimed in a conventionally stylized manner; most sentences end with the mournfully prolonged vowels of the copula verb *sōrō*. Other sections, though in poetry, are in a low key, conforming to the prescription that the *jo* section of a play be slow and serene. The structural requirements of the plays, as established by Zeami himself, also tend to confine the poetry of greatest intensity to a few sections, generally at the close of the *ha* division of the work.

An analysis of a typical play of the *waki* (first) category, *Takasago*, by Zeami, may illustrate the structure and the uses of different kinds of poetry.

The play opens as the *waki*, a Shinto priest, embarks with his companions on a journey. They sing the *shidai*, a passage in three lines of 7+5, 7+5, and 7+4 syllables, the first two lines being identical:

ima wo hajime no	*tabigoromo*	Now first we wear our travel robes,
ima wo hajime no	*tabigoromo*	Now first we wear our travel robes,
hi mo yuku sue zo	*hisashiki*	How long are the days of travel ahead.

After singing this passage the *waki* speaks the *nanori*, a passage in prose identifying himself, and relates his intention of making a journey. He and his companions now sing the *michiyuki* (travel song) in seven or eight lines of 5, 7+5 syllables, etc., ending with the statement of their arrival at Takasago. The poetry is in the restrained tone appropriate to the *jo* section, which concludes at this point.

The *ha* section opens with the appearance of the *shite* and *tsure*, an old man and an old woman. Their entrance song, known as the *issei*, consists of lines in 5, 7+5, and 7+5 syllables.

takasago no	At Takasago
matsu no harukaze fukikurete	A spring breeze in the pines blows as dusk falls,
onoe no kane mo hibiku naru	And the temple bell on the peak echoes the close of day.

Next come passages known as *ninoku* (second stanza) and *sannoku* (third stanza), each a line in 7+5 syllables:

nami wa kasumi no isogakure	The waves are hidden at the misty beach,
oto koso shio no michihi nare	Their sound tells of the ebb and flow of the tide.

The scene having been set, the *shite* describes his situation in the *sashi*, usually a passage in about ten lines of 7+5 syllables each:

tare wo ka mo	Whom shall I take

shiru hito ni sen takasago no	As my friend? Even the pine
matsu mo mukashi no tomo narade	Of Takasago is not a friend of old;
sugikoshi yo yo wa shirayuki no	The years on years I have lived through
	are forgotten, but the snows
tsumori tsumorite oi no tsuru no	Keep piling, piling; the aged crane
negura ni nokoru ariyake no	In his nest, a spring moon lingering
haru no shimoyo no okii ni mo	In the frosty dawn, awakens:
matsukaze wo no mi kikinarete	I hear nothing but the familiar pine wind,
kokoro wo tomo to sugamushiro	But making its song my friend, as I lie
	on my rush mat,
omoi wo noburu bakari nari	I tell my griefs, my only solace.

Apart from the extra line in five syllables, a common variation, this *sashi* is quite regular. But what complications are involved in the poetry! The passage opens with a *tanka* from an imperial collection, quoted in a slightly altered form: "Whom shall I make my friend? Even the pine of Takasago is not a friend of old." The next line contains a *kakekotoba*, *shirayuki*, meaning "I do not know" (or "do not remember") with what precedes, but "white snow" with the following words *tsumori tsumorite* ("piling, piling"), alluding to the white hair of the speaker, so old that he no longer has any friends and has even forgotten the past. "The aged crane" is used metaphorically for an old person, but leads also to "nest." These different images coalesce: piled-up snow lies in the nest of the aged crane; the aged crane wakes in a nest lit by the moon lingering in the frosty sky of a spring dawn; the crane becomes a metaphor for the old man who, wakening at night, hears the wind through the pines and makes this poetic sound his friend; and finally, the old man is comforted by expressing his grief in poetry.

Granted that some in the audience could follow these complexities, most spectators probably caught no more than the general drift. The clusters of images, blending imprecisely in their minds, produced an impression of beauty.

Takasago is a calmly majestic play, suitable to the category of god plays. The *sashi*, which occurs at the opening of the *ha* section, was not the place for displaying powerful emotions; nevertheless, Zeami's poetry builds a gradual intensification of interest. The first part of the *ha* section concludes with the singing of the *sageuta* (three or four lines of 5, 7+5, 7+5 syllables) and the *ageuta* (up to ten units of 7+5 syllables). At this point the *shite* encounters the *waki* for the first time.

The second part of the *ha* section begins with exchanges of dialogue in prose between the *shite* and *waki* about the Takasago Pine. The prose rises into poetry that continues the dialogue. Now the chorus enters for the first time, singing a passage in nine lines. This *ageuta*, often sung on auspicious occasions, begins:

shikai nami shizuka ni te	The waves of the four seas are calm,
kuni mo osamaru toki tsu kaze	The land at peace; favorable winds
eda wo narasanu mi yo nareya	Disturb not the branches in this holy era . . .

The third part of the *ha* section, the central episode of the whole play, describes the glory of pines and of poetry. It begins with the *kuri*, a short passage in no fixed meter. A *sashi* follows, also in free rhythms, and then the *kuse*, a long section describing how each sight of nature inspires poetry. All three passages are sung by the chorus with occasional interpellations from the *shite*. The irregularity of the meter reflects the importance of the music and dance in this part.

The *kuse* is followed by the *rongi*, a dialogue between chorus and *shite* in regular meter, terminating with the *shite*'s departure from the stage. A Kyōgen actor, identified as "a man of the place," appears, and after a few brief exchanges with the *waki*, recites the history of the Pine of Takasago. In some plays the *ai* section merely repeats in simpler language information already given; probably it was necessary for spectators who failed to understand the plot from the difficult sung passages.

After the *ai* is completed, the *kyū* section of the play begins. Usually this occupies only a page or two in print, but in performance it often takes twenty or more minutes mainly because it contains the final dance of the *shite*. The *kyū* section usually (but not in *Takasago*) begins with the *waki*'s song of waiting, seven or eight lines in 5, 7+5, 7+5 meter, followed by the second appearance of the *shite* to a *sashi* of three lines in 5, 7+5, 7+5 syllables. In *Takasago* the *shite* reveals himself as being in reality the god of the Sumiyoshi Shrine. Next ensues a dialogue between *shite* and chorus on the miraculous nature of the god, followed by the *shimai*, the final dance. A last *rongi* (dialogue) between *shite* and chorus, generally in about fifteen lines, ends most plays; in *Takasago* it is an expression of awe and delight over the revelation of the god Sumiyoshi.

Hardly a single play fits this formula exactly. Zeami himself cited *Yumi Yawata* as a model work, attributing its regularity to its sacred character. But even though the elements of most plays are somewhat at variance with the ideal pattern, perhaps to avoid monotony, their overall construction generally corresponds closely to that of *Takasago*.

Plays of the first category are the least rewarding dramatically. *Takasago* is one of the most interesting examples; a more typical work, like *Shirahige*, requires the *shite* to sit motionless in the middle of the stage through most of the performance as the chorus recites events associated with a shrine.

Plays of the second category, the warrior plays, are distinctly more dramatic. Because they belong to the slow section of the program, they do not approach the violence or emotional intensity of plays about warriors presented later in the program; of the sixteen *shuramono* (warrior plays) in the current repertory, thirteen are by Zeami, a sure indication that these plays are more likely to be poetic than realistic depictions of martial deeds.

Many warrior plays were derived from *The Tale of the Heike*, that repository of stirring or pathetic incidents from the wars between the Taira and the Minamoto. Zeami declared in his critical writings that texts based on this work must be faithful to the original, but his own are free, not only in language but in emphasis. *Atsumori*, for example, retains little of the original dramatic tension; the source is in fact more theatrical than the play. In *The Tale of the Heike* we are told how the Minamoto captain Kumagai challenges a fleeing enemy general to an encounter. They fight, and Kumagai fells his opponent. Tearing off the man's helmet, he discovers a boy of sixteen, a noble, and decides to spare his life, remembering how grieved he had been that day when his own son, also sixteen, was wounded. In polite, almost deferential language, Kumagai asks the boy his name, but the boy insolently recommends that Kumagai show his severed head to men on his side. The superbly dramatic dialogue is broken by the approach of other Minamoto soldiers. Kumagai, resigned now to killing Atsumori, the young man, promises to pray for his repose. He kills the boy and strips his armor, only to find a flute, a further reminder of the boy's aristocratic lineage. In the end Kumagai abandons his career as a soldier to become a priest.

In the play *Atsumori*, Kumagai appears as the *waki*, the priest Renshō. He tells of his intention to pray for Atsumori's repose at Ichinotani, the site of the Heike defeat. There he encounters some reapers and hears one play a flute. This reaper remains after the others go and tells the priest that he is of Atsumori's family. After the interlude the young man reappears as a ghost in armor, this time identifying himself as Atsumori. He relates the disasters that struck the Taira family, and recalls how he played his flute the night before the battle. Finally he relives his mortal struggle with Kumagai, but at the moment that he raises his sword to strike, in the gesture of a *shura*, a still resentful ghost, he sees that the priest Renshō is praying for his salvation. "Pray for me again, oh, pray for me again," are the concluding words of the play.

Comparing the two stories we see that almost every element of pathos or drama in *The Tale of the Heike* has been deleted from the play. Atsumori's youth, his resemblance to Kumagai's son, his insolence in response to Kumagai's solicitude, Kumagai's regret when forced to kill Atsumori—all are eliminated, leaving only the story of a man unable to forget his defeat at an enemy's hands.

Of course, the audience was familiar with the story as told in *The Tale of the Heike*, but Zeami's play does not depend on this knowledge; instead, he chose to delete everything particular about the two men in the interests of achieving a stylized, universal tragedy. One man kills another; by this act he brings salvation to both. Kumagai's remorse over killing Atsumori leads to his taking Buddhist orders, and this act in turn ultimately brings Atsumori salvation. The attention of the author of *The Tale of the Heike* was focused on the dramatic contrasts between the two men: the grizzled warrior and the boy-soldier, the rough frontiersman and the flute-playing aristocrat, the compassionate old man and the insolent youth. In the play, however, the central theme is Atsumori's release from the torment of being a *shura*. His ghost has lingered on earth in the guise of a reaper because, unable to attain salvation, his attachment to the world makes him relive again and again the moments of his final battle. Only his flute, the symbol of his youth and noble aspirations, brings solace to this tortured spirit. When Renshō promises the unknown reaper to pray for his soul, Atsumori appears in his true form. He repeats the motions of his mortal encounter with Kumagai, raising his sword with the cry, "Here is my enemy!" But at that moment he is saved. He cries, "We shall be reborn on the same lotus!"

Zeami chose not to dwell on the contrasts found in *The Tale of the Heike*. Atsumori's inability to renounce his memories of this world does not stem from his youth, his courtly accomplishments or his pride; only when he recognizes that Renshō is not his enemy can he be saved. The play, though telling of warriors, neither glorifies nor condemns the military life. Zeami wrote that plays dealing with soldiers of the Heike wars must be elegant: "In plays of this type especially, a brilliance of effect is desirable." In *Atsumori* the boy's youthful beauty and the music of his flute impart *yūgen*, as in *Tsunemasa* the music of the *biwa* or in *Tadanori* the cherry blossoms on the strand of Suma give a haunting beauty to the stories of defeated warriors. The more powerful *Kanehira*, on the other hand, has little of this quality:

hakujin hone wo	Horror of naked blades
kudaku kurushimi	Smashing on bone,
gansei wo yaburi	Scenes of eyes gouged out,
kōha tate wo nagasu yosōi	And shields floating on crimson waves
yanagui ni	Like scattered blossoms
zanka wo midasu	Breaking against a weir.*

Kanehira belongs to the world of the *shura*; the characters are proud of their hours of glory and need no priest to pray for their salvation. *Kanehira* is more exciting than *Atsumori*, but it fits poorly into the *jo* section of a program, and its lack of *yūgen* suggests that Zeami, despite traditional attributions, was not the author.

Plays of the third category, the woman plays, contain the most beautiful poetry. Love, when treated in this category, has a bittersweet fragrance, though apt in plays of the fourth category to be an obsession powerful enough to derange a woman. The story of Lady Rokujō, derived from *The Tale of Genji*, is described touchingly in the third-category play *Nonomiya*, where we see her at a lonely shrine in the fields awaiting her last meeting with Genji; in the fourth-category play *Aoi no Ue*, Rokujō's love for Genji is depicted as the demonic instrument of the death of Aoi, Genji's wife. The poetry in each case creates the mood. In *Nonomiya* we find:

nonomiya no	My carriage is bright
aki no chigusa no	With the thousand autumn grasses
hanaguruma	Of the Shrine in the Fields.
ware mo mukashi ni	The wheels turn; I too
meguri kinikeri	Have returned to the past.

The hollow sound of the drum accompanying the poetry suggests with unspeakable pathos the autumn, season of memories. When Rokujō, passing under the *torii*, the boundary between life

*Translation by Stanleigh H. Jones

and death, disappears, perhaps at last to gain release from the love of Genji which binds her still to the world of the living, we sense almost painfully the lonely, mysterious beauty of *yūgen:*

nonomiya no	Even the moon
tsuki mo mukashi ya	At the Shrine in the Fields
omouran	Must remember the past;
kage samishiku mo	Its light forlornly trickles
mori no shitatsuyu	Through the leaves to the forest dew,
mori no shitatsuyu	Through the leaves to the forest dew.
mi no okidokoro mo	This place, once my refuge,
aware mukashi no	This garden, still lingers
niwa no tatazumai	Unchanged from long ago,
yoso ni zo kawaru	A beauty nowhere else,
keshiki mo kari naru	Though transient, insubstantial
koshibagaki	As this little wooden fence
tsuyu uchiharai	From which he used to brush the dew.
towareshi ware mo	I, whom he visited,
sono hito mo	And he, my lover too,
tada yume no yo to	The whole world have turned to dreams,
furiyuku ato ni	To aging ruins;
tare matsu	Whom should I pine for now?
mushi no ne wa	The voices of pine-crickets
rin rin toshite	Trill *rin, rin,*
kaze bōbō taru	The wind howls:
nonomiya no yosugara	How I remember
natsukashiya	Nights at the Shrine in the Fields!

The sin of attachment, which draws ghosts back to memories they cannot relinquish, is most affectingly evoked in the woman plays, where the memories are not of vengeance, but of love. In *Izutsu,* Ariwara no Narihira's childhood sweetheart recalls their early happiness together, contrasting those days with his later deceit. She puts on Narihira's court robe and cap and, going to the well-curb *(izutsu)* where as children she and Narihira compared heights, looks at her reflection in the water.

mireba natsukashiya	She looks—how sweet the memory,
warenagara natsukashiya	Sweet the memory, though of herself,
bōfū hakurei no sugata wa	This ghost in her dead husband's form:
shibomeru hana no	A withered flower,
iro nōte	Color vanished,
nioi nokorite	Perfume only lingering.
Ariwara no tera no kane mo	The bell of the Ariwara Temple too
honobono to akureba	Tolls dimly in the dawning.
furudera no	Over the old temple,
matsukaze ya	The wind through the pines,
bashōba no	The rustle of plantain leaves,
yume mo yaburete	Broken easily as dreams;
samenikeri	Awakened,
yume wa yabure	The dream is broken,
akenikeri	The day has dawned.

The texts are replete with ingenuity—plays on words, thoughts that shift in direction, sounds echoed from one line to the next, adjectives modifying both the word they follow and the word they precede—but they do not represent virtuosity for its own sake; the complexity should suggest the shifting flow of thoughts of the characters themselves. The poignancy achieved in the poetry, rather than any display of femininity in performance, gives the woman plays their heart-breaking beauty.

The fourth category includes the widest variety of works, ranging from plays hardly distinguishable from the poetic dramas of the third category to realistic plays almost devoid of poetry. *Hagoromo*, which tells of a goddess who must perform a celestial dance as the price of a fisherman's returning her robe of feathers, is sometimes classed in the fourth category, presumably because the presence of the fisherman lends a realistic note, but it by no means resembles the bulk of the *genzaimono*, or contemporary plays. *Jinen Koji* by Kannami, an early *genzaimono*, tells of a girl who has sold herself to white slavers so that she can make an offering to the memory of her dead parents. The priest Jinen Koji, discovering what has happened, rushes after her, arriving at the shore of Lake Biwa just as the men are rowing off their boat, with the girl lying in the bottom, bound and gagged. Jinen induces the men to return the girl, but in exchange they demand that he perform the songs and dances for which he is famous. The one thing common to *Hagoromo* and *Jinen Koji* (and to many other plays of the fourth category) is that the dances are identified in the play as such, and are not heightened, abstract expressions of the emotions described in the poetry.

Another important group of plays belonging to the fourth category are those dealing with mad persons. "Madness," however, is by no means uncontrolled lunacy; it embraces such emotions as the overpowering grief of the mother in *Sumidagawa* who searches the country for her kidnapped child, or the jealous despair of the woman in *Kinuta* who fears that her husband has deserted her. These women are obsessed rather than mad, but "madness" in Zeami's day, like the divine madness of the Greeks, was associated with poetry and music; the other characters in *Sumidagawa* ask the distraught mother to display her madness, as if excess of grief had made her entertaining.

Plays of the fourth category usually recount a story rather than attempt to create a poetic atmosphere. Audiences have always responded more readily to such works than to those of more remote beauty, and as a group they are highly popular. *Aoi no Ue*, *Hachinoki*, *Dōjōji*, *Ataka* and *Sumidagawa*, though entirely dissimilar in mood and plot, all engage the audience less by their beauty of language than by their theatrical effectiveness. Yet for all their comparative theatricality, they are far removed, say, from Kabuki. The plot of *Ataka* is virtually identical to that of the Kabuki play *Kanjinchō*, but it remains stylized and aloof where *Kanjinchō* is warmly human; nothing in *Ataka* has the quality of the touching moment in *Kanjinchō* when Yoshitsune, aware how painful it must have been for Benkei to strike him, his master, extends his hand towards Benkei in a gesture of affection and understanding. However dramatic a Nō play may be, its symbolic possibilities can be preserved only if a distance is kept between the play and the audience. An unadorned play like *Shunnei* is likely to drop from the repertory even if its plot is interesting.

The final components of a Nō program, the devil plays, are closely related to those of the fourth category, but their tempo is faster, as we should expect in the *kyū* section. The *shite* is often a demonic being who appears in the second part wearing an enormous red or white wig that cascades over his brilliant costume, and the frenzied movements of his dance are accentuated by the ferocity of his mask. The props too, unlike the customary bare outlines of a house, tree or gate, may be solidly constructed platforms ornamented with gold and silver trees. In the first part of these plays the *shite* is likely to appear in some pleasant guise—as a gentlewoman in *Momijigari*, a priest in *Tsuchigumo*, or an old woman in *Kurozuka*—but in the second part the demon reveals his true form, and stamps wildly, swinging a mallet. The lively tempo of the play creates a cheerful impression on the audience, despite the frightening presence of a demon, and brings the program to a satisfying close.

The demon plays were written mainly by playwrights of the century after Zeami. Though effective as theatre and sometimes moving as poetry, they fail to touch the exalted utterance of the greatest Nō plays. It has been said of *Funa Benkei*, nevertheless, that "of the two hundred works in the current repertory, it ranks as a masterpiece of the kind one can count on the fingers of one hand." It rates this praise especially because of its brilliant variety of effects. In the first scene Benkei persuades Yoshitsune to dismiss his sweetheart Shizuka, who has accompanied him on the flight from the capital. The actor playing Shizuka must suggest the grief of this ill-starred woman; but in the second scene the same actor, taking an entirely different part, must rage with masculine vigor as Tomomori, a defeated Heike warrior who rises from the sea to menace the fugitives in their boat. Between the two sections of the play an unusually absorbing *ai-kyōgen* is played by the boatman who ferries Yoshitsune, Benkei and the others across the Inland Sea. He battles with tremendous waves stirred up by Tomomori's ghost, giving vent to realistic cries and gestures that contrast with the stylization of the rest of the play.

The demands of sixteenth-century audiences for action and lively presentation probably account for such works as *Shōzon*, *Chikatō* and *Kasui* by Nagatoshi. The former two works each have nine characters, *Kasui* has thirteen. *Shōzon*, the tale of a plot against Yoshitsune's life thwarted by Benkei, is devoid of poetry, and is performed by some schools with such acrobatics as somersaults and perpendicular backward falls. *Chikatō* has four principal characters, each given a display scene, rather in the manner of an Italian opera. *Kasui*, a work not currently performed, has many changes of scene, and its plot shifts from the fable of a dragon princess who dries up a river in order to compel the Chinese court to provide her with a husband, to the more realistic scene of the courtier who volunteers to marry her, to a strange episode in which a great drum sounds of itself, presaging war, and finally to a battle scene in which the Chinese emperor, aided by the Dragon King, is victorious. The dances in these plays are no longer natural outgrowths of the poetry but arbitrary insertions, and the texts themselves are as conventional as they are flat. *Hatsuyuki* by Zempō, more poetic than most plays of the period, contains these uninspiring lines:

are are miyo ya	Oh, oh, just look!
fushigi ya na	How strange it is!
are are miyo ya	Oh, oh, just look!
fushigi ya na	How strange it is!
nakazora no kumo ka to	What seemed to be
mietsuru ga	A cloud high in the sky
kumo ni wa arade	Is not a cloud:
samo shirotae no	White as glossy silk,
Hatsuyuki no	Hatsuyuki,
tsubasa wo tarete	Lowering its wings,
tobikitari	Has flown back.
himegimi ni mukai	Its form as it dances,
samo natsukashige ni	Ever so affectionately,
tachimau sugata	Facing the princess,
ge ni aware naru	Makes a truly touching
keshiki ka na	Sight to behold.

The plays by Nagatoshi and Zempō mark the end of the creative period of Nō. It should be noted, however, that many plays are of unknown authorship, and we cannot even assign them an approximate date. *Nonomiya*, *Hagoromo*, *Utō*, *Kumasaka*, *Yuya*, *Kantan*, *Tsuchigumo*, *Hachinoki* and *Kagekiyo* are among the plays which traditionally were ascribed to Zeami but now, in the absence of firm evidence of authorship, are listed as "other works." But if *Nonomiya*, *Yuya* and the rest were actually by another dramatist, he surely ranks (despite his anonymity) as Zeami's equal. It seems improbable that so great a genius could have remained completely unknown. It may be that the reaction against unproved attributions has been excessive, and future discoveries will enable us to credit Zeami with masterpieces whose authorship is now uncertain. His genius was not likely to have occurred twice.

KYŌGEN

The name Kyōgen, written with characters meaning "wild words," seems to have originated in a Chinese phrase which derogatively described all literature as being no more than "wild words and fancy language." The phrase came to be used in a Buddhist sense, with the implication that even frivolous writings may provide the impetus to salvation. It figures in some plays as a designation for the art of Nō itself. In *Tōgan Koji* the lines occur, "One can enter the true path of giving praise to the Buddha and setting the wheel of his Law in motion by means of 'wild words and fancy language.' Let us celebrate this flower of the human heart." The farcical Kyōgen plays may have been dignified as being a path that leads to enlightenment in order to justify their innocent frivolity.

By Zeami's day both *ai* and independent Kyōgen formed part of Nō programs. Zeami mentions that performances offered at shrines customarily included three Nō and two Kyōgen. The alternation of Nō and Kyōgen became the general rule. Kyōgen actors, in addition to appearing in *ai* and in the farces themselves, performed in Nō, usually in minor roles, as servants, messengers and the like. Generally the dialogue for these parts consists merely of such phrases as "I obey your commands," but occasionally, as in *Hanjo* (where the brothel proprietress is performed by a Kyōgen actor) the roles have dramatic importance.

The different functions of Kyōgen actors on the Nō stage indicate how intimately the two arts were related. Kyōgen, however, was normally considered only a minor element in the program. Zeami's prescription for Kyōgen actors suggests he held them in low esteem: "A Kyōgen actor performing in the *ai-kyōgen* of a Nō play should refrain from attempting to make the audience laugh. His function is to relate the plot of the Nō and to address himself to the audience in such a way that they will feel he has actually seen and heard the events he describes."

The subordinate position of Kyōgen is further suggested by the fact that the texts were not recorded until the beginning of the seventeenth century. The first substantial collection, published in 1660 under the name *Kyōgenki*, included fifty plays. This edition and a much augmented later version are now dismissed as being mere explanations of the plots with snatches of dialogue, and not accurate transcriptions of the texts. But though inferior and misleading, these are the oldest versions we have; a 1578 collection, the earliest Kyōgen document, consists merely of brief summaries. The lack of authentic texts dating back to the sixteenth century forces us to depend on the oral traditions of the three schools—Ōkura, Izumi, and the now defunct Sagi. In principle, each Kyōgen teacher carefully transmits the texts word-by-word to his pupils, but minor variants exist even within a single school, and a comparison of the texts of the three schools reveals enormous differences, not only in the dialogue but even in the structure of the plays. Probably these variants are very old: the bare outlines of the plot may originally have been the actors' only guide, the dialogue being left largely to improvisation. For this reason it is foolish to search for authors of the plays. Undoubtedly someone, whether an actor or a dramatist, first conceived the plots, but the lines developed naturally over the years, successful passages being retained and others dropped, rather than originating like Nō in a single writer's imagination.

The Kyōgen plays vary so markedly in literary quality that some scholars believe it is possible to trace a progression from early, unsophisticated works to the later masterpieces. The oldest Kyōgen were probably in the tradition of *Okina*, festive plays depicting the villagers' hopes for a prosperous new year. *Sannimpu* ("The Three Farmers"), for example, describes the happy journey of the three farmers to the capital in order to pay their taxes, no hardship in a year of peace and plenty. Such works contain more singing and dancing than the more satirical Kyōgen, and the humorous elements are minor. Congratulatory Kyōgen are sometimes referred to as *waki* Kyōgen, by analogy to the *waki* Nō, because they are presented first in a program.

The later Kyōgen are marked by greater ingenuity of plot, cleverer situations and a sharp decrease in musical or choreographic elements. The parts are often referred to as the *shite* (or *omo*) and *ado*, corresponding to the *shite* and *waki* of Nō, but there is little subordination of one part to the other; in a play like *Shūron* where a priest of the Amida sect and a priest of the Nichiren sect try to outsmart each other, it is essential that they be equal antagonists. Though secondary characters tend to be stereotypes with little individuality, they certainly assert themselves far more vigorously than the *waki* or *tsure* of Nō. As dramas the Kyōgen are therefore closer to Western theatre than most Nō plays; in recent years a few medieval European farces have even been adapted to the Kyōgen stage. The later Kyōgen partake of the universal nature of farce, though never descending to the crudities typical of many Western examples. They lack the refined wit of high comedy, but they afford the actors maximum opportunities to display ringing voices and agile bodily movements.

A Kyōgen actor may appear in any part, regardless of his age, physical appearance or voice, but some prefer the part of Tarōkaja (the servant), others the termagant wife, and still others the more pathetic roles. Most parts are performed without either masks or makeup. An actor taking the part of a woman merely ties a towel around his head in an approximation of a female head-dress, but neither in voice nor in movements does he suggest femininity. Child actors may perform not only as children but in roles of indeterminate age; their high-pitched monotones do scant justice to the lines, but the childish gravity they display in reciting and dancing endears them to the audience.

Masks are used chiefly when actors appear as non-human beings—animals, demons or gods—but there are also comically ugly masks for both male and female roles. Unlike Nō, where the mask may represent the "true" appearance of the characters, Kyōgen masks are often put on as a means of deception; a character may pretend to be a god (as in *Ishigami*) or a demon (as in *Oba ga Sake*) in order to frighten another person into obeying his wishes. Masks are used only in about one-eighth of the plays of the Kyōgen repertory.

The style of the Kyōgen texts is infinitely less complicated (and less distinguished) than that of Nō. Except for occasional songs, sometimes in mock imitation of Nō, the texts are in prose, each sentence generally ending with the copula verb *gozaru*. Whole passages may be the same from play to play, and there is much repetition in the dialogue. Audiences are not bored with such repetitions; on the contrary, they provide pleasingly familiar elements close to the essence of Kyōgen. The daimyo, for example, usually summons his servant Tarōkaja with the words: *Yai, yai, yai, Tarōkaja, oru ka yai?* The translation, "Hey, Tarōkaja, are you there?" certainly gives no idea of the effect of the Japanese. Translation is even more inadequate when it comes to Tarōkaja's response, a long *Haaaaaah*, rising about two octaves, and translatable only as "Yes."

Kyōgen possesses little of the literary merit of its tragic counterpart, Nō. It occupies a position somewhere between a comedy of masks and true comedy, but relies most heavily for its effects not on the texts but on the manner of presentation—the intonation, the stylized movements of the actors, and the delightful cadences of the sentences ending in *gozaru*. A few of the plays boast plots ingenious enough to survive even in translation, and many others are enjoyable because of the glimpses they afford into the lives of the common people of the sixteenth and seventeenth centuries, but Kyōgen needs a stage for even a fraction of its pleasures to be adequately conveyed.

IV. BACKGROUND OF THE PERFORMANCES

TRAINING OF THE ACTOR

A Nō actor's training begins in his infancy and may continue until his last tottering appearance on the stage. As a small child he hears from the next room the sounds of his father rehearsing or of pupils being instructed, and he absorbs the words and intonation of Nō almost as easily as those of normal conversation. By the time he is five he makes his debut, delighting the audience with his piping in high monotones of lines whose meaning undoubtedly escapes him. He will have learned by rote every word, every gesture he so awkwardly (but winningly) performs, patiently guided by his father. Only the son of an actor is likely to receive this training from the cradle which, connoisseurs of Nō insist, is indispensable to a truly professional actor. Indeed, the pedigree of an actor of Nō or Kyōgen is so vital a consideration that it is almost unthinkable that an outsider could achieve eminence. Conversely, the actor who can boast the finest pedigree in his school may succeed to the headship even if he himself is an indifferent performer.

Gradually the boy actor moves from token appearances to *kokata* parts which require skill in both recitation and dancing. By the time he is thirteen or fourteen he may assume his first *tsure* part. It sometimes happens today, as often in the past, that a boy who has become the head of his school because of his pedigree rather than his superior talent will take *shite* parts even at ten or twelve. Save in rare instances of genius little more can be expected of so youthful a *shite* than a display of boyish charm.

Some boys, the sons of *waki* actors, are trained in the *waki* roles, resigned from childhood to the fact that no matter how proficient they may become as actors they can never hope to become the star of a play; by tradition, actors of the *shite* and *waki* schools do not cross the lines of their specialities.

At sixteen a promising young actor may be entrusted with his first *shite* role. Usually he begins by performing as a young warrior, particularly in the later Nō plays. Energy and agility (reminiscent of the flying squirrel at the bottom of Zeami's Nine Levels) are considered far easier for an actor to project than the elusive qualities of roles with little movement; the crown of an actor's career, as we have seen, is the performance of the almost motionless roles of old women. The actor gradually progresses up the scale towards roles requiring inner rather than outer display.

The young actor's training is demanding and sometimes painful. Hōshō Kurō kept as mementos of his favorite pupils their practice-books stained with the blood from nosebleeds induced by intense rehearsals. Instruction is mainly oral, though the pupil keeps the text open before him. The teacher sits before a little desk, his pupil facing him at his own desk on which the text rests. The teacher pronounces a line and the pupil, guided more by his teacher's voice than by the notations on the text before him, repeats the line again and again until the teacher is satisfied. The method of instruction in Kyōgen is entirely oral, practice texts not being available. The teacher explains neither the meaning of the words nor the mood they are intended to convey, but insists instead on exact, unquestioning conformity to his own delivery. The pupil parrots the teacher, never attempting to "get inside" the sense of the exceedingly involved poetry. The teacher aids the pupil's recitation by beating time with a small leather baton, but he never suggests that, say, the pupil "give more feeling" to his delivery. When the pupil comes to perform the dances and other movements of the roles, he is shown precisely the number of steps to take at a given moment or the prescribed manner of opening a fan, but not how he is to preserve the flow of movement necessary to a graceful performance. The pupil imitates exactly, avoiding any suspicion of making a fresh attempt to penetrate a role. Only once he has proved that he has mastered the routine techniques will he be initiated into the secret traditions, and only long afterwards will he perhaps interpret the roles slightly differently from his predecessors.

The insistence on imitation and the absence of systematic instruction in performing the texts have resulted in even mature actors at times being ignorant of precisely what they are singing or representing. In extreme cases, as we know from the biographies of distinguished actors, a veteran performer may be unacquainted with the plot of a play in which he has appeared countless times, never having deciphered the language. The Nō actors seem to embody in their voices and gestures the profound beauties of the texts, but their understanding of the parts may be physical rather than mental, and they may lack the intellectual capacity to appreciate why audiences should wish to spend their time and money to attend Nō. Iwakura Tomomi once dismissed with aristocratic disdain all Nō actors except Hōshō Kurō as "monkeys" in the tradition of *sarugaku* ("monkey music"), but even Hōshō Kurō, whose whole life was consecrated to preserving the true traditions of Nō, once expressed amazement that anyone should prefer watching a Nō play to a wrestling match. The lack of intellectual involvement, far from lowering the level of performances, has accounted for the faithful preservation of tradition. The danger today is that young actors, far better educated than their predecessors, will be distracted from a unique concern with Nō into dabbling with other dramatic styles, or may attempt to modernize and rationalize an art which has thus far withstood the assaults of change.

Some changes, however, may become necessary. Sitting in Japanese style on the wooden boards of the stage, surely never comfortable for anyone, has become agonizingly painful for the younger members of the chorus, whose daily lives (unlike those of actors of the past) are spent mainly in rooms with chairs. When at a New Year performance *Okina* is followed by *Takasago*, the chorus and the drum *(taiko)* player must remain in a kneeling position for three hours, a feat of endurance increasingly distasteful to the younger generation. Again, the arbitrary division of the roles into *shite* and *waki*, the latter even following texts of the plays which differ in details from those performed by the *shite*, has been preserved by family traditions for centuries, but ambitious young actors now seem disinclined to become *waki* and play a perpetual second fiddle to the *shite*. Eventually it may be necessary to open all roles to talented actors, and to provide some more comfortable way of sitting for the chorus.

Even more serious than changes dictated by the physical comfort or vanity of the performers are the objections, usually unspoken, against the organization of each school around an *iemoto*, or head. The *iemoto* system, established during the Tokugawa period, was favored by the government, which found it convenient and philosophically desirable to deal with the actors (like other members of the society) in a hierarchical manner, issuing its commands to the head of a school who, like the head of a family, was responsible for the transmission and execution of the order. The system is by no means absolute today, but the head of the school still possesses privileges and obligations that strike the younger generation as being "feudalistic." The head of the Kanze school, for example, is entrusted with the scrolls which explain secret traditions of performing each part. When an actor is qualified to have the secrets imparted to him, the head of the school, with the utmost display of decorum, opens the scroll and reveals only so much of it as is necessary for the particular part. The head of each school normally represents it at cultural festivals sponsored by the government, even if he happens not to be the most distinguished performer of the school, inevitably giving it a bad name among outsiders. The head of the school sometimes also disciplines actors, as a father might discipline a wayward child; two Kyōgen actors who appeared in a Kabuki play were temporarily forbidden to perform in Kyōgen because they had "abandoned their profession." It is hard to imagine an opera director refusing to permit a singer to appear on his stage because the singer had ventured for a few weeks into the domain of musical comedy, but the *iemoto* of Nō and Kyōgen is a father who worries about his children's marriage, drinking habits or lapses from the true path of the art. Needless to say, disciplinary action by the *iemoto*, however benevolently intended, is now often resented.

If the head of a school happens to be its outstanding performer, as for many years Kita Roppeita was not only the finest actor of the Kita school but of the entire world of Nō, the *iemoto* system will not weigh excessively on the actors, who will feel grateful for the prestige the *iemoto* lends to his disciples. Even at its worst, the *iemoto* system has tended to prevent economic hardships among the actors by providing each man with opportunities to perform and a fair share of pupils. The maintenance of the artistic integrity of a school would certainly be infinitely more difficult if no central authority exercised vigilance against departures from orthodoxy and offered the only criticisms which an actor genuinely respected. The five schools—Kanze, Hōshō, Komparu, Kongō and Kita—provide a welcome variety of performance, but the fortunes of the smaller schools are governed by the strength of the *iemoto*'s determination to maintain the traditions. The two largest schools, Kanze and Hōshō, play so dominant a role that the other schools sometimes have difficulty in assembling a competent chorus.

THE SCHOOLS OF NŌ

The five schools have preserved their traditions with a pride commensurate with their long histories. Actors have been known to declare that they never witness Nō presented by another school, either because they fear they may corrupt the purity of their interpretations, or simply because they are totally uninterested in divergent interpretations. The connoisseur of Nō has no trouble in distinguishing among the schools, as a Western music critic will easily identify the mellowness of Central European strings, the clarity of French woodwinds, or the overall brilliance of an American ensemble. To anyone less than an expert, however, *Matsukaze*, regardless of the school, like a Schubert symphony regardless of the nationality of the orchestra performing it, is more likely to leave an impression because of its intrinsic beauty or because of the skill of the performers, rather than by the fidelity it displays to a particular tradition. But the parallel between schools of Nō and European orchestras is far from exact; the variations in the tonal quality of orchestras are apt to be unintentional or even accidental, but the differences among the schools of Nō are so jealously preserved that, the story goes, families will refuse to give their daughters in marriage to men who have studied—even as amateurs—the wrong school of Nō!

The first difference marking the schools is the texts. Textual variants can be found for each play, especially in the prose parts. In extreme cases whole scenes are dissimilar. In presentations of the *shimogakari* (Komparu, Kongō and Kita) schools, *Dōjōji* opens with dialogue accompanying the hanging of the great temple bell, but this scene is omitted from the Kanze and Hōshō presentations. The title of the play may differ according to the school: thus, the work called *Kurozuka* by four of the five schools is called *Adachigahara* by the Kanze school. In some instances, though the title is pronounced identically irrespective of school, the characters used for the sounds differ. *Yuya* is written with characters meaning literally "bear field" by most schools, but the Kita school uses characters meaning "hot water valley."

The repertories also vary from school to school, Kanze boasting the most plays, Komparu the fewest. In 1878 Hōshō Kurō removed thirty plays at a stroke from the repertory of the Hōshō school, some because he considered them inferior, others because their special demands made it impossible for the *iemoto* to guarantee they could always be performed. (*Futari Shizuka*, for example, requires two actors whose build and style of acting will permit them to appear as doubles.) The different schools formerly clung to certain plays as their special possessions, and if another school wished to acquire one of them for its repertory an exchange would be made. This system has now broken down; a work like *Motomezuka*, formerly performed only by the Hōshō and Kita schools, has been borrowed freely for their repertories by the other schools.

Variations in the text are emphasized by special acting traditions called *kogaki* ("small writing"). The *kogaki* employed in the performance of a play is written in small print after the title in the programs, indicating some departure from standard practice. The *kogaki* were probably devised originally so as to prevent spectators from becoming bored by overly familiar representations of the plays; so well were they acquainted with each work that even a slight shift of emphasis could surprise and excite. Sometimes the variation provided by a *kogaki* consists merely of the *shite* wearing a white instead of a red wig for the part of a demon. This seemingly inconsequential difference is elevated to the importance of a major aspect of the performance. An actor deemed insufficiently senior to wear a white wig would be severely criticized. The *kogaki* are learned by the actor only at the appropriate stage of his career and on payment of the regulation fee. Their importance stems from the conviction that altering any element in a play involves a changed conception of the entire performance. For example, *Takasago* is generally performed without any stage prop, but some *kogaki* require a pine tree. In this case, the *shite*, coming to the line, "I shall rake the dust under the tree," must perform the gesture of raking fallen pine needles. The *kogaki* of some schools prescribe a rake rather than a broom for the *shite* in keeping with this change.

Such variations in performance are less important than the stylistic differences among the schools, apparent to the connoisseur. The Komparu school is considered to preserve the old style of performance most faithfully; one authority characterized its singing as "melodic in an old-fashioned way with a placid delivery." In contrast, the Kanze singing has been called "delicately melodic with a nuanced delivery," and the Kita singing "martial in its delivery." The Kongō school is noted for its vigorous, sometimes acrobatic, dancing, in contrast to the extreme restraint of the Hōshō school. The wealth of a school may accentuate its style of performance: the Hōshō school can costume ten *tengu* (demons) for a performance of *Kurama Tengu*, but the Komparu and Kita schools would be hard-pressed to costume more than two or three *tengu*. A school may also follow a particular interpretation of the unspoken implications of a play. In *Yuya*, for example, the mistress of Munemori begs permission to return home, where her aged mother is supposedly dying. Munemori at first refuses, insisting that she accompany him when he visits the cherry blossoms at Kiyomizu, but eventually he relents. She joyfully takes leave, hurrying off to her mother's sickbed. In one school, however, the actor playing the girl is supposed to suggest by almost imperceptible variations in accent that she is less concerned about her mother's health than about rejoining a boyfriend at home. The text does not readily support this interpretation, but its novelty may appeal to spectators looking for something new to admire in a work they know only too well.

Differences of school in Kyōgen are easily apparent even to the casual spectator. Not only do the texts differ markedly, as noted, but the intonation of the lines is totally dissimilar, that of the Izumi school resembling modern Japanese more closely than that of the Ōkura school. Differences in the repertory are also considerable.

THE MASKS

Masks are the lifeblood of a performance of Nō. A great actor may move us even if the mask he wears is inferior, but a beautiful mask can make his performance immortal. Some masks have been registered as national treasures and are displayed in museums, but as the late Kongō Iwao wrote, "The true value of a mask is revealed only when worn by a performer on the stage. There a superior mask can become a part of the actor's body by dint of his superior artistry; it is alive and his blood courses through it. The true beauty of a mask may be sensed at just such moments, and it is just such masks that teach us the spirit of Nō.''

It is not easy for an actor to make the audience believe that the mask he wears is part of his flesh. His success is the culmination of efforts begun as a boy of twelve or thirteen. This was the age when, prior to the Meiji Restoration, he would undergo the "coming of age" *(gembuku)* ceremony, and it is still the age when a mask is fitted to the boy's face for the first time, generally the sacred mask of the old man in *Okina*. This is his initiation at once into the world of adults and of Nō. The young man is permitted afterwards to perform with any mask, excepting only those of the middle-aged woman or the old person. At first he is likely to perform roles in which he previously appeared without a mask, like the youthful god in *Makura Jidō*. He is trained to keep the mask steady, avoiding jerky movements or abrupt (and therefore ugly) raising and lowering of the head. By fifteen or so he is ready to put on a young woman's mask, not as a *shite* but as a *tsure*. The *tsure* roles are generally not especially difficult, but it is no small task to wear the mask in a manner evocative of feminine beauty. The apertures in the eyes of the mask are merely holes which permit the actor at best a glimpse of the customers in the balcony. If he wishes to discover where on the stage he stands he has only the nostril-openings in the mask to look through. The young actor has all he can do to keep from bumping into the others onstage even without attempting to suggest by his use of the mask feminine loveliness.

By twenty the actor, having overcome the initial difficulties of wearing a mask, will take the part of a *shite*, appearing as a young woman and wearing a *ko-omote* mask. At the same time he may appear as a young warrior in such plays as *Tsunemasa* or *Kiyotsune*, wearing the *chūjō* mask. Next he moves on to roles requiring the *heita* mask—the powerful, mature warriors of such plays as *Tamura* or *Yashima*. In his thirties he will study female *shite* roles of the fourth category, wearing the *shakumi* mask in *Fujito* or *Sakuragawa*. He may then progress to the roles of gods and demons, wearing the appropriate masks, to the great female *shite* roles of the third category, and finally, when past sixty, to the parts of old women, wearing the *yase-onna* mask in such works as *Sotoba Komachi*.

The progression from one category of role to the next implies increasing difficulty in interpreting the roles but also increasing beauty in the masks used. It might seem more logical for a young man to appear as the beautiful Matsukaze rather than a man in his fifties—probably in Zeami's day a young actor in fact took the part—but it is assumed today that an actor could not evoke the full poetry of the role unless he had spent many years on the stage. He could not, for that matter, employ the mask to the full effect, adumbrating the shades of emotion by causing shadows or glints to fall on his mask. He would also be unworthy of wearing a mask of the highest dignity *(kurai)*. Not only do the masks differ in dignity according to their category (whether for a young general, a young woman or a devil), but also according to the quality of a particular mask within the same category. Sometimes this is a matter of artistic excellence: many masks, particularly of the Muromachi period, rank as masterpieces of carving, and to perform with such a mask is not only an honor but a responsibility. The story is told of Hōshō Kurō's visit to Kyoto with his disciple Matsumoto Nagashi. The young man was to appear in *Tenko*, and Kurō asked the head of the Kongō school if he might borrow a *koujijō* mask for the occasion. The mask offered him was so magnificent that Kurō refused it, saying that young Matsumoto was not yet sufficiently accomplished to merit such an honor.

Even among masks of approximately equal artistic value a difference in "dignity" may arise because one is almost imperceptibly older, severer in expression or more dreamlike than another. The different schools are known for their preferences in these matters: the Komparu actors prefer *ko-omote* masks of a childlike innocence, the Kongō actors a slightly more sensual face, and at the other extreme, we find the almost voluptuous expression on the *ko-omote* masks used by the Kanze school. When Hōshō Kurō appeared twice within a short time in *Sumidagawa*, an admirer remarked that one interpretation had seemed quite astringent, the other almost youthful. Kurō, pleased to find such acuteness of appreciation, took out the two *shakumi* masks he had worn, one aged, the other youthful. The different interpretations of the role had grown from a week or more studying each mask. The slightly different "dignity" had inspired different performances. That is why an actor desires several masks of the same category. As Kongō Iwao put it, if an actor has only one *magojirō* he can express only one level of dignity *(kurai)* in the role, but if he has five *magojirō* masks he can perform five different interpretations of *Matsukaze*. The *kurai* of the mask also determines the costumes used, and it is said that unless the musicians and the members of the chorus know the *kurai* of the *shite's* mask they cannot perform.

The actor's greatest problem in the use of the mask is giving it expression. The female masks especially are virtually blanks as far as the expression goes. Scholars have argued over whether this "intermediate expression" was intended to represent feminine beauty at its most evocative, or to be a straightforward depiction of a lovely face in a moment of repose, or a symbolic representation of the essential nature of a woman's character; but the researches of Gotō Hajime indicate that the neutral expression of the female masks much antedates the age of Zeami, when the ideal of *yūgen* might have inspired symbolic delineation of the features. No doubt the "intermediate expression" was adopted for masks in order that the actor might suggest without changing his mask the joy or grief of the character. Certainly the female masks are so used today. A lowering of the mask *(kumorasu)* casts shadows suggestive of grief, a raising of the mask *(terasu)* lightens it, giving an expression of happiness. Needless to say, the use of the mask is far more subtle than a mere raising and lowering. In *Nonomiya*, for example, at the lines "Whom should I pine for now? The voices of pine-crickets trill *rin, rin* . . .," the actor, who must not resort to any obvious gesture of listening, lowers his gaze to the chirping insects, then gently moves his head laterally in the gesture known as "seeing a voice." The effective use of any mask is difficult, but in comparison to the delicacy required in *Matsukaze* or *Nonomiya*, the warrior plays are relatively uncomplicated in expression, the masks less demanding. The ascending order of the roles is also an ascending order of difficulty in using the masks, culminating in the great plays *Sotoba Komachi* and *Sekidera Komachi*, in which the actor must convince us by the way he uses his mask that beneath the skin of the aged crone there is still a beautiful woman.

Some roles, especially in the *genzaimono*, are performed without mask. In these cases it is hardly an exaggeration to say that the actor's face becomes a mask, that there is hardly more individuality in the face of a great actor performing without mask as Benkei in *Ataka* than in a warrior mask. The Kyōgen actor appearing as Sambasō in *Okina* who repeats again and again the meaningless, incantatory syllables *yo hon ho*, by the end of the performance becomes as impersonal an embodiment of good fortune as the masked old man Okina himself. In the parts performed without mask the *kurai* comes from the innate personality of the actor. The effect is the opposite of the masked roles where the actor endeavors to infuse a carved piece of wood with expression; here the actor must drain the expression from his face into his voice and body. In either case the effect achieved is a stylized and evocative beauty remote from the representational effects of actors on other stages.

Though the roles without masks may be as demanding as those performed with masks, the mask is the symbol of the Nō actor, and the moment when he puts on a mask before a performance marks the transition from his daily existence to the special realm of his art. Before the actor places the mask on his face he stares at it intently, holding it at the two small holes of the ears, the only part of the polished surface which should be touched. The actor's face is padded with wadded cotton wrapped in soft paper so that the mask will fit snugly and securely. The mask is attached to his head by ribbons passed through the ear-holes. The color of these ribbons varies with the mask: white for *okina*, red for *kokushiki*, purple for a woman's mask worn by a *shite*, dark blue for a woman's mask worn by a *tsure*, and so on. The ribbons from the left and right ears must be attached with equal tautness if the actor is to see at all. Originally, it seems, the ribbons holding the mask to the face were concealed by the wider bands attached to the wig, but today the wig is fastened below, leaving the mask ribbons exposed.

The masks are made of *hinoki* (Japanese cypress), a wood easily worked yet durable. The bark side of the wood is fashioned into the inside of the mask; in this way any resin which might seep to the surface will not harm the mask. Ideally, the *hinoki* wood for the masks should come from trees felled in the Valley of Kiso, floated down the Kiso River to Tokyo, and kept there for five or six years in mingled fresh and sea water before being cut into the blocks used by the mask-carver. Wood of this quality is scarce today, but the best available is always used, for the Nō mask is a work of art.

Most masks are about eight and a half inches in length, the width varying somewhat according to the variety. They are too small to cover the actor's entire face, but generally leave a disillusioning sallow or reddish fringe of jowls around the lovely contours of the painted wood. The smallness of the mask may have originated in an aesthetic ideal of a small head on a large body, though Japanese more often have large heads on small bodies. Audiences in the past, seated at a distance from the badly lighted stage, were undoubtedly far less aware of the actor's jowls than we are today from our seats a few feet from a stage brightly lit with fluorescent lamps.

Aesthetic ideals apparently also gave rise to the extraordinarily high foreheads of the masks of young women. The proportions of the forehead are accentuated by the shaved eyebrows and the false eyebrows painted almost at the hairline. The Muromachi fashion for a high forehead and shaved eyebrows, curiously coincidental with the similar fashion in Europe of the time, is perpetuated in the masks, along with the severe part of the hair in the middle. New masks have been devised and the prevailing tastes of later ages have found unconscious expression, but for the most part the masks, like the Nō itself, adhere to models created in the fifteenth century.

The earlier masks, as we know from examples preserved in temples and shrines, showed far greater variety. Some are startlingly realistic, the faces of men and women one might encounter today. No doubt these masks reflect the plebeian origins of Nō. Unlike *gigaku* or *bugaku*, Nō in the thirteenth and fourteenth centuries was a popular entertainment, performed at inconspicuous temples in the hills—anywhere an audience could be attracted—as well as at the great monasteries. The plays surely lacked the exalted manner of Nō in its full glory, and the countrified expressions on the masks suggest little of *yūgen*. Indeed, the masks may originally not have been intended to afford greater beauty than the commonplace face of the actors; they may have been intended instead to make the actors resemble the characters they portrayed, whether a girl, a middle-aged woman, a general or a demon. The old masks usually have a definite expression. Those for young women have smiling mouths and eyes crinkled with merriment, indications that the plays themselves were not the melancholy vehicles now associated with the name Nō. The features, it should be noted, are distinctly Japanese, unlike the *gigaku* and *bugaku* masks, which were faithful copies of prototypes from the Asian continent. The techniques of carving the early Nō masks may have been borrowed from those of the *bugaku* masks—*bugaku* was widely performed when the Nō masks were being created in the thirteenth and fourteenth centuries—but the faces are entirely dissimilar. Even the devils represent peculiarly Japanese conceptions rather than the leonine *bugaku* features. The old masks are true products of the lively theatricals performed before Nō acquired its unique dignity as a court entertainment and the categories of masks were formalized.

The masks today may roughly be divided among the three roles mentioned by Zeami—the old person, the woman, and the warrior—plus the demons. Within each category numerous variations occur. The young woman, for example, may be a girl between sixteen and twenty, as in *Yuya* (*ko-omote* mask), or between twenty and twenty-five, as in *Eguchi* (*magojirō* mask); she may be possessed by a demon like Rokujō in the first part of *Aoi no Ue* (*deigan* mask), or a divine being like the angel in *Hagoromo* (*zō no onna* mask); she may be brooding like Kiyohime in the first part of *Dōjōji* (*Ōmi onna* mask) or griefstricken like the mother in *Sumidagawa* (*shakumi* mask). Each school maintains different traditions and sometimes different names for the masks. The individual actor, moreover, is at liberty to experiment somewhat in the choice of mask for a role in the interests of a slightly altered emphasis. A few masks are used for a single role only, like that for Yorimasa, a man aged but still warlike; for Shunkan, emaciated and deeply embittered; or for Yoroboshi, a blind young man of haggard appearance. (The masks for the roles of blind persons have long, downcast slits for the eyes instead of the usual tiny apertures, paradoxically affording the best visibility to the actors!)

The most distinctive masks are those of the demons. *Beshimi* masks have mouths tightly shut in a frown, and lines in the face denoting strength cluster around the forehead and cheeks. The effect, however, is more comic than frightening, and the mask is used for *tengu*, the rather genial demons. By contrast, the small *beshimi* (*ko-beshimi*) masks, much closer to normal human features, are marked with evil unrelieved by exaggeration. Most terrifying are the different varieties of *hannya*, a horrible grinning mask with horns, the incarnation of feminine possessiveness. The name *hannya*, ironically, means "wisdom" (from the Sanskrit *prajna*), but here it probably comes from the maker, Hannyabō.

The names of sixteen celebrated mask-makers have been preserved from Muromachi times, some mentioned in Zeami's writings. Prized masks today are almost all attributed to these men, but clearly many attributions are legendary, and others refer to a workshop rather than to an individual. The profession of mask-maker was recognized only in the Tokugawa era. Until then, we may gather, masks were often made by priests or general artisans rather than by special artists. Many superlative masks are undoubtedly old copies of even older works. Such makers as Kuoji, Tokuwaka, Himi, Echi and Shakuzuru are solemnly credited with many extant masks, but probably no more can be said about these revered names than that they represent characteristic styles. Certainly the degree of sophistication in the carving of many masterpieces does not accord with the early dates—some in the Kamakura period—assigned to these men. Kongō Magojirō (1538–64), whose name was taken for the female mask typifying the Kongō school, is one of the earliest mask-makers we can date.

Three *ko-omote* masks attributed to the legendary Ishikawa Tatsuemon acquired special fame as prized possessions of Hideyoshi. The masks, known as the "snow," "moon," and "flower" *ko-omote*, were left by Hideyoshi to the head of the Komparu school, the Shogun Ieyasu, and the head of the Kongō school respectively. The "moon" mask was lost in a fire, the "flower" mask has been disfigured by clumsy restoration, but the "moon" mask, now owned by the Kongō school in Kyoto, is a particularly lovely *ko-omote*, considered by some experts to be the most perfect mask of all.

Kyōgen masks, far fewer than those for Nō, fall into four main categories: Shinto and Buddhist divinities, spirits, human beings, and animals. The deities include the god of good fortune, Bishamon (a Buddhist protective divinity), Lightning, and Dragons; the spirits include Buaku and Usobuki, two typical Kyōgen figures; the human beings include Grandpa, the Ugly Woman (Oto), and the Nun; the animals consist of the fox, the badger, the monkey, the ox, the dog and birds. Buaku, a comic villain, wears a grotesque version of the Nō mask *beshimi:* the eyes droop, the cheeks are extraordinarily broad, the teeth protrude and bite the lower lip. The *usobuki* mask has pursed and twisted lips and great goggling eyes; it is used to represent the spirit of a mosquito (in *Kazumō*) or of a cicada (in *Semi*) or of a mushroom (in *Kusabira*) or, occasionally, a pathetic-looking robber (in *Uri-nusubito*). Normally the Kyōgen actor does not resort to using a mask in order to indicate that he is playing the part of a woman, but for comically ugly women the *oto* mask is used. Oto has a bulging forehead and cheeks, a nose squashed almost flat, and a comically twisted mouth. The *nun* is sometimes an older version of *oto*, sometimes amusingly lachrymose in expression.

The Kyōgen masks are far from realistic, but just as the Nō masks seem to symbolize the essential traits of a role, the Kyōgen masks exaggerate and distort them. Ugliness, timidity and even ferocity become funny thanks to the masks.

The masks, whether Nō or Kyōgen, are never worn without a wig or head covering. In Kyōgen a towel or a simple hood (zukin) will serve as covering, but the Nō masks require a wig in one of three lengths: katsura, tare or kashira. Katsura, not generally used for male roles, are black wigs parted in the middle, covering the ears and pulled back. Tare are longer, falling to the shoulders; they are always worn with a kammuri or head ornament, which may be a hat, a crown, or another kind of headgear. Some tare are white rather than black, and are used for aged gods or warriors. The third variety of wig, kashira, hangs down in back as far as the hems of the robe or even to the floor, in front to the actor's chest. The kashira exists in black, white and red: black is for a wide variety of male roles, white for aged persons, red for demons. The wigs are fastened to the head by a broad, decorated cloth band, the ends of which hang down behind. Some wig bands are exquisite examples of weaving and embroidery. The colors used with a particular wig are determined by the role. An expert, if informed of the mask, wig, wig band and headgear used for the shite's part, should be able to name the play.

THE COSTUMES

The brilliance of the Nō costumes relieves the performances from any impression of excessive severity that might be created by the astringent bareness of the stage, the harsh cries of the musicians, and the formal gestures of the dancers. In Zeami's and Zenchiku's day the costumes were probably far less elaborate than today, and possibly even in bad taste by modern standards; we can infer this from the description of a costume worn in Bashō ("The Plantain Tree"), which was to be suitably ripped here and there to suggest the easily torn leaves of the plantain tree.

The oldest surviving Nō robes, dating from the reign of the Shogun Yoshimasa in the fifteenth century, may have been woven for the Shogun himself, as their sober but elegant taste indicates. One owned by the Kanze family, a jacket (happi) of dark green material woven with gold thread in designs of paired dragonflies, is a lovely but unassertive robe. We can imagine Yoshimasa removing his jacket and throwing it to the actors in admiration, rather in the manner of a Spaniard throwing some article of clothing into a bull ring by way of homage to a toreador. The presentation of robes by way of reward goes back at least as far as Zeami's day. By the seventeenth century it came to be a gesture of affluence on the part of daimyos towards the actors they maintained. During the Tokugawa period the robes attained a degree of elegance and luxury unparalleled in theatrical costumes elsewhere. Some were woven or embroidered in silks with breathtakingly bold patterns of plantain leaves, enormous butterflies, wisteria sprays, or ships riding the waves; others were covered with finely figured designs in geometric or floral patterns; still others had patches of contrasting, brilliant colors and designs. The robes were woven in heavy brocades or translucent gossamer silks, and the blend of the colors, whether on the surface of the robes, between one layer and the layer underneath, or between the surface and the lining, was in flawless, though sometimes daring, taste.

The Nō costumes are without exception splendid, whether the actor appears as a princess or a fishergirl, a general or a priest, but the colors and designs are modified according to the roles. The costumes for the female roles are divided between those with and without "color" (iro). By "color" was meant red, associated with young women and worn with the ko-omote, waka-onna or magojirō masks in such plays as Matsukaze or Yuya. Roles performed with the shakumi or fukai masks (like the mother in Sumidagawa or the jealous wife in Kinuta) are costumed in robes without "color." Color is not, of course, used in costuming old women, though there are a few exceptions: the shite in Sotoba Komachi, though a woman of a hundred years, wears a touch of red in her sash or cloak to suggest that something of the beautiful woman lingers about her. If red is used for the outer robe the color is usually echoed in the wig band, the sash and even in the fan. These hardly visible touches of color help to create a unified impression. On occasion, as when a young god is portrayed, a brilliant red sash, contrasting with the white or pastel color of his robe, produces an effect of youthful vigor.

The colors of the under-kimonos, visible at the neckline, are also important indications of the "dignity" of the role. The colors may be single, double or triple, each variation signifying a difference in character. White, red, light blue, dark blue, ultramarine, light green, russet, yellow-brown and brown are the chief colors used. White is the most dignified, green and brown the least dignified. Red stands for youth, high spirits, good fortune; light blue for a quiet temperament; dark blue or ultramarine is used for strong roles; light green is generally reserved for menials, and the browns for old people. The use of white under-kimonos in a play of the third category marks the role as of the highest "dignity"; more commonly, the neckline will show one white and one red under-kimono. In *Shōjō* two red under-kimonos are worn by the auspicious red-maned demon, and as acted by the Kongō school the demon is further graced by red *tabi* on his feet. Because red is somewhat less dignified than white it is the invariable color of youthful female *tsure*, of some male *tsure*, and of all *kokata*. The *waki* usually wears a light blue under-kimono. A combination of one white and one light blue under-kimono adds dignity to a role.

Each actor before appearing onstage chooses the costume for the part according to the emphasis he desires to give the role, the mask to be worn, and the holdings of his school. Strong traditions dictate the costumes to be worn for certain roles: the snake-lady in *Dōjōji* always wears a robe with a lozenge pattern suggesting a snakeskin. Nevertheless, the actor enjoys some leeway in his shading of most roles. When a play is revived after long absence from the Nō stage the costuming is particularly important. At the revival of the rarely-performed *Ochiba* ("Fallen Leaves") by the present Kongō Iwao, the entrance of the *shite*, wearing a *chōken* (long-sleeved jacket) of a mingled green and brown, evocative of fallen autumn leaves, created an unforgettable impression. This superb garment was a modern reweaving of a *chōken* originally presented the school by the Shogun Yoshimasa.

The articles of clothing worn, including the many varieties of headgear, reveal the function and dignity of the persons. No less than twenty-eight costumes have been distinguished for the male roles performed without mask. Twenty or so distinct types of attire for female *shite* and *tsure* exist, and there are comparable numbers for all other parts, including the Kyōgen. The Nō robes, originally derived from the costumes of the court and military nobility (and the priesthood), were later modified so noticeably that they came to constitute a distinct variety of dress seen only on the stage. A typical robe worn by men and women alike is the *mizugoromo*, a kind of cloak. The *mizugoromo* occurs in white, black, gray, violet and most pastel shades, depending on the role. Most often it is unpatterned and woven of raw silk into a thin gauzy material. When worn in a male role a sash is tied over the *mizugoromo*, but in female roles it is held together by a silken cord. Each detail of the costuming is governed by usage, down to the type of fan carried and whether or not it can be tucked into the sash of the *mizugoromo*. Details of the costumes are discussed elsewhere in connection with the accompanying photographs.

The mask and costume used by an actor in a particular role reveal almost as much about his interpretation of the part as his singing and dancing. The mask and wig give him the face of his choice, the voluminous robes, all but blotting out the outlines of his own figure, give him the shape prescribed by aesthetic ideals, and the most glorious colors ever used to adorn the human form surround him in beauty. The eyes of the spectators are dazzled by the sight of the *shite*, but the purpose of the mask and costume is not so much to attract attention and praise as it is to allow the spectator, undistracted by ugliness, to take these exquisite passages into a realm of absolute beauty.

V. MUSIC AND DANCE IN THE PLAYS

MUSIC

For the hundreds of thousands of amateurs who study the singing of the texts Nō is primarily a vocal art and the actors are above all singers. Amateurs who devote themselves to the *shimai*, the climactic dances in the plays, may disagree about the importance of song, but they recognize equally that music is essential to their dances. The scholar of literature, it is true, may read the Nō plays as if they were verse dramas, not thinking of the music he is missing, but a performance without music would be unthinkable. The stranger to Nō may nevertheless find that the music, though hypnotically impressive, lacks the variety common to most other music for the stage, a variety stemming both from alternations of mood and tempo and from the distinctive styles of different composers. The music in Nō lacks obvious contrasts of mood, and it would be almost impossible to identify the composers. Its importance also seems to be thrown in doubt by the tolerance of the poor voices of many actors. The great Hōshō Kurō went so far as to deplore the tendency, prevalent in his day, for actors to rely on the beauty of their voices to win acclaim; this, he insisted, was contrary to the emphasis on interpretation characteristic of Nō. Even at their most lyric, the songs of the *shite* rarely attain an independent existence as melody; only in the sections sung by the chorus is it easy to detect the melodic element, which sounds—to the non-musician at least—rather like the Gregorian chants. The man witnessing Nō for the first time may find the music to be the most elusive aspect.

The difficulty of Nō music comes both from its complexity and its dissimilarity to familiar Western music. The texts used by the actors are marked with dots, curved and angular lines, and letters of the Japanese syllabary, each indicating the manner in which a particular syllable is to be delivered. A rise or fall in the voice, a shift from declamation to recitative or to full voice, can be prescribed, but these markings (dating back to the sixteenth century) give only the relative pitch and length of the notes, not absolute values. A mark indicates that a sound is held twice as long as the preceding one or that it is higher in pitch, but not the note that might be played on a piano. Neither is the tempo of the successive notes stated except vaguely, in recommendations that a passage be "quietly" rendered and the like. The annotations serve as a guide or reminder to students of Nō, but they must turn to their teachers for instruction. Even then they will discover that ultimately the singing of a role, like the dance, depends on the actor's understanding of its "dignity" *(kurai)*, and his ability to suggest by means of vocal techniques unknown in the West the inner natures of the characters he portrays.

The simplest parts of the play are those in prose, sometimes a third or more of the whole. These passages, which bear almost no musical notation, are declaimed in a style marked by regular cadences; in particular, the second note after each pause in a sustained utterance is delivered at a noticeably higher pitch. In some schools the pattern of declamation depends on whether the actor is representing a man, a woman or an old person; in others no distinction is made. Despite the mournful prolongation of the words the prose parts are in general intelligible to the audience. They are delivered without musical background.

It is rather misleading to speak of the "accompaniment" for the sung parts. The "name saying" (*nanori*) at the start of the play is sometimes "accompanied" by a flute, but the flute neither blends with nor opposes the singer's vocal line; its music proceeds virtually independently, decorating or heightening the passage, but not commenting on it. Even the drums "accompanying" the singer may not play at his tempo. Indeed, one feature of all Nō music is its irregularity; the range required of the singer's voice being extremely limited and the musical patterns established by long tradition, slight differences in tempo or accent assume great importance, and the mood evoked by the musician's hand against a drum or by his inarticulate cries evokes the poetry better than would an accompaniment which merely echoed or reinforced the vocal line.

Two styles of singing Nō are distinguished, *yowagin* (weak) and *tsuyogin* (strong). Different styles of singing apparently existed even in Zeami's day, but the present distinction of "weak" and "strong" dates only from the late seventeenth century. Previously, *yowagin* was used exclusively. *Yowagin* can be rendered with reasonable accuracy in Western musical notation, but *tsuyogin*, closer to declamation, hardly goes beyond two distinguishable tones. In contrast to the rich melodic patterns of some passages delivered in *yowagin*, in *tsuyogin* "accent, dynamic stress, tone color, and a special vocal technique are more important than melodic movement itself."* *Yowagin* predominates in most plays, especially in scenes of heightened emotional content, but *tsuyogin* occurs in auspicious or festive plays like *Takasago*.

The vocal music includes sections like the *issei* or *kuri* in free rhythms, and others in fixed rhythms, such as the entrance song (*shidai*) of the *waki*, the travel song (*michiyuki*), and passages of dialogue between the *shite* and chorus. There are three basic rhythmic structures: the first, a majestic, regular beat called *ō-nori*, links each beat to a single syllable; the second, the fast *chū-nori*, links one beat to two syllables; and the third, the *hira-nori*, distributes the twelve syllables of a normal line of Nō poetry (consisting of two verses of seven and five syllables respectively) among eight beats. Of these three rhythmic patterns the last, the *hira-nori*, is by far the most common. Its pattern tends to fall into two sections: the first fits a seven-syllable verse into four and one-half beats, the second fits a five-syllable verse into three and one-half beats. This is done by giving the first, fourth and seventh syllables double the duration of the others. The final beat is usually a pause, plus the beginning of the next beat. The counting of the beat therefore begins not at "one" but at "eight," taking over from the end of the previous section. Many variations exist, but adequate discussion involves technicalities beyond a layman's competence. The rhythms of Nō in any case are flexible, not metronomic; indeed, musicians avoid metronomic regularity as carefully as some Western musicians cultivate it.

Nō gives pleasure to many solely as music, but to the actors the music is the natural outgrowth of the sounds and meanings of the words and of the overall "dignity" of the play. The melodies, whether in such purely instrumental sections as the opening flute solos or in the sustained passages of choral singing, are rarely unique to a particular play, though the combinations form peculiarly appropriate patterns. There is never any improvisation in the performance—every sound, to the last cry from a drummer and the part of his drum he strikes, is noted in the score—but flexibility in the rhythm and tempo enables the actor to impart to his singing an individual interpretation of the roles.

The statements by the great actors on their preferred way of singing the roles afford some clues to their interpretations. Kanze Sakon (1895–1939) wrote about the *waki* part in *Takasago*: "The *waki*, being a minister of state, should sing forcefully and clearly, without faltering. His entrance song, this being a Nō play of the first category, should be delivered with greater forthrightness

*From the excellent article "Japanese *Noh* Music" by Tatsuo Minagawa in *Journal of the American Musicological Society*, Vol. X, No. 3, (1957).

than a normal entrance song. In general, the actor should attempt in singing the *waki* role to preserve a smoothly flowing line." Sakon went on to describe the entrance song *(shin no issei)* of the *shite* and *tsure* in the same play: "The *shite* enters, accompanied by the *tsure*, and sings the entrance song. This passage, as the first song by the *shite*, determines the *kurai* of the piece and is therefore most important. It should be sung loudly and firmly with a relaxed but solemn feeling. The actor must not impart to it sticky, heavy or listless feelings."

The manner in which the music may affect the actor's performance is indicated by remarks of Umewaka Manzaburō (1868–1946) concerning the "woman" plays: "By the time the *waki* has made his entrance the "dignity" of the play should already have been established. Of course, a clear distinction must be made between the music accompanying the *waki*'s entrance song and that found in a god play or a warrior play. This distinction is all the more essential for the entrance of the *shite*; the musicians must exercise sufficient care so that there will be plasticity in the accompaniment. Any lack of understanding on the part of the musicians will make it extremely difficult for the actor even to step out on the *hashigakari*, let alone to travel along the *hashigakari* to the stage. If the musicians let the tempo get out of hand, the *shite* will be forced to race down the *hashigakari*, for he has no choice but to move his feet ahead in step with the *ya ha* of the accompaniment."

Specific recommendations on the manner of singing Nō are apt to be unintelligible to the layman, and even the devoted student of Nō can hardly be guided much by the constant injunctions to maintain grace and dignity. The present head of the Kanze school, Kanze Motomasa, suggests the great emphasis given today to the psychological analysis of a play like *Kagekiyo*: "Even if I were to attempt to treat each problem involved, I could not hope to explain everything. The student has no choice but to follow his teacher's instructions. He should practice the opening passage again and again until satisfied." Motomasa added, "If a student has been able to analyze exhaustively the character of Kagekiyo, he has already succeeded eighty percent with the opening song. Of course, the musical line here is one of unusual difficulty even within the entire repertory, and any belief that analysis of the character alone suffices would lead to serious mistakes. But if the student combines with an adequate command of the melodic line a complete understanding of the role, then practices beyond all normal demands, he will probably pass as a fair singer of *Kagekiyo*."

The delivery of the Nō actor cannot be judged by the standards of Western singing, for no attempt is made to delight by the beauty of sound alone. The different voices—tenor, baritone or bass—are not distinguished intentionally, and certainly there is no exploitation of the extremes of the voice, whether the ringing high notes of the tenor or the growling depths of the basso. A hoarse, quavering or thin voice is not considered a flaw in an older actor, and a younger actor will also be forgiven an inadequate voice if he manages somehow to convey the inner meaning of the texts. The Hōshō school insists that singers produce a "lower voice" together with their normal tones, a complexity in vocal production intended, no doubt, to parallel the complexities of meaning in the text, which easily results in a strong vibrato. The voice, regardless of school, is produced in the back of the throat, altering the quality of the vowels and contributing to the obscurity of the words. A novice taking his first lesson from a teacher of the Komparu school is likely to be informed that it is a feature of the singing of this school to open the mouth wide but never show the teeth; what this does to the diction can be imagined. The peculiarities of the delivery certainly interfere with intelligibility, but the spectators (who either know the texts by heart or consult printed versions) expect the actors to interpret the words rather than enunciate them. The voice itself becomes a special kind of musical instrument, no less than the drums and flute.

Of the instruments used in the Nō ensemble the flute is closest to its Western equivalent. It is some fifteen inches long, made of bamboo, and has seven apertures in addition to the mouth-hole. The flute is the only instrument capable of sustaining a melody, but the thin, sometimes shrill notes are apt to produce an effect of disembodied sound rather than the sweetness associated with the Western flute; the two are as dissimilar as the mad women in Nō and the unhappy heroine of *Lucia di Lammermoor*, who goes mad to a flute accompaniment.

The *kotsuzumi* and *ōkawa* are quite unlike any Western instrument. Each is shaped like a diabolo, the *kotsuzumi* being covered with coltskin, the *ōkawa* with ox or horsehide. The drums, made of lacquered cherry wood, are kept in tune by six hempen cords fastened to holes in the metal rims at the two ends. The *kotsuzumi* is about eight and a half inches long, the *ōkawa* nine and a half inches; but it is less the difference in size than the difference in the skins drawn over the drum-frames that causes the two drums to sound so dissimilar. The *ōkawa* produces a loud and resonant crack, the *kotsuzumi* a more delicate thump. The *kotsuzumi* is grasped by the cords with the fingers and palm of the left hand and held on the right shoulder, where the drummer strikes it with the fingers of his right hand. The quality of the sound depends on the tension of the cords and the place on the skin struck, whether the center or the edges. The *ōkawa* is grasped in the left hand by the cords and placed on the left knee, where the drummer strikes it with the fingers of his right hand. The index, middle finger and palm of the hand are protected by leather coverings against the smart from the taut skin. Unlike the *kotsuzumi*, the *ōkawa* cannot be tuned in performance; this means that the only differences in sound possible are loud and soft, but the expert can recognize whether or not a new drumskin has been used for each performance, as tradition prescribes (but as economic realities rarely permit).

The *taiko*, a large drum, is used in perhaps a third of the plays. It is beaten, like a Western drum, with sticks held in both hands. The *taiko* rests on a low stand placed on the stage, and the drummer, less fortunate than the *kotsuzumi* or *ōkawa* player who sits on a folding stool, must kneel on the bare stage, sometimes striking the drum from high above his shoulder, sometimes bending to cut off reverberations. The *taiko* is about eight and a half inches in diameter, but the only place struck is a round patch of deerskin about two inches wide pasted at the center.

The sounds of the instruments are accompanied by cries from the players. In general, a player utters a cry *(kakegoe)* before the half-beat. The variety of the cry and the strength of his beat give character to the sound. There are four basic varieties of cries: *ya*, delivered before the first and fifth beats, indicating that it divides the eight beats of a measure in two; *ha*, delivered before the second, third, sixth and seventh (and sometimes the eighth) beats; *iya* and *yoi*, delivered with odd-numbered beats, to demarcate the rhythmic patterns or serve as signals to points of tension.

The music for Kyōgen is far simpler. Most lines are delivered to a rhythmical, though not specifically musical, intonation. The standard opening line of a Kyōgen, "I am a person who lives in this vicinity," is delivered by actors of the Ōkura school as:

kore wa/ kono atari ni/ sumai/ itasu mono de/ gozaru.

This passage is in prose, but as the contemporary Kyōgen actor Shigeyama Sennojō explains, a rhythmical quality is imparted by giving each group of syllables, whether three or six, about the same length of time and a single accent, without ever slurring the pronunciation of unaccented syllables. Most important to the effect is the ringing Kyōgen voice, which Sennojō's great-grand-father Sengorō Masatora (1810–1886) once compared in vigor and clarity to the sensation of slicing vertically through a piece of green bamboo.

Occasional songs, called *kouta*, are interpolated in the plays. These popular songs of the Muromachi period are far lighter both in content and delivery than the music for Nō; they are, moreover, always identified as songs by the characters and not utterances which are sung. Usually, too, the *kouta* are not accompanied, but in some plays, especially those of a festive nature, drums accompany the dance of a god. In other plays Nō is parodied by having the foolish hero make his entrance to the conventional accompaniment of a flute and drums only to intone such unpoetical lines as, "I am glad to be returning home and I am eager to see my wife and children again." But musical accompaniments of whatever variety are exceptions: the Kyōgen plays are prose, spoken dramas with only occasional outbursts of song.

DANCE

Dance is no less close to the heart of Nō than music. By "dance," however, one should not imagine anything resembling even the stateliest of Western ballets. Some movements called "dance" in Nō seem hardly more than a solemn circling of the stage; others are so slow and so devoid of choreographic ornamentation that it is hard to tell when the dance begins or ends. With the exception of a handful of special dances, like the *rambyōshi* ("wild rhythm") of *Dōjōji*, the dances consist of familiar elements, repeated from play to play, on the surface little related to the actions or the characters. Instruction in performing the *shimai*, regularly published in the magazines directed at students of Nō, is likely to consist of a few diagrams depicting simple triangular or semi-circular patterns of movement and statements such as: "Stand when the chorus sings *the lightning flashing in the trees*; stamp the left foot at the syllable *re* at the end of the phrase *hi ka to koso mire*; at the words *truly the world is like a lightning flash glittering on the morning dew* take four steps forward, beginning with the left foot," and so on. The exact moment to open the fan or to sing a phrase, taking over from the chorus, is clearly stated, but if the dance were no more complex than these injunctions imply, it could not rank as an important part of Nō.

Our experience is quite otherwise. The dances in Nō dominate remembrances of the plays to such a degree that some critics have insisted that the plays themselves are little more than preparations or justifications for the dances. These dances never startle by their pyrotechnics; they are so rarely athletic that, like the singing, they are best performed by aged actors even in the roles of young women or warriors in their prime. An unearthly beauty pervades the dances. Oswald Sickert, writing in 1916 his impressions of the final dance in *Hagoromo*, declared, "The divine lady returned on her steps at great length and fully six times after I thought I could not bear it another moment. She went on for twenty minutes, perhaps, or an hour or a night; I lost count of time; but I shall not recover from the longing she left when at last she floated backwards and under the fatal uplifted curtain."

The movements of the dance are unassertive but they express and epitomize the texts, not by crude miming (though in a few realistic plays the actor's gestures may suggest actions described by the chorus), but by evoking the ultimate meaning, the "dignity" of the work. Kita Roppeita's performance as the angel in *Hagoromo*, even when he was a man in his sixties, enchanted audiences by an atmosphere of remarkable charm. Even at eighty his performance as the *shite*, a white heron, in *Sagi* was filled with a haunting, other-worldly beauty, though he appeared without a mask. By tradition this role is danced only by a boy under twelve or a man over sixty, someone untouched by worldly passions, and as Roppeita danced he communicated a magic power surely partaking of *yūgen*, a quality that could exist only in Nō.

The higher the "dignity" of a play, the fewer and simpler tne movements of the dances; unable to distract by mere virtuosity, the actor must transmute each gesture into symbolic utterance. Some roles, it is true, require great agility. The Kongō school in particular maintains a tradition of acrobatic display in a few plays. But though people still reminisce admiringly about the late Kongō Iwao turning somersaults as the demon in *Tsuchigumo*, even when in his fifties, the Kongō school itself prizes this skill less than the ability to execute with authority the unassertive movements of a *Matsukaze*. The audiences too attend Nō not for brilliance of footwork but for absolute assurance in every gesture of the head, arms, body and legs, an inevitability that expresses the nature of a role better than the most literal display.

We are often told about the glories of the actors of former days, which are contrasted unfavorably with contemporary performances. Normally it is impossible to prove or disprove these assertions, but the film of *Aoi no Ue* made in 1936 by Sakurama Kintarō (1889–1957) reveals an almost unbelievably accomplished performer whose every motion glows with controlled fire. In his later years Kintarō once advised amateurs how they should go about learning the *shimai*: "You should stand erect, your head perfectly straight, pulling your chin back as far as possible. If you pull back your chin your whole body—not only the line of your neck—will naturally be straight. The shoulders should be relaxed, but the arms kept at the sides and held in a gentle arc so that the elbows will not sag. This is worth noticing; most people, when told to stand erect, at once throw back their shoulders and their body freezes. You should let your strength flow into your abdomen without making any conscious effort to do so. As long as you maintain a steady posture your strength will naturally flow there . . . The small of the back, like the chin, should be pulled back somewhat, but you must avoid protruding the buttocks. The exact posture to be held can only be demonstrated on the stage.

"The first thing the actor must remember while onstage is to walk on his heels. Ordinarily one begins a step with the toes, but in Nō the actor puts his strength into his heels and walks from the heels. If he puts his strength into his heels his toes will naturally curve upwards somewhat. If he were deliberately to attempt to curve the toes it would look unnatural, but if he concentrates on his heels the toes seem to curve upwards of themselves. It is ugly if the actor permits his knees to bend excessively when walking.

"Movements of the eyes are also important. There is nothing less attractive than an actor with unsteady eyes. It sometimes happens that a single glance reveals the emotions of a character."

Dance in Nō has been defined as any action made by the actors on the stage, for not one motion is unpremeditated. In a narrower sense, dance can be defined as movements by the actor to the accompaniment of a flute at a time that the chorus is not singing. Dancelike movements executed while the chorus is singing and which may or may not be related to the words of the song are known as *kata*, or forms. These highly stylized gestures are best considered in terms of photographs. They provide much of the element of *monomane* ("imitation of things") in a performance, though far removed from literal representation. The *kata* provide intermittent clues to the texts, but the dances of Nō, usually abstract patterns, are almost synonymous with the art itself.

The varieties within each of the five categories of Nō dramas are distinguished as much by the dances as by the subject matter; indeed, the dances and subject matter are inseparable and affect the entire structure of each play. Two main divisions are made: *mai* and *hataraki*. *Mai* are recognizable as dance by their length, solemn atmosphere and complexity of movements, but *hataraki* may be so simple as hardly to seem dances. Often the *hataraki* consist of vigorous, even wild, steps, and are used especially for fierce gods or demons. The *hataraki*, unlike the *mai*, are generally not performed to the same rhythm as the accompanying flute. The *mai* contain no elements of representation, but the *hataraki* may embody *kata* which refer to the texts.

Seven varieties of dance can be found in plays of the first category, the god plays, alone: *kami-mai* ("god dances"), *hataraki*, *gaku* (dances derived from *bugaku*), *shinnojonomai* (especially slow and stately dances), *chūnomai* (dances performed by female deities), plus *kagura* and *shishimai* ("lion dance") used in one play each. A play with a *kamimai*, for example, contains such features as: (1) two scenes, the first consisting of the *jo* and *ha* sections of the play, the second of the *kyū*; (2) a dance occurring in the second scene; (3) the *shite* in the first scene appears as an old man of lowly occupation, normally accompanied by another man who does not wear a mask; (4) the *shite* in the second scene appears as a youthful god and performs a vigorous dance to express his appreciation of the worshipers' sincerity, a token of his desire for the protection of the imperial family and the nation; (5) the *waki* as a rule is a courtier, accompanied by two to four attendants.

Obviously the nature of the dance grows out of the plot, which in turn must be made to fit smoothly into the pattern of expression provided by the dance. If the story tells of an aged god rather than a youthful one, the dance performed in the second scene must be a *shinnojonomai*. In this case the *waki* will be a Shinto priest rather than a courtier. Again, if there are two dancers a *hataraki* will be used; the *shite* of the first part, whether a man or a woman, will wear a mask of less exalted "dignity" than for a *kaminomai* or *shinnojonomai* role; and the costume will be plebeian. A mixture of the elements proper to different dances does not occur.

The typical dance in the warrior plays is called *kakeri*, a relatively short and simple dance usually performed by the *shite* as he enacts his confession of the sins of violence which have brought him torture.

Plays of the third category are almost all about women, though in two the *shite* is the poet and great lover Narihira. The dances are slow and elegant; more than half are *jonomai*, a dance of the slowest tempo. In these plays the *shite* of the first scene is a village woman of humble birth, but normally the same mask is retained for the second scene where she appears as a noblewoman. The *waki* is an itinerant priest. In some works a *taiko* is added to the accompaniment. This creates a somewhat livelier atmosphere, and the "dignity" is therefore lower than that of plays without the *taiko*. Another group of third category plays is of a more realistic nature and in one scene, like *Yuya*. Here the dance is a *chūnomai* of a faster tempo.

The fourth category contains the greatest variety of plays and dances, including those like *Hanjo* with a graceful *chūnomai* for the *shite*, a woman; or like *Semimaru* with an agitated *kakeri*; or like *Sotoba Komachi* with a brief *iroe*, a gliding about the stage rather than a dance; or like *Kanawa* with a fierce *inori* ("prayer") dance by which a demon is subdued; or like *Shunkan* with no dance at all. These plays rely less on the beauty of the dance (which may be the core of a work like *Matsukaze* or *Hagoromo*) than on what it contributes to the dramatic tension. It might be said of certain plays of the first or third categories especially that they are excuses for dances, but in plays of this category if the action does not require a dance, none is performed.

Plays of the fifth category, belonging to the fastest section of the program, almost all have *hataraki* rather than *mai*, regardless of the plot. A typical work concludes with the furious prancing of a demon, but in the special case of *Funa Benkei*, the *shite* of the first part is given a *chūnomai*, performed in the semblance of Shizuka, the beautiful sweetheart of Yoshitsune, as well as a *hataraki* in the second part, performed as the fierce ghost of Tomomori.

In addition to the *mai* and *hataraki* mentioned above, which figure in almost every Nō play, a few dances are performed in one work only, including the three different dances of *Okina* and the *rambyōshi* in *Dōjōji*.

The effortless lines described by a master actor's body as he moves in a dance are the despair of the amateur. Though the movements are simple in themselves, they approach a perfection that can be sensed though not measured in terms of the height of a leap, the number of entrechats, or the other obvious exhibitions of virtuosity in Western ballet. The depth of communication—the ability of the actor to express with his whole body the torment, serene joy or bittersweet longing felt by a character—is the only touchstone of his powers. Every passage in the text is given overtones by the actor's movements, though none may directly represent the words. Criticism of the dances by experts in Nō sometimes suggests to the amateur the emperor's new clothes, a beauty more in the eye of the beholder than in the performance, but repeated experiences in this theatre breed a virtuoso audience no less than virtuoso actors. The Nō actors, with the barest economy of means, achieve in song and dance a grandeur of expression fully intelligible only to spectators who have made comparable efforts to understand this endlessly rewarding art.

VI. THE NŌ STAGE AND ITS PROPERTIES

THE STAGE

The interior of a Nō theatre is unlike any other in the world. It is dominated by the large, gleaming stage projecting into the auditorium, a stage which by its size and majesty seems to assert that even without actors it would have sufficient reason to exist. Its ornate curved roof confirms this impression of independence: the stage, as we have seen, was formerly a separate building, and at the very beginning of its history may have served as the scene of ritual observances before the gods. Today, when the theatre building housing the Nō stage may be fashionably modern, and the audience attired mainly in business suits and Paris-inspired dresses, the stage still imposes its authority, hushing the voices of those entering its presence, even before the performance begins. The absence of a curtain, the unvarying lighting before and during a performance, the great pine painted on the back wall, all suggest less a Western stage—shabby and bare until it takes on life from a play—than a church, itself an architectural masterpiece but ready for the drama of the mass.

Each event that takes place in a performance emphasizes the presence of the stage. In a Western theatre, whether an ornate opera house or an intimate theatre-in-the-round, the stage itself is no more than the platform on which the actors perform. It may be chalk-marked to show the actors where to stand, or grimy with the residue of a thousand nights, or pockmarked with holes. Nothing in the world is so forlorn as a Broadway theatre after a performance, the abandoned set lit by a single, naked lamp. The Nō stage, by contrast, is a superbly finished object of art whose surface is polished rather than scuffed by the actors, their feet shod in white cloth *tabi*. The boards are immaculate. A famous anecdote tells of an actor who was complimented by an expert in Japanese fencing for having maintained an *en garde* position throughout a performance—except for one fleeting moment of uncertainty. "Yes," answered the actor, "that was when I noticed a speck of dust on the stage."

The importance of the stage to the plays is underlined by the precise nomenclature for the different areas and the equally precise functions that have been assigned to each. The *hashigakari*, an extension of the stage, affords superb possibilities for entrances and exits, whether the uncertain steps of the blind Yoroboshi, guided by an inner light, or the precipitous departure of one Kyōgen actor in pursuit of another. Some scenes take place entirely on the *hashigakari*, the actors disposed at the first, second and third pines to form a pleasing composition. The railing of the *hashigakari* may also serve a function in the play, as when a demon vaults from it onto the stage. Even the entrance of the musicians at the start of a play is given a solemn dignity by their passage along the *hashigakari* that no entrance from the wings of a conventional Western theatre could approximate.

Once on the stage from the *hashigakari*, the *waki* and the *shite* will each go to his appointed place, and though they move away from time to time, they will presently return. It is not merely that the actors are so strongly bound by traditions that they cannot make innovations; the stage no more permits the *shite* to stand in the *waki*'s place than the rituals of a church would permit the

83

officiating priests to alter their stations in the interests of more powerful dramatic effects. The actor's appearance on the Nō stage presupposes that he will obey its demands.

The actor acknowledges the importance of the stage by his pounding on it during climactic moments of his dances. Unlike the ballet dancer who attempts to create an illusion of weightlessness, the Nō actor insists that he tread the stage. If he leaps in the violent movements of a dance, he deliberately lands with a reverberating thud. Even the ghosts in Nō proclaim their reality by their footfalls.

The stage imposes its aesthetics. The plays, with few exceptions, can be acted without props, but even when props are used, they are never permitted to clutter the clean expanse of the Nō stage or to usurp the audience's attention. The prop—whether a boat, a tree, a hut or a carriage— is hardly more than an outline of the object represented. The boat in *Funa Benkei* is so small that only the boatman, Yoshitsune and Benkei can board it; the other soldiers sit on the stage outside the white frame of the boat in an attitude of being aboard. Of course it would be possible to build a more commodious boat, but the larger the prop the less easily it could be brought on by the stage assistants and removed when no longer needed; moreover, it would break the beautiful lines of the stage.

The present form of the Nō stage dates from the mid-Tokugawa period, when Nō achieved what may have been its final evolution. The earliest stages consisted of pieces of level ground, perhaps beaten earth like the rings for *sumō* wrestlers. Even today the torchlight Nō performances at the Kasuga Shrine in Nara take place on a stage consisting merely of boards over the bare ground. Originally—as at the Kasuga Shrine today—there was no *hashigakari*. The actors made their way to the stage from the dressing room, a curtained-off enclosure some distance away, entering the stage from the rear-center. The pines now planted along the *hashigakari* may be a memento of the trees passed by the actors in former days as they walked through the precincts of a shrine to the stage; similarly, the curtain that shields the mirror room from the *hashigakari* may be the descendant of the curtains around the original makeshift dressing room.

The bridge to the stage gradually developed into a formal architectural feature. At the time of the performances given in 1464 under the patronage of the Shogun Yoshimasa a passageway similar to the *hashigakari* extended from the dressing room to the stage-rear, meeting it perpendicularly. A curtain hid the backstage area beyond the *hashigakari*. Seats were arranged in a large circle around the stage: the area directly in front of the stage was reserved for the gods, and the best seats (adjacent to the gods') were occupied by the shogun (to the left) and his consort (to the right). Less favored guests sat at the opposite side of the circle, near the *hashigakari*. The presence of an audience on all sides suggests a style of performance dissimilar to that of Nō today, but the actors probably concerned themselves with pleasing the spectators directly before them— the gods and the shogun.

In the early Muromachi period the *dengaku* stage had two *hashigakari*, one on either side, presumably in imitation of the practice of *bugaku* dancers of entering from both left and right. Not long after the 1464 performances the Nō actors began to experiment with attaching the *hashigakari* to a side of the stage rather than to the rear. At first the *hashigakari* extended to the stage at stage-left, by the flute pillar, but presently it was switched to stage-right, by the *shite* pillar, perhaps because the side closer to the shogun's seat was considered more important. When stages came to be built within the compound of a daimyo's palace, less spacious than a Shinto shrine, the angle made by the *hashigakari* and the stage, at first almost forty-five degrees, steadily decreased. Today the horizontal boards of the *atoza* merge almost imperceptibly with those of the *hashigakari*.

By good fortune two magnificent old Nō stages have been preserved. The first, at the Itsukushima Shrine on the Inland Sea, was built in 1568 as an offering to the shrine by Mōri Motonari (1497–1551), a powerful warlord who found time amidst his more than two hundred military campaigns to become expert in poetry and the arts. The stage at Itsukushima is built so close to the sea that high tide flows between the stage and the spectators, creating the illusion that the realm of the plays is separated from our own not only by time and space but by the sea. The stage stands about three and one-half feet above the water. Its pointed roof thatched with *hinoki* bark and its unpainted pillars (unlike the satiny gleam of the pillars at other Nō stages) have a weather-beaten look that makes the contrast with the brilliant costumes all the more striking. The *hashi-gakari* from the dressing room meets the stage at rather a steep angle and its boards, instead of joining those of the *atoza*, cut across to those of the stage proper. The *hashigakari*, thatch-roofed like the stage, stands on stone posts, the better to resist the erosion of the sea water.

The stage at the Nishi Honganji Temple in Kyoto was originally constructed for Toyotomi Hideyoshi about 1595 and moved to its present site in 1626. It is still in use, together with a smaller practice stage which is slightly older. Seated in the temple hall surrounded by magnificent gold screens along the walls, it is easy for the spectator as he watches the plays today to imagine himself a daimyo. Beneath the eye-level of those seated in splendor within the hall stand the ground-lings on the gravel of the area around the stage. The elaborately carved horizontal beams under the stage roof are a further reminder of the grandeur of Hideyoshi's palace and of his great devotion to Nō. The *hashigakari* joins the stage, a separate building, at an angle conspicuously less acute than that at Itsukushima. The Nishi Honganji Temple stage may have been the first provided with large jars underneath for resonance—seven under the stage proper, two under the *atoza*, and three under the *hashigakari*. These jars are suspended by copper wires over pits in the ground to provide the maximum effect.

The conservatism of the Nō theatre accounts for its retaining the roof for the stage, the gravel bed around it, the steps leading down—all meaningless today in terms of function. Even the number and shape of the metal rings used to hold up the curtain at the end of the *hashigakari* have been carefully prescribed. Yet there have also been many changes, some unconscious, others re-flecting almost imperceptible shifts in taste. A modern Nō theatre is equipped with the latest com-forts, including an up-to-date restaurant that has largely replaced the lacquered lunch-boxes of the past, and the pine of the backdrop may be distinctly of the twentieth century, an angular tree that startles us by its unconventionality.

Some innovations have been adopted only after a long struggle. When it was first proposed that electric lights be installed in the Nō theatres, the conservative Hōshō Kurō and Umewaka Minoru were flatly opposed. Kita Roppeita, a younger *iemoto*, was willing to experiment, but at first allowed only one small light bulb and insisted that the audience be warned in advance that electricity would be used. Umewaka Minoru's son (who took his father's name) later recalled, "My father, a man of the old school, was curiously obstinate in some respects. In 1905 Mr. Iwasaki Yanosuke had complained that the stage was too dark when lit by candles only, and pro-posed that electric lights be installed, but my father was absolutely opposed. At the time, the theatre had two candles on either side of the steps at stage front, two before the *waki*'s seat, three on the *hashigakari*, and two thick candles in square glass boxes at the *kōken*'s seat and by the flute pillar. Mr. Iwasaki kept urging that these candles be replaced by electricity, and finally won the day when he pointed out that the glass boxes we were already using were no less foreign than electric lights."

The stage itself has changed little in recent years, but if future members of the chorus are unable to sit for prolonged periods on the wooden boards it may become necessary for stools or chairs to be provided, undoubtedly entailing some modification of the entire stage.

THE PROPS

Many plays are performed without props, but when used they add much to the visual pleasure of Nō. Yuya's journey to the blossoming cherry trees at Kiyomizu is given special brilliance by the carriage in which she travels. This prop is no more than a rudimentary evocation of the wheels and hood of a real carriage, but when Yuya stands inside to the accompaniment of music of suddenly heightened intensity, we feel poignantly the contrast between the loveliness of the blossoms and the sad thoughts of Yuya, who fears her mother may be dying. The prop lends a charm and pathos to the scene all out of proportion to the simple means employed.

Props are usually brought in along the *hashigakari* by the stage assistants before the play begins. In some plays, however, the prop is used only in the second part. It is particularly effective if the *shite* is first revealed to us when the wrappings of the prop, which represents a hut or a palace, are removed by the stage assistants. In *Kagekiyo* the wrappings drop away to disclose the old warrior in his hut, blind and despondent. If the character made his entrance along the *hashigakari* in the normal manner, the overpowering impression of withdrawal from the world would be much diluted. The hut in which Kagekiyo sits is barely large enough to hold a seated man. Once the wrappings are removed all that is left is four bamboo poles holding up a tiny thatched roof. The actor's appearance at that moment should be a clear indication of his interpretation of the entire role, whether he will emphasize the pathetic fate of the defeated warrior or the dignity of a man proud even in adversity. When at last Kagekiyo, having rejected his daughter, emerges from the hut, the prop makes this moment intensely moving. Of course the adept of Nō could easily visualize the pathos of the moment, even without the prop, but the flimsy little structure is more affecting than the hut that might be conjured up by the imagination.

Some elaborate props are used, like the great bell in *Dōjōji* into which the snake princess leaps, the platform ornamented with huge peonies used for the demons' dance in *Shakkyō*, or the chrysanthemum garden evoked by the prop in *Makura Jidō*. A few plays require props representing mountains or grave mounds from which the *shite* makes his appearance; usually these props are wrapped round with cloth and covered at the top with leaves to suggest the mountain vegetation. Pines, cherry trees and plum trees are represented by a standing branch held up by a square or circular frame. In *Izutsu* a frame with a spray of pampas grass represents the well-curb, and in *Hachinoki* the prop represents dwarf trees in their pots.

In addition to the stage props the actors often carry swords, halberds, sickles, Shinto wands, flower baskets, and a large variety of other objects intended to heighten their appearance in particular roles. Unlike the stage props which are dismantled after a performance, the accessories are solid, if often smaller-than-life, objects. The actor sometimes carries an accessory in his hand from his entrance, but in many plays he goes to the *atoza* and accepts the sword or cloak he will use from a stage assistant, returning it in the same manner when no longer needed. The stage assistants also produce the lacquered cylindrical cask which serves as a seat for the *shite* during moments of repose. This cask is commonly used in Kyōgen too, where it may represent a great variety of objects.

By far the most important of the accessories is the fan. Hardly a role in Nō does not require a fan. The signal for a dance by the *shite* is his lifting of the fan he keeps at his waist and opening it. The fan is not only indispensable to the dances of the *shite* but may be used, especially in Kyōgen, to represent other objects—a flask of saké, a saké cup, or a deadly weapon.

The importance of the fan in Nō reflects its peculiar role in Japanese life. A fan formed a part of formal attire in the past, and even today it is customary at New Year for ordinary citizens to carry a fan when making their first calls. As early as the eleventh century a fan was carried by military men when in attendance at court, and there are numerous accounts of court ladies, priests and others giving and receiving fans as presents on special occasions. The pictures painted on the fans include some counted among the masterpieces of Japanese art.

Three types of fans are used in Nō. The first, called *uchiwa*, is round and does not fold. A Chinese invention, it is carried only by Chinese personages in the Nō plays. (A variant, the enormous feather *uchiwa*, is carried by *tengu*, the feathered demons, as part of their outlandish getup.) The fan most commonly used in Nō is the *chūkei*, a folding fan. The folding fan was a Japanese invention—it was in fact a principal article of export to China during the Muromachi period—and its association with Japanese dance goes back at least to the twelfth century, when the *shirabyōshi* dancers beat time for their dances with a folding fan. *Chūkei* means something like "spread out from the middle," referring to the flaring out of the upper part of the fan. The *chūkei* used in Nō has fifteen ribs, either black or white (actually, the natural yellowish color of the bamboo). Black-ribbed fans are used for all female roles and for many male roles; white-ribbed fans for the roles of old men and priests. Fans with white ribs have monochrome paintings on white paper, but the fans with black ribs are decorated with brilliant colored scenes, the subjects determined largely by the category of the play. Fans used in plays of the first category in which the *shite* is a god are likely to bear a painting of phoenixes sporting among paulownia leaves and flowers. If the *shite*'s role is that of an old man, the painting on his fan may be a *sumie* representation of the Seven Sages of the Bamboo Grove. The design of fans used in plays of the second category, the warrior plays, depends on whether the *shite* is victorious or vanquished. The victorious warrior's fan has a design of the rising sun amidst pine branches; the defeated warrior's shows the sun rising amidst the waves, reminiscent of the Heike clan, which perished at sea. Plays of the third category, the woman plays, often use fans with brightly colored pictures of carriages filled with flowers or of court ladies carrying sprays of blossom in a "flower tournament." However, if the *shite*'s role is of an old woman the design may be of autumnal flowers or camellias. The obsessed women depicted in plays of the fourth category carry fans with a double design of profusely blossoming clematis and pine branches, no doubt to suggest the warring emotions in the *shite*'s mind. Fans carried by the demons in plays of the fifth category usually depict a peony in full blossom against a vermilion ground. The *waki* if a priest carries a fan with a design of the moon among the clouds, an allusion to the peripatetic life of the traveling monk. Certain roles require special designs, and variations exist from school to school. The *chūkei* used in Kyōgen are less rigidly prescribed in subject, but tend to be parodies of the beauties depicted on the Nō fans, showing for example a huge turnip on a golden ground.

Another variety of fan, called *shizumeori*, is more like the fan used in daily life. It is carried by actors in some roles performed without mask, and also when dancing the *shimai*, the climactic dances of the plays, in "concert versions," wearing an ordinary formal kimono instead of the costume for the role. Members of the chorus also carry these fans, placing them on the stage before them until about to recite, then raising them as in ceremonial utterance. The *shizumeori* fans bear different designs for each of the five schools of Nō: a pattern of swirling water for Kanze, five-fold clouds for Hōshō, five "dumplings" for Komparu, nine "dumplings" for Kongō, and three-fold clouds for Kita. The Kyōgen *shizumeori* also indicate the school: a design of young pines in the mist for Ōkura and usually a design of snowflakes in a circle for Izumi.

The handling of the fan is an essential part of the dancer's art, and each motion is as carefully prescribed as the steps of the feet. The fan accentuates the motions of the arm and lends grace to gestures, particularly the characteristic sweeping movements found in the Nō dances. Of all the stage props and accessories it is the most pervasive, and so indispensable that Nō has been spoken of as a kind of drama performed with fans.

Compared to theatres elsewhere in the world and even to other varieties of Japanese theatre, Nō and Kyōgen depend very little on props and accessories. The stage offers nothing to distract the audience, certainly nothing in the nature of the facile realism of representational theatres. Even such accessories as swords or spears are not intended to convince by any realistic glint of metal. The stage props help create the illusion of a particular place or atmosphere; the accessories help to distinguish the persons, rather as a wheel, tower or handkerchief may distinguish a medieval saint and tell us the nature of her suffering or triumph. But however effective the props may be in their functions, they are dispensable; representation in Nō depends far less on the props and accessories and even the costumes than on the basic elements, the stage and the masks.

PLATES

COLOR PLATE 2.
A scene from *Sōshi Arai Komachi* performed by Kanze Motomasa and other
actors of the Kanze school. The brilliance of the *karaori* robes gives a warm
coloring to the otherwise austere Nō stage.

COLOR PLATE 3.
Hanjo, performed by Umewaka Rokurō and actors of the Kanze school. The *shite* wears the *waka-onna* mask and a *karaori* robe bared from one shoulder to indicate the character is deranged.

PLEASURES OF NŌ

THE FIRST PLAY: *Okina*   Kanze School
Okina: Kanze Tetsunojō
Senzai: Nomura Shirō
Sambasō: Nomura Manzō

Okina has no plot, but consists of dances by three characters: an old man, apparently a god of longevity; a young man; and a third man who dances once without a mask and later with an old man's mask. The text, when not utterly obscure, promises happiness, peace, and prosperity. *Okina*, the oldest Nō play, is performed on felicitous occasions such as the New Year, always at the beginning of a program.

1–2. The ceremony in the "mirror room" before the performance. The mask to be worn by the actor appearing in the role of Okina is placed on the altar to the left, together with saké, salt and rice. (1) When the actors and musicians have assembled, the chief actor drinks some saké, eats a few grains of uncooked rice, and is purified by a handful of salt sprinkled over him. (2) Next, the other performers partake of the saké and rice, and are purified with salt.

3. After the actors and musicians have seated themselves, Okina begins to sing the cryptic but auspicious words *Tōtō tarari* . . .
4. Senzai dances to the music of flute and drums.

5. Senzai twirls his sleeve in his second dance after singing the words, "May this place last a thousand ages! We shall serve you a thousand autumns. The roar is the water from the falls. The sun shines but never ends. *Tōtari aryū dō dō.*" This passage is typical of the text.
6. During Senzai's second dance the mask-bearer offers Okina the mask, and an assistant helps him put it on. Okina wears a *hakushikijō* mask.

5

6

7

7–8. Okina's dance. (7) He spreads his arms in the *kata* called *hiraki* and opens his fan. (8) He voices a prayer for "Peace in the world, tranquillity in the land."

9. The Okina actor, having completed his dance, removes his mask and leaves the stage, accompanied by Senzai. Sambasō, who has been sitting at the Kyōgen pillar, rises and performs a lively dance, called *momi no dan*, which he punctuates with meaningless cries of *yo, hon, ho*.

10

10. Sambasō puts on a *kokushikijō* mask for his second dance. He shakes a
small bell to accentuate the movements of the dance. Here he performs the
gesture of scattering seed, symbolic of prayers for a bountiful harvest.

98

THE GOD PLAY: *Takasago*   Kongō School

shite: (first part) An old man, guardian of the Takasago Pine; (second part) the god of Sumiyoshi. (Kongō Iwao)

tsure: An old woman, wife of the old man. (Teshima Michiharu)

waki: A Shinto priest of the Aso Shrine. (Takayasu Shigeo)

ai: A villager. (Inoue Reinosuke)

A priest of the Aso Shrine in Kyushu, on his way to the capital, visits the Bay of Takasago, renowned for its great pine tree. He finds an old couple sweeping fallen pine needles, and learns eventually that this man and woman are the spirits of the pines at Takasago and Sumiyoshi. After they leave a villager tells the priest the legend of the pines. He offers to take the priest aboard his boat to Sumiyoshi. When the priest reaches Sumiyoshi the god appears, and after telling of his age-old protection of the Imperial House, he dances, promising to dispell wicked demons and bring joy to the people.

11. Entrance of the *waki*. "I am Tomonari, a priest of the Aso Shrine in Kyushu." He wears a dark blue *kariginu* cloak, white divided skirts, and a courtier's hat *(daijin eboshi)*.

11

99

12. The old woman, the spirit of the Takasago Pine, enters carrying a broom, followed by the old man, the spirit of the Sumiyoshi Pine, with a rake. Facing each other on the *hashigakari*, they sing:

"At Takasago
A spring breeze in the pines blows as dusk falls,
And the temple bell on the peak echoes the close of day."

The old man wears a *koujijō* mask, a brown *mizugoromo* cloak, blue plaid kimono, and white divided skirts. The old woman wears an *uba* mask, patched-silk *mizugoromo*, and russet *karaori* kimono.

13. The old man, in response to the priest's questions, tells the story of the Takasago Pine. "Like the pines, we have spent all these years together, husband and wife."

100

14. The actors remain seated as the chorus sings
of the glories of the Takasago Pine:
"Though the winter comes,
The green of a thousand years
Deepens with the snow."

15. The old man rises and mimes the action of
raking pine needles:
"Morning and evening
Though I rake the fallen needles,
They never cease to fall."
The ever-renewed pines are a symbol of longevity.

16. The old man and old woman disclose their true identities to the priest. The old man says, "Now to Sumiyoshi I shall go, and there await you." His fan points the direction he will travel.

17. "So saying, he boards a little fishing boat
Moored in the evening waves by the shore."
The old man performs the *kata* of boarding a boat *(norikomi)* as he departs for Sumiyoshi.

18. During the interval between the two parts of the play the *ai*, a man who lives by Takasago Bay, tells the priest about the Takasago Pine.

102

19. The *shite* appears in the second part wearing a *kantan otoko* mask as the god of Sumiyoshi. He stands by the first pine of the *hashigakari* and sings:

> "Long has it been since first
> I saw the pine on Sumiyoshi shore;
> How many ages has it lived?"

20.   "Breaking a bough of plum blossoms,
>   I hold it over my head;
>   The spring snow falls on my robe."
>   The god looks at the snow fallen on his outstretched sleeve.

103

THE "GOD" KYŌGEN: *Ebisu Bishamon*   Izumi School
shite: Ebisu, a Shinto god of good fortune. (Nomura Mannojō)
ado: a gentleman. (Nomura Matasaburō)
ko-ado: Bishamonten, a Buddhist protective divinity. (Nomura Mansaku)

A certain gentleman with a beautiful daughter is looking for a son-in-law. Two suitors present themselves—the Buddhist divinity Bishamonten and the Shinto god Ebisu. Each asserts his own importance and abuses the other. The gentleman asks that the suitor who really wishes to marry the girl prove it by the presents he bestows. The two gods try to outdo each other in their gifts to the man.

   This Kyōgen has a full accompaniment of flute and drums, in keeping with its designation in the Izumi school as a "god" Kyōgen *(waki kyōgen)*.

21. Bishamonten (at right) has already presented himself as a suitor, but now Ebisu also appears (on the *hashigakari*). The gentleman respectfully kneels in addressing him. Bishamonten wears a *chūbeshimi* mask and carries a spear. Ebisu wears an *emmeikaja* mask and carries a fishing pole to which a sea bream *(tai)* is attached.

104

22. Ebisu enters and Bishamonten demands of the gentleman who this rival might be.

23. Bishamonten's dance displays his authority as a god.

24. He presents the gentleman with his spear "which subdues evil demons and drives away misfortune."

105

25. Ebisu begins his dance.
26. Ebisu, determined not to be outdone by Bishamonten, offers the gentleman his lucky fishhook and a fish.
27. Bishamonten removes his helmet (actually, a pierced-work *eboshi*) and gives it to his prospective father-in-law.
28. Ebisu, again refusing to be outdone, gives his *eboshi* to the gentleman.

106

29 and 30. The two gods dance together, admitting that each is equally deserving of his reputation as a god of good fortune.

107

THE WARRIOR PLAY: *Kiyotsune*   Kita School
shite: The ghost of Taira no Kiyotsune. (Kita Minoru)
tsure: Kiyotsune's wife. (Uchida Yasunobu)
waki: Awazu no Saburō, a retainer of Kiyotsune. (Mori Shigeyoshi)

Awazu, the faithful retainer of the defeated Heike general Kiyotsune, goes to Kiyotsune's wife to tell her how her husband died, a suicide when he received the oracle that his cause was doomed. Awazu gives the wife a lock of hair Kiyotsune left as a keepsake before he drowned himself in the sea. Later, the wife falls asleep and Kiyotsune appears before her in a dream. She reproaches him for having abandoned her, and he bitterly rebukes her in turn for having cast aside the keepsake he left her. Kiyotsune describes the events leading up to his death and the suffering in hell that comes from his remembrances. At the end he is promised surcease from his torments.

31. Entrance of Awazu no Saburō. He wears a lacquered hat, a *suō* cloak, divided skirts, and carries an amulet bag around his neck. Standing on the *hashigakari* he sings his entrance song, then tells of the suicide of his master Kiyotsune.

108

32. Awazu arrives at Kiyotsune's house. Bowing before Kiyotsune's wife, he tells her, "Late one night he threw himself from his boat and perished." The wife wears a *ko-omote* mask and an embroidered kimono *(karaori)*.

33. The wife lifts the bag containing the lock of Kiyotsune's hair. "Is this black lock of hair my husband's? My eyes dim, my heart grows faint, my longing grows the stronger."

34. The ghost of Kiyotsune appears in his wife's dream. "Ever since I saw my love in daytime slumber, I have begun to place my hopes in dreams," he says, reciting an old poem. He wears a *chūjō* mask, a tall black hat (*nashiuchi eboshi*), white headband, black *happi* cloak, gold brocaded kimono, and figured silk divided skirts.

35. Kiyotsune addresses his wife:
    "Death was bitter,
    But your words make it bitterer still:
    Your sullen tears wet the pillow.
    Tonight we lie together—
    How sad that rancor makes us sleep alone."
36. Kiyotsune weeps in the *kata* called *shiori*.

110

37. Kiyotsune, seated, tells of the downfall of the Heike clan: "Dismayed to think the gods and buddhas had abandoned us . . ."

38. He rises from his seat. "Dejected, unsteady as a lame-wheeled carriage, the Emperor left the shrine, a heart-rending sight." Kiyotsune falls strengthless to his knees, and touching the floor with his right hand, brushes away his tears with his left.

39. Kiyotsune, opening his arms in the *hiraki* gesture, resumes his tale. "We boarded ship again and pushed off, ignorant even of our destination."

111

40. He holds his fan horizontally, pretending **to** be playing a flute. "Drawing the flute from my waist, I blew clear notes."

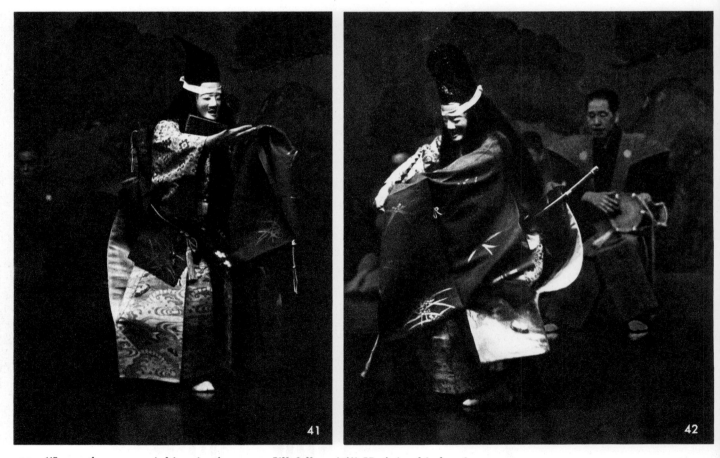

41. "I see the moon sinking in the west. I'll follow it!" He joins his hands in prayer, facing westwards, the direction of Amida's paradise. He cries, "Hail Amida Buddha! Lead me to your paradise!"

42. Kiyotsune leaps into the sea. "With this final cry I leapt into the ebbing tide."

112

THE SECOND KYŌGEN: *Kirokuda* ("Six Loads of Lumber")   Ōkura School
shite: Tarōkaja, a servant. (Shigeyama Sensaku)
ado: a teahouse proprietor. (Zenchiku Yagorō)
ado: a gentleman. (Zenchiku Kōshirō)
ado: the uncle of the gentleman. (Zenchiku Keigorō)

A certain gentleman has an uncle who needs some lumber. The gentleman decides to send his servant Tarōkaja with six ox-loads of lumber and a cask of saké. In the meantime, the uncle, impatient for a reply to his request, sets out for the nephew's house. The uncle is obliged by a heavy snowstorm to take shelter at a teahouse in the mountains. Tarōkaja also stops there. Frozen with the cold, he drinks some of the saké to warm himself. Before long, he and the proprietor have consumed the whole cask, and Tarōkaja, in drunken good spirits, presents the man with the lumber. The uncle finds out when it is already too late.

43. The master gives Tarōkaja a letter for the uncle.

113

44. "Look how the snow is falling!" Tarōkaja says, looking up at the sky.

45. Tarōkaja drives his oxen through the falling snow.

46. Tarōkaja and the owner of the teahouse get thoroughly drunk on the saké intended for the uncle. The owner asks Tarōkaja to perform the "quail dance."

47. Tarōkaja mimes the words, "I think I'll shoot a quail to make a snack for us."
48. "I'm going to shoot you—don't move now, quail!"

115

49. Unsuccessful at shooting the quail, he cries, "I'll grab it in my arms instead!"

50. The uncle, who has been resting in a back room, decides to leave. He looks for the owner but finds Tarō-kaja, dead drunk. The latter, recognizing the uncle, hands him the letter with which he was entrusted.

THE WOMAN PLAY: *Hagoromo*   Komparu School
shite: A celestial being. (Nishikawa Michio)
waki: The fisherman Hakuryō. (Kaburagi Mineo)

A fisherman finds a robe of feathers hanging upon a pine tree at the beach of Miho. He announces his intention of keeping it, but a beautiful woman appears and begs him to give back the robe, saying that without it she cannot return to heaven. The fisherman, moved by her grief, agrees to give her the robe if she will dance for him. She performs several dances before she disappears into the heavens.

51. The fisherman Hakuryō (to right) arrives at the beach of Miho with his companions. He carries a fishing pole, and wears a *noshime* kimono, a striped *mizugoromo* cloak, and white divided skirts. Here he sings the *issei*, his opening song:
> "The wind quickens, the fishermen
> Riding by Miho's curving strand
> Shout as they crest the waves."

117

52. Hakuryō finds the robe on the pine branch. The celestial lady, entering, begs him to return her robe. He refuses, saying that he intends to keep it as a treasure of the nation.

53. The angel weeps in the *shiori* gesture. She wears the *zō-onna* mask, a pierced headdress, a *karaori* embroidered kimono folded over from the waist downwards, to suggest she has bathed in the sea, and a white under-robe. The chorus sings for her: "When shall I return to the sky? How I envy the passing clouds!"

54. The fisherman, moved by her grief, gives back the robe. He insists that she dance for him.

118

55. The angel, going to the back of the stage with the robe (a *chōken*), puts it on, then comes forward. She sings:

> "The maiden dons her robe and dances
> The Rainbow Skirt and Cloak of Feathers."

55

56. As the angel performs the *kata* called *sayū* ("left and right"), the chorus sings for her:

> "From this time began the Suruga dance,
> The music of the East."

56

57. The *kata* called *yūken*, expressing joy, is performed as the chorus sings:
"I left the moon, the laurel tree,
And briefly descending to the East,
Danced the Suruga dance,
My gift to the world of men."

58. She performs the *kata* called *ageha*, her opened fan gradually being lifted over her head:
"Our Lord's reign will still endure,
Though a rock but rarely rubbed
By a heavenly robe of feathers
Crumbles to powder."

59. In this *kata*, performed during the second section of the *jonomai*, a stately dance, the actor twirls both sleeves over his arms.

120

60. The angel lifts her left sleeve over her head as the chorus sings:

"The blossoms of her headdress nod,
Her feathery sleeves turn over."

61. The *kata* of looking down from a height signifies that the angel has risen into the sky.

"Over the mountain of Ashitaka,
Over the high peak of Fuji,
Her form grows indistinct.
She mingles with the mists of heaven,
She is lost to sight."

THE THIRD KYŌGEN: *Hanago*   Izumi School
shite: A gentleman (Miyake Tōkurō)
ado: His wife (Nomura Manzō)
ado: Tarōkaja, a servant (Nomura Mannojō)

A certain married gentleman has fallen in love with a woman named Hanago and is desperately anxious to visit her. His domineering wife, however, foils his every strategem. He finally hits on a successful plan: he says he will spend the night in Zen meditation, and she consents. The man summons his servant Tarōkaja and intimidates him into becoming a substitute in the meditation hall. After he leaves, the wife discovers the ruse and forces Tarōkaja to let her sit in his place. The gentleman returns and recounts his amorous adventures, only for the wife to reveal herself.

62. The husband (left) is dejected by his wife's stern refusal of every suggestion he makes. He tearfully pleads: "Everything I say you oppose. It's just for one day and a night. Please, I beg you, let me do it."

63. Having at last won his wife's consent, the husband compels Tarōkaja to take his place. The servant, fearful of the wife, at first refuses, but the master threatens him: "I'll beat you to a pulp!" "Wait, I beg you, sir!"
64. In order to prevent the wife from uncovering the deception, even if she should peep, the gentleman has Tarōkaja cover his face with a cloak.

65. The wife, curious as always, feels sorry for the husband under his stuffy hood. She removes it, to discover Tarōkaja. The servant prostrates himself in terror.

66. The wife learns what has happened. "When I think that he told me he was going to sit in Zen meditation, then went instead to that dreadful Hanago, I seethe with rage! I'm furious!"

67. The wife forces Tarōkaja to let her take his place. He puts the cloak over her head.

68. The husband returns from Hanago's place singing, "When shall I ever forget how she looked, her hair dishevelled by sleep?"

124

69. Not realizing that his wife is sitting there, the husband relates what happened at Hanago's. He describes their parting: "Thinking it was time to be going, I bade her a tearful farewell."

70. The husband tells how, when Hanago asked what his wife looked like, he replied, "If you saw my wife she would remind you of a skinny monkey deep in the mountains."

71. Still supposing the figure under the cloak is Tarōkaja, the man is puzzled why he remains covered. He removes the cloak himself, only to discover his wife.

72. The wife chases the husband. "I am furious!" "Forgive me, please," he begs, running away.

126

THE MADWOMAN PLAY: *Semimaru*   Kanze School
shite: Sakagami, daughter of the Emperor Daigo. (Kanze Motomasa)
tsure: Semimaru, younger brother of Sakagami. (Takeda Takashi)
waki: Kiyotsura, a courtier. (Hōshō Yaichi)
ai: Hakuga no Sammi, a rustic. (Satō Usaburō)

Semimaru, the fourth son of the Emperor Daigo, is blind. His father orders that he be taken to Ōsaka Mountain and abandoned there. Semimaru has become a priest, and he is convinced that his father's action is intended to assure his happiness in the future life, but he is beset by loneliness. His sister Sakagami, hearing him play his lute, discovers him. She is believed to be mad because of her unruly hair *(sakagami)* and distraught actions, but the mad sister and blind brother experience a moment of recognition and affection before they must part.

73. Entrance of Semimaru (right) and the courtier Kiyotsura. The latter explains that the Emperor has commanded that Semimaru be abandoned because of his blindness. Semimaru wears a *semimaru* mask, a *kariginu* cloak, and a kind of *hakama* called *sashinuki*. Kiyotsura wears a *kazaori eboshi*, a *chōken* cloak, and white divided skirts, indicating that he is a nobleman.

74. After their arrival at Ōsaka Mountain, Kiyotsura expresses his surprise at the Emperor's harsh command. Semimaru replies that his blindness was due to sins in a previous life; his abandonment in the mountains, though it appears an unkind act, is actually the Emperor's far-reaching plan to ensure that his son will enjoy happiness in his next incarnation.

75. Semimaru removes his nobleman's attire and puts on the robe and hat *(sumbōshi)* of a Buddhist priest. Kiyotsura departs, and Semimaru is left alone with his lute and his blindman's stick.
76. A rustic, Hakuga no Sammi, appears. Taking pity on Semimaru, he offers to build a shelter for him. Here he guides Semimaru to the hut.
77. Semimaru sits in his hut.

78. Sakagami enters. Standing at the first pine of the *hashigakari*, she identifies herself, "I am Sakagami, the third child of the Emperor Daigo." She wears the *waka-onna* mask, a long wig which hangs down in front, an embroidered outer robe bared from the right shoulder to indicate her distraction, and a figured silk under-robe.

Sakagami then strokes the long, unruly hair which has given rise to her sobriquet. "Though I stroke it, my hair will not lie flat."

79. Sakagami journeys from the capital to the Barrier of Ōsaka. She catches sight of herself in the water of a well. "My unruly hair is reflected: water, they say, is a mirror—how wild and disordered I look in the waves!"

80. Arriving at Ōsaka Mountain, Sakagami catches the sound of Semimaru's lute *(biwa)*, and listens as he sings, "In this world we become as we are destined; whether we live in a palace or a hut, it will not be our home forever."

81. Sakagami calls to Semimaru through the door of the hut. He rises. "Is that you, my sister?" he cries. He opens the door, and steps out.

82. Brother and sister take each other's hands in affection.

83. Semimaru plays his lute. The fan serves to represent the instrument.
"He tunes the music of the lute to the sound of the spring rain, and as he
plays, his own voice rises in tears."
84. Sakagami, grieving over Semimaru's loneliness in his hut, weeps to
think of him "neglected even by the moon, unable even to hear the rain."
The *kata*, called *shiori*, indicates weeping.

85. The parting of brother and sister. Sakagami, still weeping, leaves;
Semimaru gazes off in the direction of her voice.

THE CONCLUDING KYŌGEN: *Utsubozaru* ("Quiver and Monkey") Ōkura School
shite: A daimyo. (Shigeyama Sensaku)
ado: Tarōkaja, a servant. (Zenchiku Chūichirō)
ado: A monkey trainer. (Ōkura Yatarō)
ado: A monkey. (Ishihara Hajime)

A certain daimyo, meeting a man with a trained monkey, demands that the man give him the monkey's fur so that he can cover his quiver with it. The trainer is too fond of the monkey to agree. The daimyo, though at first enraged, is eventually touched by this affection, and in turn becomes entranced by the monkey's pranks. He finally joins him in a joyful dance which appropriately concludes the Kyōgen section of the program.

86. "I am a daimyo, famed far and wide. Having long resided in the capital, I feel oppressed and in poor spirits. I think that I shall divert myself today by hunting in the fields."

132

87. The daimyo and Tarōkaja encounter a man with a performing monkey. After ascertaining through Tarōkaja that the trainer will perform a service for him, the daimyo addresses the man directly: "It is kind of you to offer to do me a service the first time we meet."

88. When the daimyo asks the trainer for the monkey's fur, the man refuses. The daimyo, angered, threatens him. "I'll teach you a lesson!" The trainer replies, "No matter how you may try to frighten me, I am not a man to be intimidated." He lifts his stick, meaning he intends to defend himself.

89. The daimyo, infuriated by this obstinate refusal, orders Tarōkaja to stand aside so that he can shoot both trainer and monkey. But Tarōkaja throws himself before the daimyo and implores him to wait.

90. The trainer finally yields, but insists on killing the monkey himself with a stick, so that his fur will not be torn by an arrow. The monkey, thinking this is part of a stunt, snatches away the stick and pretends to be poling a boat, his latest trick. The trainer, moved, decides he cannot kill the monkey after all, even if his own life is taken.

91. The daimyo is touched and spares the monkey's life. In gratitude, the trainer has the monkey perform a dance. The delighted daimyo gives the monkey his fan.

134

92. The daimyo, more and more carried away, next gives the monkey his sword and outer robe, and finally joins the monkey in a dance.

93. The daimyo and the monkey perform a rice-planting dance.

94. At the end the trainer sings the praises of monkeys as the emissaries of the gods, and the daimyo, lifting his quiver high, strikes an impressive pose.

135

THE DEMON PLAY: *Funa Benkei*   Kanze School (Umewaka Branch)
shite: (First part) Shizuka, the mistress of Yoshitsune; (second part) the ghost of Tomomori, a defeated Heike
        warrior. (Umewaka Rokurō)
waki: Benkei, Yoshitsune's loyal retainer. (Hōshō Yaichi)
kokata: Yoshitsune. (Takenaka Tetsuya)
ai: A boatman. (Nomura Mannojō)

Yoshitsune, a brilliant general of the Genji clan, has fallen out with his brother Yoritomo, the commanding
general. He flees the capital together with his mistress Shizuka and some retainers headed by Benkei. When they
reach Daimotsu Bay and are about to sail across the Inland Sea to Shikoku, Benkei persuades Yoshitsune that he
must send Shizuka back to the capital. Shizuka, heartbroken, reluctantly consents, and performs a dance by way
of farewell. Yoshitsune and Benkei put out to sea. From the rough waves rises the ghost of Tomomori, who
menaces the Minamoto heroes. By dint of Benkei's prayers, however, the vengeful ghost is overcome.

95. Entrance of Yoshitsune (right) and Benkei. Benkei relates how Yoshitsune, having fallen out with his
brother, is fleeing to the western provinces. Yoshitsune is played by a boy actor: he wears a tall black hat
(nashiuchi eboshi), white headband, brocade sleeveless cloak *(sobatsugi)*, heavy silk kimono, blue divided skirts,
and a sword. Benkei, dressed as a *yamabushi* priest, wears a small black hat *(tokin)*, *suzukake* surplice, *mizugoromo*
outer robe and white divided skirts.

136

96. Shizuka, told by Benkei that she must return to the capital, weeps in the *kata* of *shiori*. She wears a *waka-onna* mask and a robe of embroidered silk over a gold-painted under-kimono.
97. Shizuka is commanded to dance for Yoshitsune before his departure. She puts on a tall golden hat for her dance.

98. Shizuka dances. The beat of the accompanying drums is agitated, suggesting the impatience of Yoshitsune and his party to be on their journey; but Shizuka moves slowly, suggesting her reluctance to leave Yoshitsune.
99. Shizuka, unable to continue with her dance, retires to the *hashigakari* and weeps. After weeping for a while, she returns to the middle of the stage to resume her dancing.

100. In a gesture of despair, Shizuka unfastens and drops her dancing-hat. "Choking with tears, she takes her leave."

101. The boatman rushes onstage in response to Benkei's command that the boat sail immediately. He carries the prop that serves to represent the boat. The boatman wears a Kyōgen *kamishimo* (a starched, hempen outer garment and wide, pleated trousers) over his kimono.

139

102. Yoshitsune and Benkei sit in the boat as the boatman poles. Another retainer sits on the stage outside the prop, but it is understood that he is also aboard.

103. The ghost of Tomomori appears from the waves to threaten Yoshitsune's boat. Standing on the *hashigakari* he proclaims himself: "I am the ghost of Taira no Tomomori, the ninth generation descendant of the Emperor Kammu." He wears an *ayakashi* mask with a long black wig, a white headband, a heavy silk sleeveless jacket *(happi)* with brocade trousers *(hangiri)* over his brocade kimono. He carries a halberd.
104. Tomomori advances against the boat with his halberd.

140

105. He menaces Yoshitsune, his violent movements taking the form of a dance *(hataraki)*.

106. "Yoshitsune, not the least perturbed,
Draws his sword, challenging the ghost,
And fights as with a living man;
But Benkei pushes him aside:
'Your sword is useless,' he cries,
And tells his rosary, calling the gods in prayer."

141

THE CONGRATULATORY PLAY: *Midare*   Hōshō School

shite: Shōjō, an auspicious, mythological being known for its love of saké. (Hōshō Fusao)
waki: Kōfū, a saké merchant. (Matsumoto Kenzō)

A congratulatory play is sometimes staged at the conclusion of a full program. *Midare*, essentially the same work as *Shōjō* (except for its *midare* or "wild" dance), tells of Kōfū, an unusually filial Chinese merchant. One night he dreams of going to market to sell his saké. A stranger comes who drinks enormously without showing any signs of intoxication. The merchant asks the man's name and learns that he is a *shōjō*, a creature who lives in the sea. The man goes to the seashore with his wine, and is rewarded by the appearance of the *shōjō*, who drinks, dances, and finally gives Kōfū an inexhaustible jug of wine, a reward for his filial piety. Kōfū awakens from his dream, but the jug is still there, and he grows extremely rich.

107. Shōjō appears, singing his praises of saké. He wears a *shōjō* mask, a long red wig, an embroidered *karaori* outer robe, red divided skirts, and a red kimono. From the moment of his entrance his fan is opened, contrary to the normal practice of opening it only before a dance.

142

108–110. The first section of the *midare* dance. This extremely difficult dance abounds in sudden variations of tempo and in complicated movements for the feet. (108) In the *kata* of *uchikomi*, the fan is lowered from above, then brought in towards the body. (109) The *kata* of *agehaōgi*: the opened fan, held at first before the dancer's face, is lifted above his head. (110) Conclusion of *agehaōgi*: the raised fan is moved to the right, then lowered.

143

111. Shōjō glides backwards sinuously, as if treading on the waves of the sea.

112. He shifts his grasp on the fan as he moves backwards, still in the *midare* dance.

113. A special feature of this dance is the violently energetic prancing of the feet.

144

114. End of the *midare* dance. Shōjō
offers saké to the merchant Kōfū.

115. The *kata* of *yūken*, an expression
of joy, The chorus sings, "The prosperity of his house will never end,
let us rejoice."

145

116. Plays performed today at Nakorn Pathom in Thailand suggest what the purposes of drama may have been in Japan many years ago. The actors perform on tiny stages facing the great stupa. The plays are paid for by donors as acts of piety, and the audiences tend to consist entirely of small children or old people. Even if no one is present—hardly anyone is watching the play being performed on the far stage—the show goes on, for the real audience is the deity.

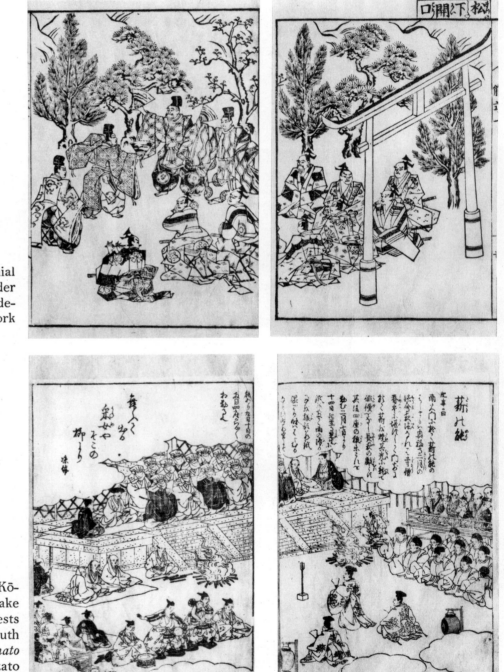

117. The opening ceremonial dance *(kaikō)* performed under the Yōgō Pine in Nara, as depicted in *Nō no Zushiki*, a work published in 1697.

118. Torchlight Nō at the Kōfukuji in Nara. The actors make their salutations to the priests assembled beneath the South Great Gate. From *Yamato Meisho Zue* (1791) by Akizato Ritō, illustration by Matsumoto Nobushige.

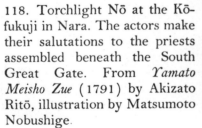

119. The *shishimai* ("lion dance"), a prominent part of *gigaku* entertainments, is still popular today. Two men cavort inside the skin of the curious beast. From *Shinzei Kogaku Zu*, attributed to Fujiwara Michinori (1106–59).

120. A *gigaku* mask, used for the *shishimai*. It is characteristic of *gigaku* masks in that they cover most of the performer's head, unlike the small Nō masks.

121. This *bugaku* mask is used in performing *raryōō*.

122. This screen by the great artist Tawaraya Sōtatsu depicts various kinds of *bugaku*. These are (from left to right): *konron hassen*, performed by four dancers wearing bird masks; *genjōraku*, a kind of snake-taming dance; *raryōō*, about a triumphant king; *nasori*, performed by two men; and *saisōrō*, an old man's dance, performed before the traditional great drum of *bugaku*.

147

124. A *sangaku* entertainment depicted in *Shinzei Kogaku Zu.* Women with high *geta* on their feet walk over tightropes; two juggle balls, the third holds a lighted lamp. Clowns perform antics below.

123. A bow preserved in the imperial collection at the Shōsōin in Nara is decorated on the inner surface with monochrome drawings of *sangaku* performers. These sketches of acrobats, jugglers, and other entertainers were drawn in the eighth century or earlier.

125. This drawing of an *ennen* performance at the Kōfukuji is attributed to Tosa Mitsunobu (1469–1533)

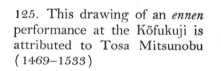

126. *Dengaku* performance, depicted in the fourteenth-century scroll *Urashima Jin Emaki.* The musicians play flutes, drums, and the *binzasara*, a horseshoe-shaped instrument. In the background a priest juggles knives, balls, clogs, etc.

127. A portrait of Ashikaga Yoshimitsu (1358–1408), painted around 1424. Artist unknown.

128. This huge *kusunoki* (camphor tree) at the Imakumano Shrine in Kyoto was already standing when Zeami danced before Ashikaga Yoshimitsu in 1374.

129. Texts of both plays and critical works in Zeami's handwriting are still preserved. This is a page from *Yoroboshi*.

130. This mask is owned by the Rinnōji, a temple in Nikkō. According to the inscription on the back of the mask, it was presented to the temple by a certain Tsuruwaka Tayû, an actor, in the year 1469; presumably the mask was made a few years earlier. The forehead is much lower than in female masks used today. The old masks in general more closely resemble human features, and this example preserves characteristics of the female masks used prior to the crystallization of Nō.

149

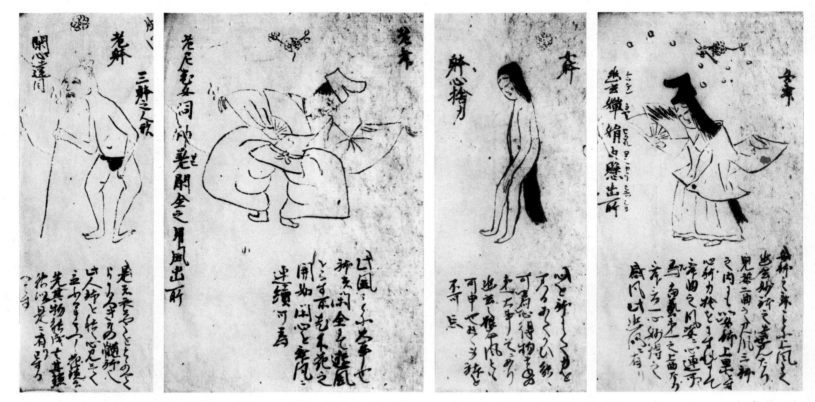

131. Details of illustrations to *Nikyoku Santai no Ezu*, a work of criticism by Zeami. Human figures, some clothed and some naked, provide hints as to how the body should be held in performance. The plum blossom designs above symbolize the degree of *yūgen* of the figures illustrated. The title of the work means "dance and music" (*nikyoku*) in "three forms" (*santai*), the latter designating the old person, the woman and the warrior. From left to right are: the "figure of an old person," "dance by an old person," "female figure," and "dance by the female." This illustration is believed to be in the hand of Komparu Zenchiku, Zeami's son-in-law.

132. The celebrated "Scenes Within and Without the Capital Screen," painted 1622–24, depicts many forms of popular entertainments presented in Kyoto, including this Nō play staged by the Kanze school.

150

133. This Nō stage at the Nishi-Honganji Temple in Kyoto is one of the oldest. It was built for Toyotomi Hideyoshi about 1595, and was moved to its present site from his castle at Momoyama.

134. These screens, depicting performances at a samurai's residence towards the end of the sixteenth century, indicate the popularity Nō and Kyōgen then enjoyed among that class. The screen on the left shows the audience watching *Igui*, a Kyōgen. The stage and performers are left of the pillars, the audience to the right. The screen on the right shows a performance of the Nō play *Miwa*, with the actors in the center, the musicians to the right, and the audience to the left.

151

135. The oldest texts of Kyōgen are the brief summaries found in this 1578 manuscript.
136. A drawing of the play *Utsubozaru* found in a scroll of the late sixteenth century. Artist unknown.

137. The most famous and beautiful texts of Nō are those prepared by Honnami Kōetsu (1558–1637). The bamboo design on the cover of this text of *Kantan* was printed with a mica paste on the heavy paper (left). The pages of the texts themselves have designs of autumn grasses. The words and musical notations were printed from moveable types.

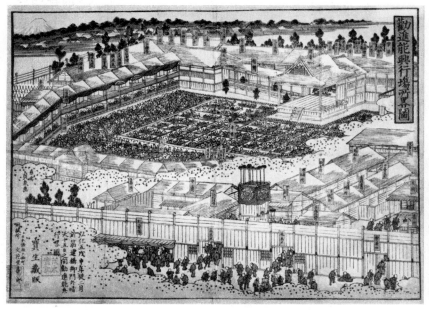

138. This print by Ikeda Eisen (1790–1848), executed shortly before his death, depicts the scene of the Subscription Nō of the Hōshō school, the last important performances of the Tokugawa period. Crowds pack the open-air stalls; the gentry have places upstairs in roofed boxes. The *yagura*, a tower with nine sheathed arrows, symbolizes official permission to hold the performances.

152

139. Umewaka Minoru (1827–1909), more than any other actor, was responsible for preserving Nō during the critical period after the Meiji Restoration of 1868.
140. Hōshō Kurō (1837–1917) was the greatest actor of the Meiji era.

141. This print by Hashimoto Chikanobu (1838–1912) shows a performance of *Takasago* in the presence of the Emperor Meiji and his consort, performed at the newly-opened Kōyōkan in Shiba Park in 1881. The scene is fancifully portrayed, but captures the festive atmosphere of the performance.

142. Kita Roppeita (born 1874) performs as the white heron in *Sagi*. The last of the great actors of the Meiji era, Roppeita displayed an uncanny, supernatural beauty in this role, which is traditionally danced by a boy or an old man, persons free of worldly passions.

153

REGIONAL NŌ AND KYŌGEN

Wakamiya Festival at the Kasuga Shrine
The Wakamiya Festival is held in December. It is a pageant of Japanese drama from its traditional inception at the base of the Yōgō Pine to its maturation as Nō and Kyōgen.

143. The head (center), standing under the pine, re-enacts ceremonially the dance of the god.

144. Later in the day Nō is performed on a temporary stage. The audience sits on matting laid on the ground. Here *Kayoi Komachi* is acted by the Komparu school.

145. Kyōgen is also performed before the shrine building. Actors of the Ōkura school present here *Kagamiotoko*.

154

Torchlight Nō at Kōfukuji

Torchlight Nō *(takigi* Nō*)* has a history going back a thousand years to performances given by priests of the Kōfukuji Temple in Nara. For centuries actors considered it so great a privilege to be allowed to take part in these performances that bitter disputes occurred.

146. As it grows dark an attendant stirs up the fire in the brands stacked before the stage. Lanterns bearing the inscription *takigi* Nō are also lit.

147. An hour later, when *Kurozuka* is being performed by the Komparu school, the torchlight and lanterns are the only illumination for the stage

155

148. At high tide the waters of the Inland Sea flow in, surrounding the stage and lapping under the pavilions where the spectators are seated.

149. The play being performed here by actors of the Kita school is *Tomoe*. To the right the Great Torii of the Itsukushima Shrine is faintly visible in the water.

150. Spectators seated in the pavilion to stage right can see over the heads of the chorus the corridors of the magnificent buildings of the shrine.

156

Nō at Kurokawa
Ōgi-matsuri, the annual festival of the village of Kurokawa, begins at dawn on the first of February. The two sacred images worshiped at the Kasuga Shrine are taken to the houses of the two oldest villagers, who are designated respectively as the hosts *(tōnin)* at the *kamiza* (upper) and *shimoza* (lower) residences of the gods.

151. The performances begin at dusk, after a day of feasting and entertainments. Huge candles are lighted, and after god plays are staged by the two rival residences of the gods, boys from each take turns in executing the steps of *Daichifumi*, a ritual stamping on the earth. The boys are dressed as Shinto priests and carry wands with sacred streamers.

153. A view of the Nō stage fashioned inside the Kasuga Shrine of Kurokawa. In place of the usual pine tree, the background is furnished by the symbols of the two gods.

152. Sambasō performs his bell dance in *Okina*. The Okina actor is chosen from among the *kamiza* players, the Sambasō actor from the *shimoza* players.

157

Ennen at Mōtsūji
A short distance from the Chūsonji stands the Mōtsūji, a mere suggestion of its former grandeur as a monastic center. The annual *ennen* performances include *dengaku* dances, Nō, *bugaku* and various Buddhist rites. *Ennen*, which enjoyed great popularity in Nara and Kyoto during the middle ages, now survives mainly at these two isolated temples.

154. *Ennen* is held in the *jōgyōdō*, a hall used by priests of the Tendai sect for perpetual recitations of the invocation to Amida.

156. *Hanaori* ("Picking Flowers") is danced by two boys in the manner of *bugaku* to the accompaniment of a chorus.

155. *Rōjomai* ("The Old Woman's Dance") is the dance of a woman one hundred years old. She manages, despite her bent back, to prance vigorously around the stage.

Nō at Chūsonji
In the twelfth century the Chūsonji, a temple situated in far northern Japan, became for three generations of the local rulers an isolated outpost of Kyoto culture. Later it slipped back into the obscurity and silence of the majestic trees surrounding the old buildings. Today, as a relic of past glories, *ennen* and Nō plays are presented at the annual festival in May

157. Through most of the year the Nō stage of the Chūsonji stands deserted, often covered by snow.

158. An overall view of the stage and surroundings during the performance of Nō at the Chūsonji.

159. The opening *ennen* play, called *kaikō*, consists of a recitation by an Okina-like character explaining the felicitous nature of the occasion.
160. *Jakujo* ("The Young Woman") is performed with a mask similar to the *waka-onna* of Nō. The actor dances with bells and a fan, in the tradition of the priestesses (*miko*) at the Shinto shrines

159

Nō at Nōgō
The survival of a distinctive form of Nō in the remote hinterland of Gifu Prefecture, at the village of Nōgō, was first reported in 1956. Though the texts performed—whether Nō or Kyōgen—clearly were written after the perfection of Nō under Zeami, the performing techniques may go back much earlier.

161. The stage, a temporary platform erected before the *torii* of the Hakusan Shrine, has for its backdrop a curtain (dated 1807).
The actors make their entrances from behind the curtain rather than along a passageway, as in a modern Nō theatre. All dialogue and songs are rendered by a chorus seated on the stage with the musicians. The actors depict with gestures, stylized or naturalistic, the meaning of the texts.

162. *Rashōmon*, a Nō play of the demon category, is danced with a mask and wig quite distinct from those used in metropolitan performances.
163. Kyōgen also is performed. This scene is from *Kanehiki* ("The Bell Puller"), a work peculiar to Nōgō.

160

Mibu Kyōgen
For ten days every April, Kyōgen plays are staged at
the Mibu Temple in the southern part of Kyoto. Mibu
Kyōgen is distinctive in that it is mimed throughout
with no recourse to dialogue. The accompaniment is
provided by a drum, flutes and a gong whose sound of
gan den den is much beloved by the people of Kyoto.
Some scholars claim that Mibu Kyōgen is older than
Nō, but in its present form it unquestionably owes
much to the more evolved art.

164. The stage is in a building separate from the
audience. To the left is a *hashigakari* used by the
actors for entrances and exits. A partition running
along the base of the stage prevents the audience from
seeing the lower part of the actors' bodies.

165. Each day's performance begins with *Hōrakuwari* ("Smashing the Pans"), a play about
two merchants, one a dealer in unglazed earthen-
ware pans, the other in drums. They quarrel
over which one will obtain a preferred stall at
the market. The merchant of pans sets out his
ware while the other merchant dozes, but the
latter wreaks vengeance by smashing the pans.

166. The plays are performed at the Mibu Temple as
part of a religious observance called *Dainembutsu*,
intended to invite good fortune and ward away misfortune. Many, however, are farces with no apparent
religious meaning. In *Hana Nusubito* ("The Flower
Thief"), a man catches a thief and holds him while
his foolish servant slowly twists together a rope to
bind him. At the end the servant mistakenly ties up
the master and the thief escapes.

161

THE MASKS OF NŌ

The attributions of the masks presented here, the traditional ones, are often supported by inscriptions written on the inner surfaces, but modern scholars have cast doubts on their authenticity. It would probably be safer in each instance to say "in the style of," for we cannot be certain that a particular artist was responsible for a mask.

Masks designated by the Japanese government as "important artistic properties" are distinguished by an asterisk*; those which are "important cultural properties" by a dagger†

167. †*Okina (hakushikijō)* by Miroku. Kanze Collection. $7\frac{1}{8}'' \times 6\frac{7}{8}''$.
The *okina* mask, used only in the play *Okina*, is the oldest type of mask still worn. The *okina* mask is characterized by the *kiriago* (split jaw), meaning that the mask is in two pieces tied together with string, presumably in order to facilitate movements of the mouth. The eyebrows, cotton pasted on the wooden surface, are also peculiar to this mask. The three main categories of *okina* mask are associated with the legendary mask-makers, Miroku, Nikkô and Kasuga. A further division is made by color: *hakushiki* (white), *kokushiki* (black) and *nikushiki* (flesh-colored). A passage in *Sarugaku Dangi* by Zeami seems to refer to this mask: "The *okina* mask used by this troupe was by Miroku. It was found and presented to the troupe when it was organized at Obata in Iga."

162

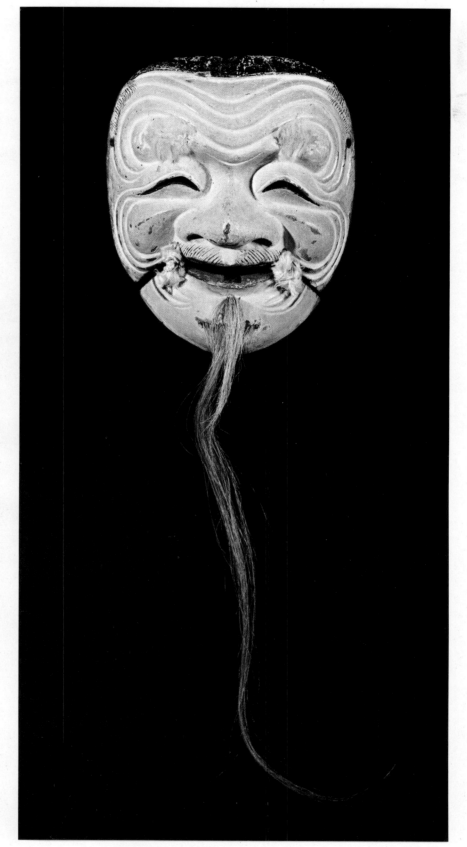

COLOR PLATE 4.
Okina (nikushikijō) by Miroku.   Kanze Collection.
$6\frac{7}{8}'' \times 6\frac{1}{2}''$.
This mask, attributed to Miroku, is flesh-colored
(*nikushiki*). It is believed to have been carved about
the end of the twelfth century.

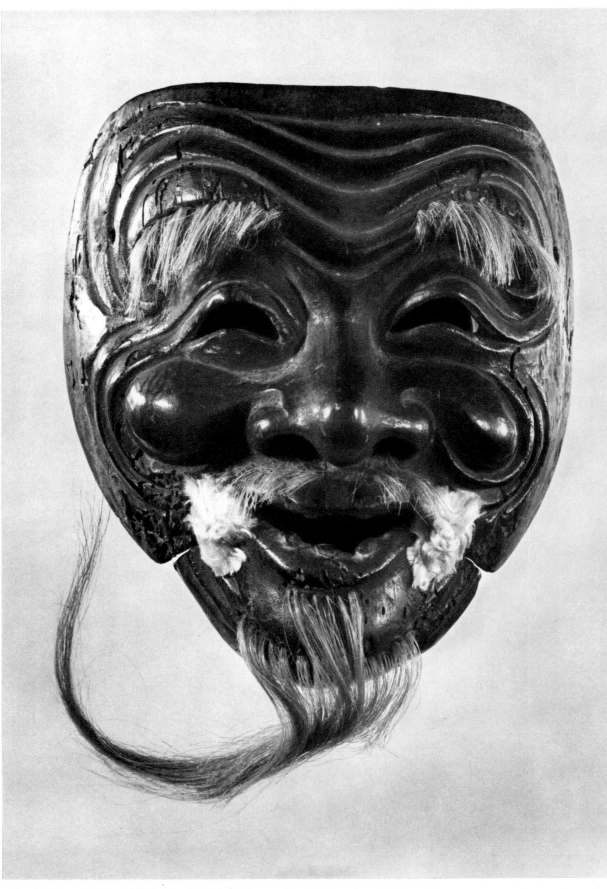

168. †*Okina* (*kokushikijō*) by Nikkō. Umewaka Collection. $6\frac{1}{4}'' \times 5\frac{3}{4}''$.
This *okina* mask, used only for Sambasō in *Okina*, is of the black variety (*kokushiki*). Less aristocratic in features than the other two types of *okina* mask, it is well suited to the comic nature of the Sambasō role.

169. †*Chichinojō* by Miroku. Kanze Collection. 6¾″ × 5¼″.

Okina originally included characters other than those who appear in the present versions, as we know both from the masks and old documents. The *chichinojō* mask is today worn only in certain variant performances of *Okina*. It has the split jaw of the *okina* mask but lacks the beard.

170. †*Emmeikaja* by Bunzō. Kanze Collection. 7⅛″ × 5½″.

This mask, though worn by a youthful character who no longer appears in *Okina*, is obviously of a later date than the preceding ones, perhaps fourteenth century. The small holes in the chin were probably intended for inserting a beard. The mask is used today in special performances of *Okina*, and occasionally, for the roles of divinities, in Kyōgen.

165

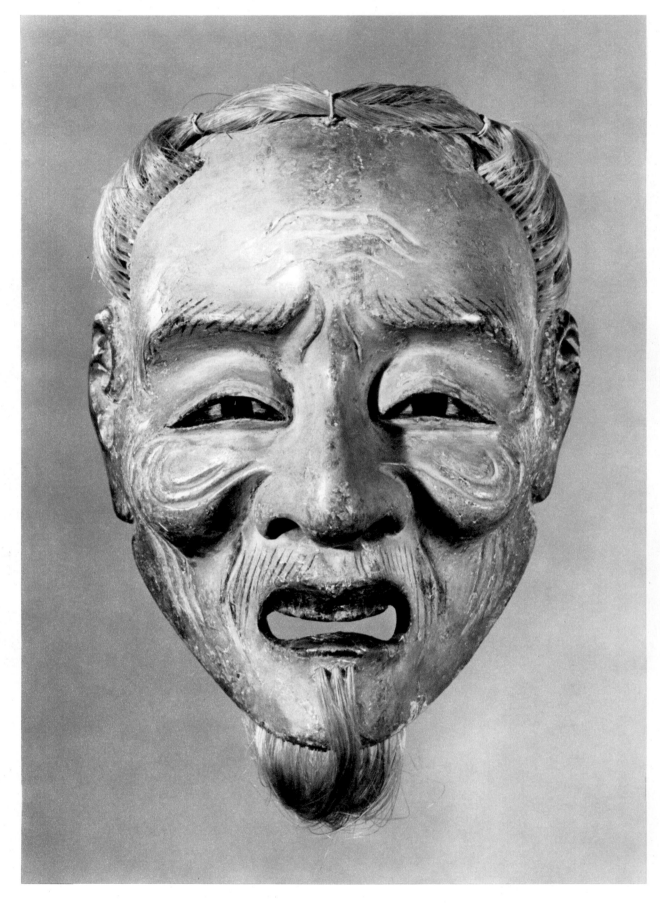

171. *Koujijō* by Kouji. Kongō Collection. 7⅞″ × 6¼″.
This mask derives its name from the maker, Kouji. It is known also as *kojō*.
Unlike other masks used for the roles of old men, the cheekbones are not especially prominent. The face is rather thin, and the features are at once grave and noble. Its dignity makes it an appropriate mask for the roles of old men who prove to be earthly manifestations of the gods, like the *shite* in the first part of *Takasago*.

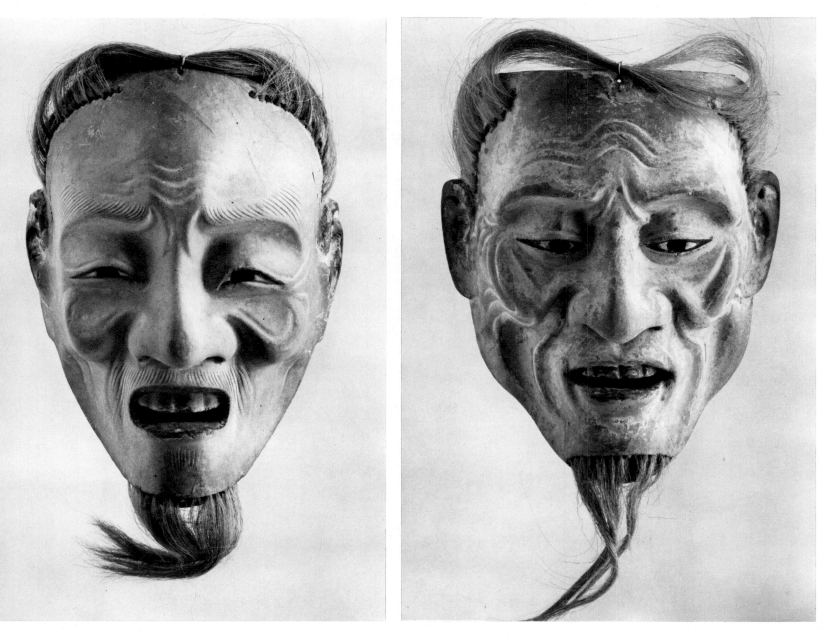

172. †*Akobujō* by Kouji. Kanze Collection. $8\frac{5}{8}'' \times 6\frac{1}{2}''$.
This mask is used mainly for the roles of old men in such emotional dramas of the fourth category as *Tōsen*. The old man in such works is a human being, not a god; the mask therefore lacks the dignity of the *koujijō*.
173. †*Shiwajō* by Fukurai.   Kanze Collection. $8'' \times 6\frac{1}{8}''$.
The characteristic feature of this mask is its deep wrinkles, extending from the outer edge of the eyes to the lower cheeks. The name itself is derived from *shiwa*, meaning wrinkles. The *shiwajō* mask is used by the Kanze school only in such plays as *Saigyō Zakura*.

167

174. †*Ōakujō* by Shakuzuru. Kanze Collection. 9″ × 7¾″.
This was the original form of the *akujō* mask, but when similar masks later came into use, it was distinguished by being called *ōakujō* (large *akujō*). As in other masks attributed to Shakuzuru, the influence of the *gigaku* and *bugaku* masks is apparent. This mask is used for powerful, frightening old men in such works as *Tamanoi*.

175. * *Omoni Akujō*   by Fukurai.   Kanze Collection. $8\frac{7}{8}'' \times 6\frac{3}{4}''$.
This variety of *akujō* mask is used only in the second part of *Koi no Omoni*, a work peculiar to the Kanze school. Both the plot of the play and the character represented by the mask resemble those of *Aya no Tsuzumi* ("The Damask Drum"), a work performed by other schools.
176. * *Beshimi Akujō*   by Shakuzuru. Kanze Collection. $7\frac{7}{8}'' \times 6\frac{3}{4}''$.
This is another variety of *akujō* mask, but the tightly clamped jaws, characteristic of the *beshimi* masks, makes it a cross between the two. It is used mainly in such *beshimi* roles as the white-wigged demon in the variant of *Kurama Tengu*.

177. * *Ōbeshimi* by Shakuzuru. Hōshō Collection. 8⅝″×6¾″.
This mask is used for the demons called *tengu*. Appropriately, the nose and mouth are prominent, giving an expression of arrogance tinged by a slightly comical quality. It is used in such plays as *Kurama Tengu* and *Zekai*.

178. * *Kumasaka* by Bunzō. Kanze Collection. 8⅛″×6¼″.
This mask belongs to the category of *ōbeshimi* masks, but because it is used especially for the *shite* role in *Kumasaka* it has been given this name. It has greater human warmth than the ordinary *ōbeshimi* mask.

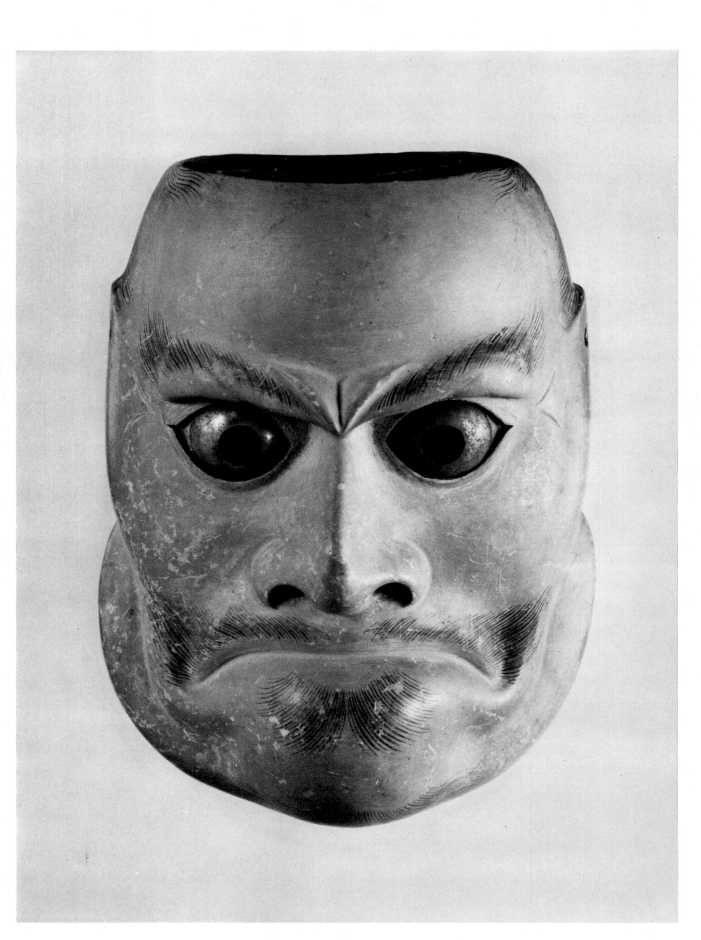

179. †*Kobeshimι* by Shakuzuru. Kanze Collection. $8\frac{1}{8}'' \times 5\frac{7}{8}''$.
Similar to the *ōbeshimi*, but smaller, is the *kobeshimi* mask. The humorous exaggeration is gone, and we have instead a fierce, malicious being, like the
demon in *Ukai*. This variety of mask was first used by Zeami, as we know from
his writings.

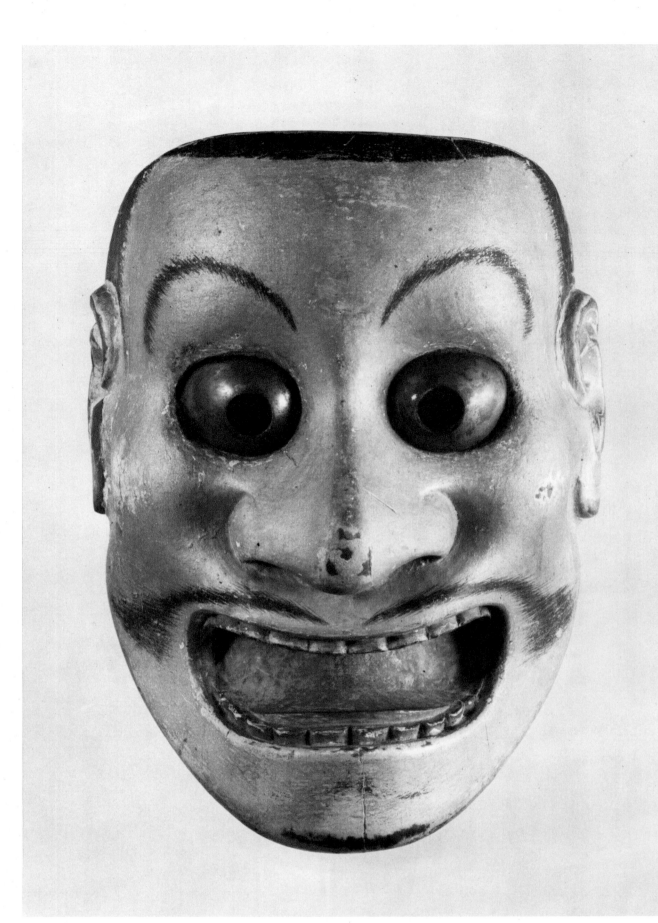

180. †*Ōtobide* by Shakuzuru.   Kanze Collection. $9'' \times 6\frac{1}{4}''$.
Tobide means protuberance, referring in the case of this mask to the eyeballs.
The expression, evocative of the strength and severity of a being invested with
divine powers, makes it suitable for the thunder god in *Kamo*.

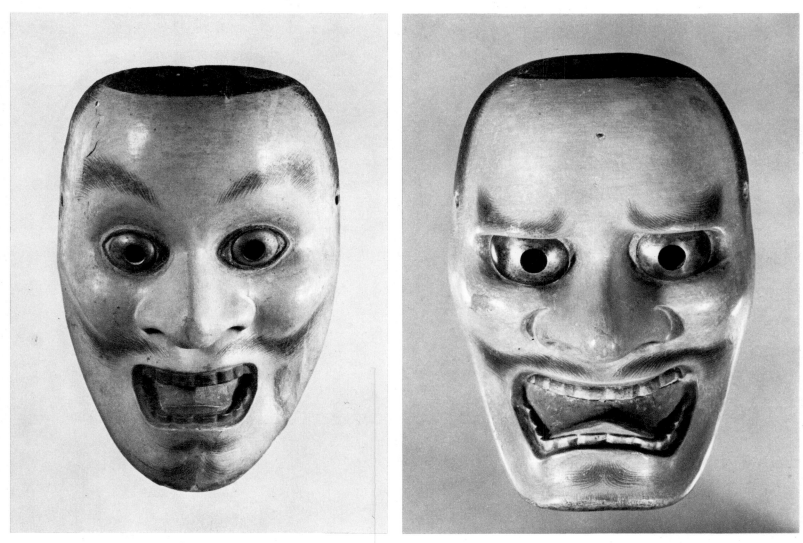

181. * *Kotobide* by Shakuzuru. Kanze Collection. $8\frac{1}{8}'' \times 5\frac{1}{2}''$.
This smaller version of the *ōtobide* mask lacks ears, and is flesh-colored rather than gold. Unlike the *ōtobide*, which emphasizes the strength of divine beings, this mask depicts their alertness and intelligence. It is used for the fox-god in *Kokaji*.

182. *Kurohige* by Kawachi. Kongō Collection. $8\frac{1}{8}'' \times 5\frac{7}{8}''$.
This mask represents the Dragon God *(ryūjin)* in such plays as *Chikubushima* and *Kasuga Ryūjin*. The features suggest a flattened-out version of *ōtobide*: the mid-section is low, and the forehead and jaw protrude. The eyebrows are unusually close to the eyes. The name *kurohige* ("black beard") apparently derives from the painted moustache.

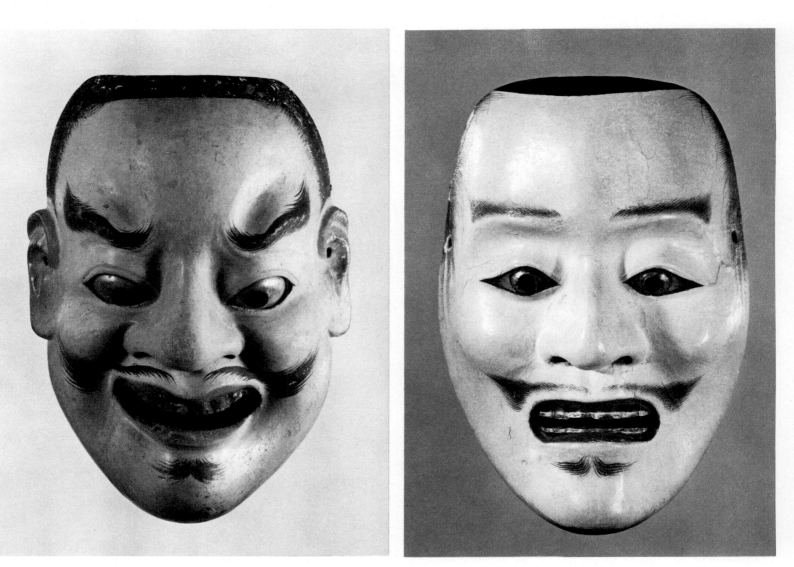

183. ✝*Tenjin* by Shakuzuru. Kanze Collection. 9¼″×7″.
This mask is said to depict the rage of the great statesman Sugawara no Michizane on being betrayed. The name Tenjin was given to Michizane after his death, when he came to be worshiped as a god. Although the *tenjin* mask has metallic eyeballs, characteristic of supernatural beings, the expression is distinctly human. The mask is used in *Raiden*.

184. *Ayakashi* by Tokuwaka. Kongō Collection. 7″×5¾″.
Ayakashi is the name given to a phantom who appears on the sea. Its features resemble those of the *mikazuki* mask, but the expression is human rather than supernatural, and is tinged by hatred. It is used for ghosts, especially of warriors like Tomomori in *Funa Benkei*.

174

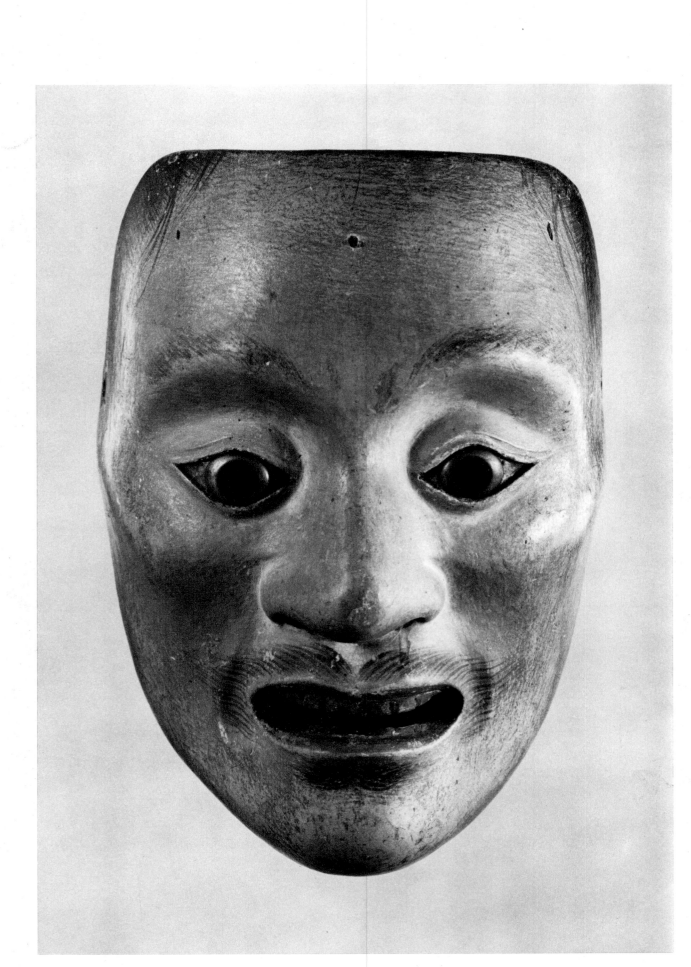

185. * *Mikazuki* by Fukurai. Kanze Collection. $8\frac{1}{4}'' \times 5\frac{3}{4}''$.
This mask represents not a human being but a powerful spirit. As is true of the
akujō, *beshimi* and *tobide* masks, metal is used for the eyeballs. The *mikazuki*
mask formerly was used in *Takasago* and *Funa Benkei*, works now performed
with the *kantan otoko* and *ayakashi* masks respectively. It is now used only when
an effect of special dignity is required. A metal pin used to hold a headband in
place can be seen in the forehead, suggesting that the mask was also used in
warrior plays.

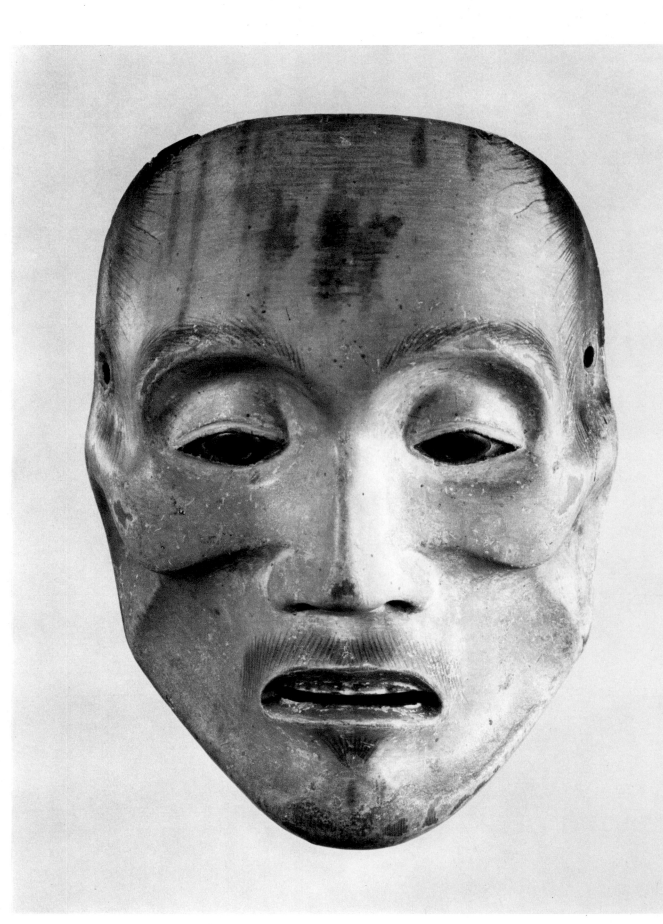

186. * *Yase-otoko* by Himi. Kanze Collection. $8\frac{1}{4}'' \times 6\frac{3}{8}''$.
The expression on the *yase-otoko* ("thin man") mask is extremely sad, like that
of a dead man whose spirit is suffering the torments of hell. However, it retains
a greater air of dignity than other similar masks. It is pale yellowish brown
in color, with metallic inserts in the eyes. The mask is used in such plays as
Kayoi Komachi and *Fujito*.

176

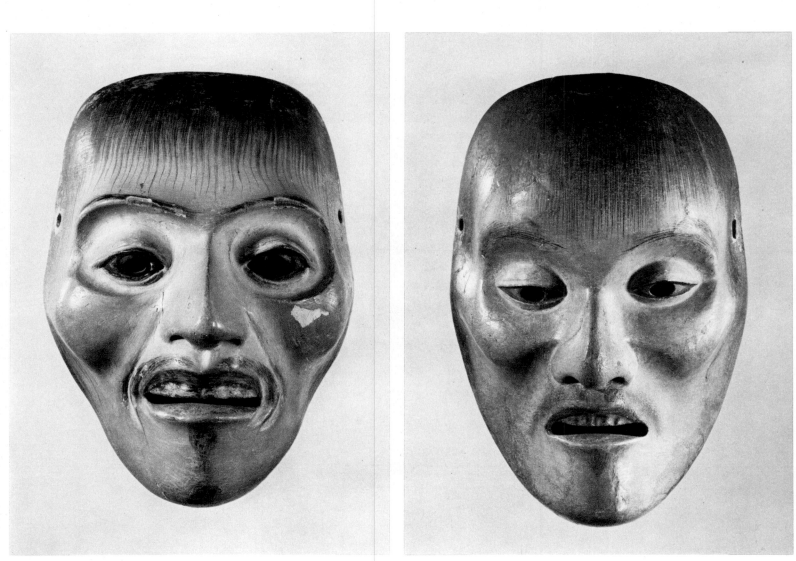

187. * *Kawazu* by Himi. Umewaka Collection. $7\frac{3}{4}'' \times 5\frac{3}{4}''$.
This mask also depicts the gaunt features of a man experiencing the tortures of hell, but it lacks the dignity of the
yase-otoko mask. The name *kawazu*, meaning frog, derives from the frog-like appearance of the eyes and cheekbones.
The mask is used for ghosts being punished in hell for the sins of a former life, like the *shite* in *Utō* or *Akogi*.
188. * *Hatachi Amari* by Himi. Hōshō Collection. $7\frac{7}{8}'' \times 5\frac{1}{2}''$.
This mask is used only in *Fujito*, as performed by the Hōshō school. The name, literally "over twenty," comes from
a passage in the text describing the *shite*. Metal is not used in the eyes; the expression is therefore more human.

177

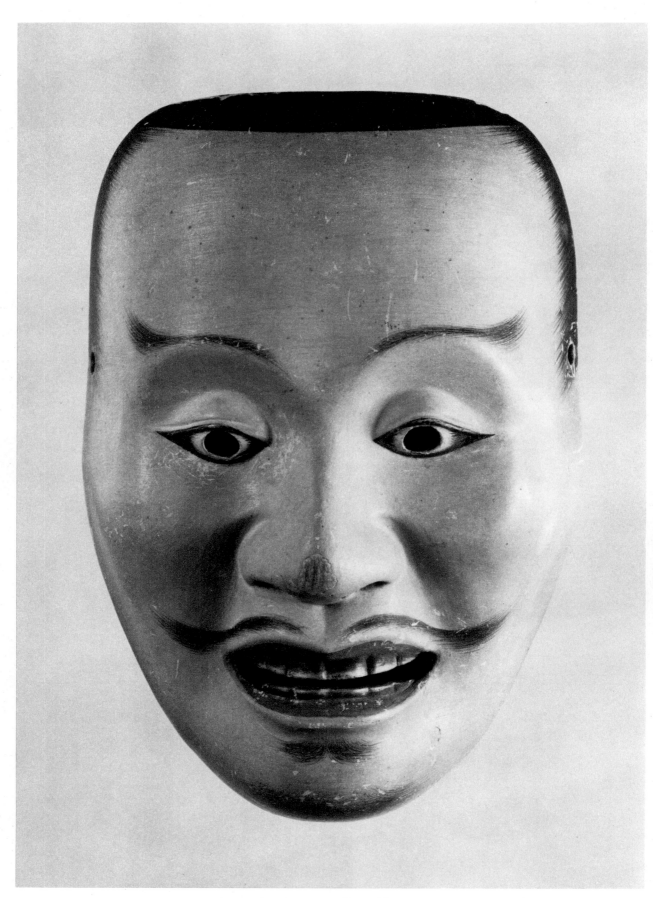

189. * *Heita* by Tokuwaka. Kanze Collection. 7¾″ × 5½″.
The mask represents a middle-aged warrior. Unlike *ayakashi*, used for warriors
who have become demons (as the metallic eyes indicate), *heita* is used in warrior
plays for brave and admirable men, like the *shite* of *Tamura* or *Yashima*.

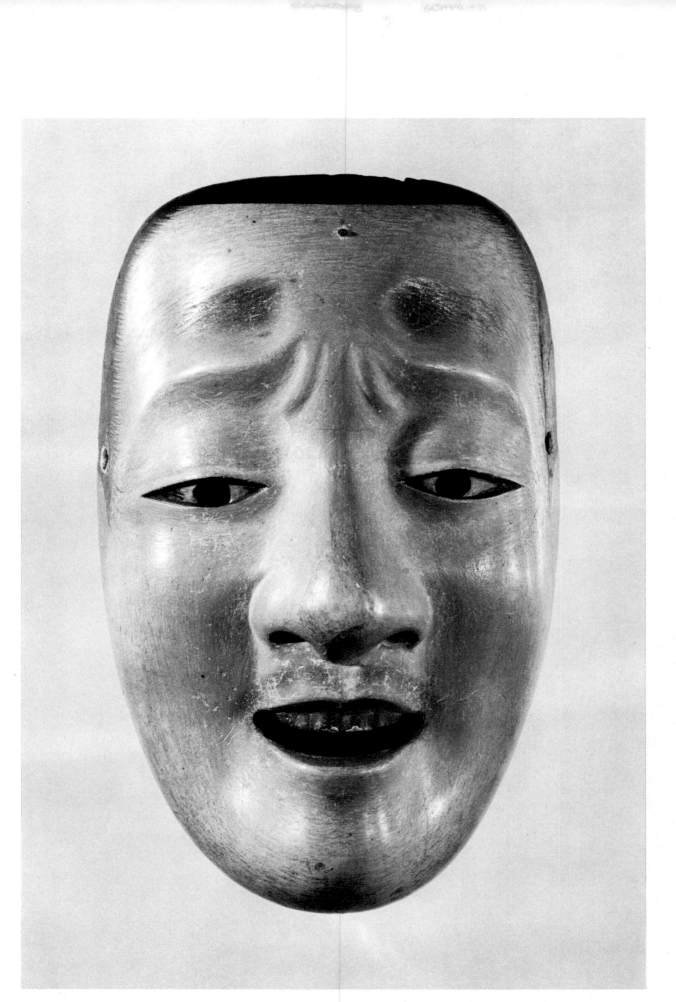

190. * *Chūjō*   Maker unknown.   Umewaka Collection. $8'' \times 5\frac{1}{8}''$.
Chūjō designates the military rank of a certain Heike nobleman. The special
feature of this mask is the deep furrow between the eyes, lending a shadow of
sadness to the elegant and beautiful face. The mask is used for noblemen both
in the warrior plays (like *Tadanori*) and in certain demon plays (like *Tōru*).

179

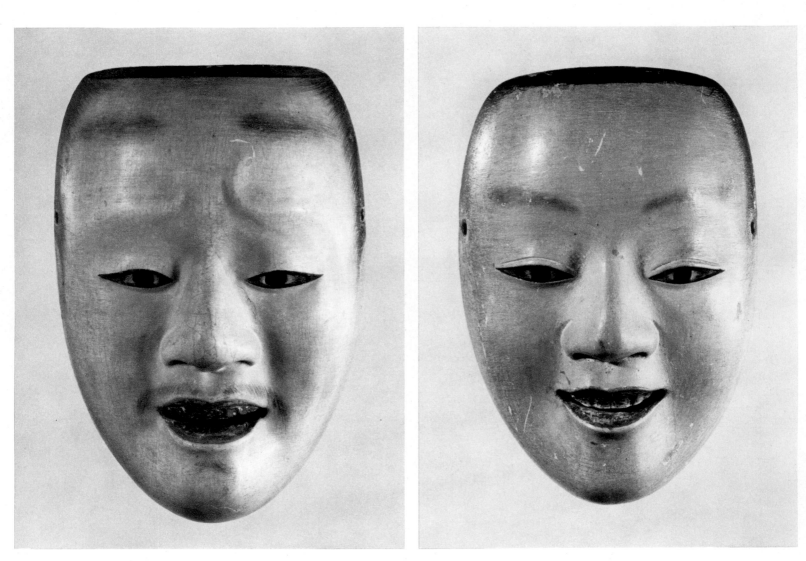

191. * *Imawaka* by Yasha. Kanze Collection. 8″ × 5½″.
Like the *chūjō*, this mask is of a young nobleman, and it bears a similar look of sadness. The *imawaka* mask is used by the Kanze school in most instances where the *chūjō* is used by other schools.
192. *Atsumori* by Kawachi. Kanze Collection. 7¾″ × 5½″.
The mask is named after Atsumori, the Heike general who died in battle when only sixteen. Originally it was used only in plays about Atsumori—*Atsumori* and *Ikuta Atsumori*—but today it is used for other young noblemen also. Except for the eyebrows and hair, it resembles a female mask, no doubt because of Atsumori's youth.

180

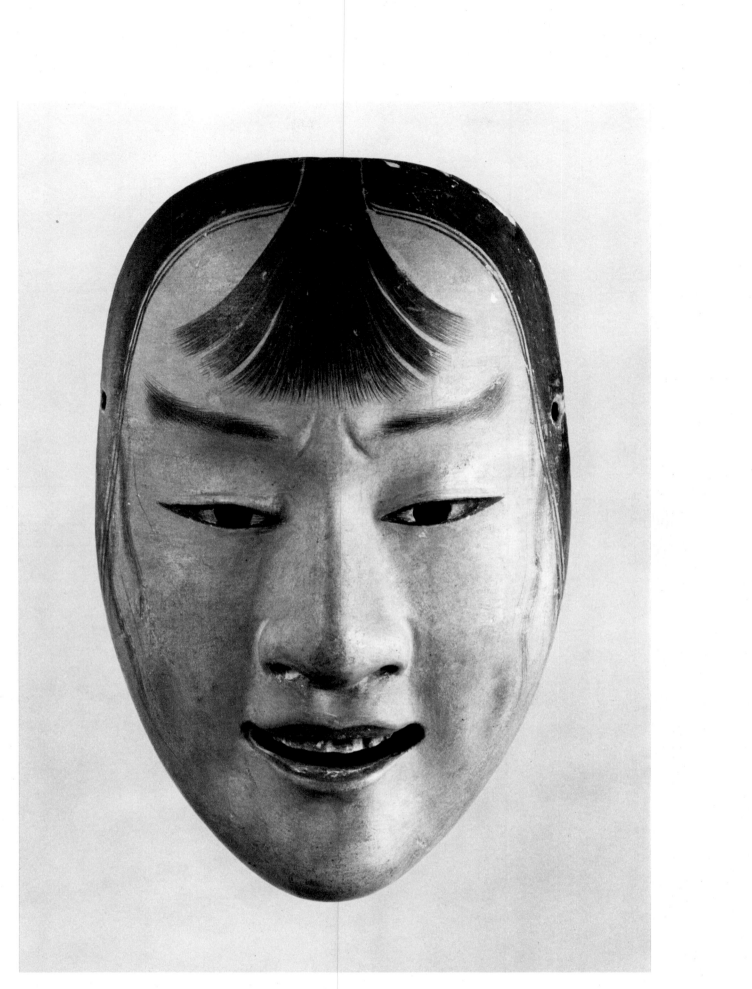

193. * *Kasshiki* by Tatsuemon.   Kanze Collection. $8'' \times 5\frac{1}{4}''$.
This mask with boyish features is worn in such plays as *Jinen Koji* and *Tōgan Koji*. The word *kasshiki* refers to an acolyte at a Zen temple who is still not a full-fledged priest and therefore retains his boyish forelock. The mask is distinguished by the forelock and the dimples.

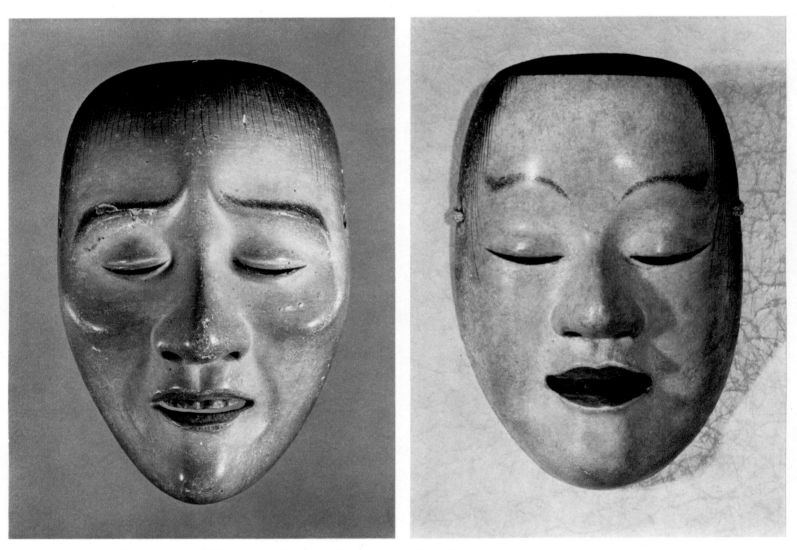

194. *Yoroboshi* by Yamato. Kongō Collection. $8\frac{1}{8}'' \times 5\frac{1}{2}''$.
This mask of a blind boy is worn by the *shite* in *Yoroboshi*. An innocent boy, falsely accused and disowned by his family, goes blind through grief and must beg for a living. The mask powerfully suggests the boy's tragic fate.
195. *Semimaru* by Mitsuteru. Kongō Collection. $8\frac{1}{8}'' \times 5\frac{1}{2}''$.
This mask, also of a blind young man, is worn by the *tsure* in *Semimaru*. The character is a prince, rather than a beggar (as in *Yoroboshi*), and the modeling is therefore much more elegant. Though blind, the prince's expression is serene. In both masks of blind men the aperture for the eyes is a long slit, rather than holes for the pupils, making it easier, paradoxically, for an actor to see when appearing as a blind man.

182

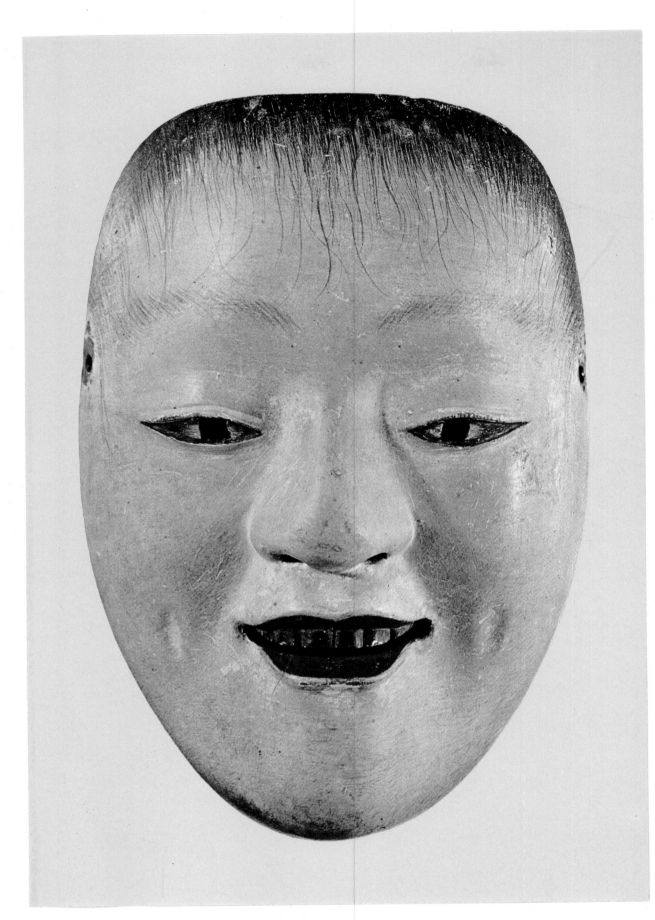

COLOR PLATE 5. †*Jidō* by Tatsuemon. Kanze Collection. $7\frac{7}{8}'' \times 5\frac{3}{4}''$.
This mask represents a young boy, and suggests eternal youth. It is used only
by the Kanze school in such plays as *Kiku Jidō* for which the other schools use
the *dōji*. The mask has a more pronounced sprite-like quality than the *dōji*.

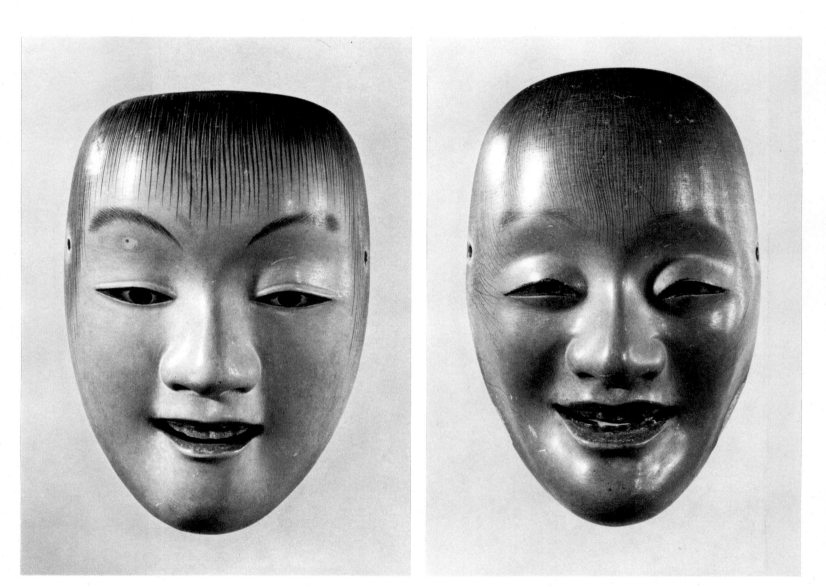

196. * *Dōji*   by Kouji.   Umewaka Collection. $7\frac{7}{8}'' \times 5\frac{1}{2}''$.

This boyish face has a sprite-like quality. The eyes, nose and mouth closely resemble those of the elegant *chūjō* mask, but the eyebrows suggest a young boy, and there is no furrow between the eyes. The overall impression is light and cheerful. The mask is used by schools other than Kanze for the roles of young boys who later in a play are revealed as gods or ghosts, as in *Kokaji* or *Ōeyama*.

197. * *Shōjō*   by Tatsuemon.   Umewaka Collection. $7\frac{7}{8}'' \times 5\frac{1}{4}''$.

The *shōjō* is a fabulous creature who lives in the water, loves to drink saké, and frolics when intoxicated. The mask, named after the creature, is used solely in such plays as *Shōjō* and *Taihei Shōjō*. Its features resemble those of the *dōji* and *jidō* masks, but it is red instead of white.

184

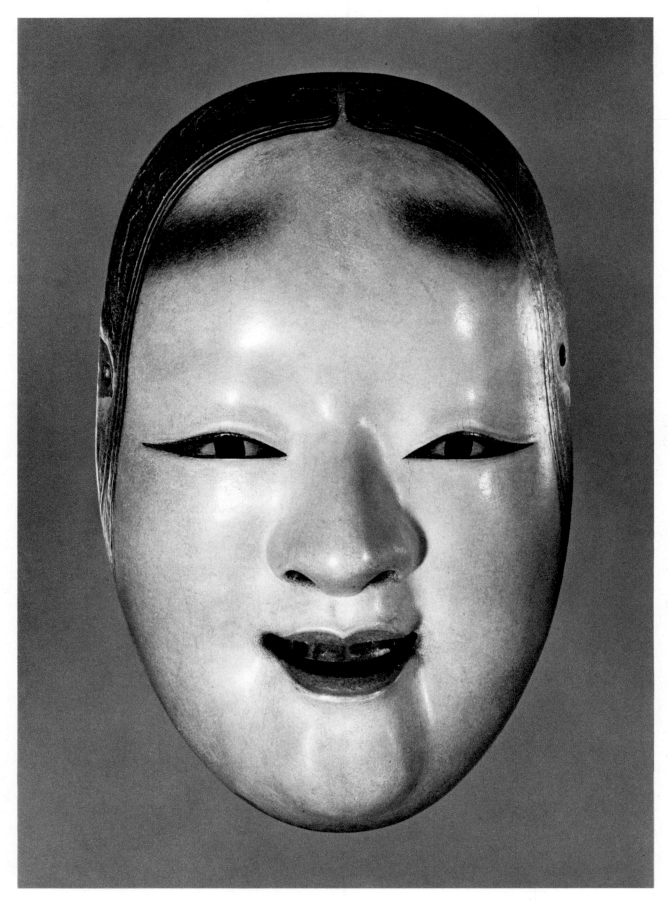

198. * *Kō-omote* by Tatsuemon. Kongō Collection. $8\frac{1}{4}'' \times 5\frac{3}{8}''$.
The Komparu and Kita schools use the *ko-omote* mask for most roles depicting young women. The cheeks of this mask are full, the forehead wide, and the face suffused with youthful beauty. This particular mask is commonly known as the *yuki* ("snow") *ko-omote*; it was one of three *ko-omote* masks by Tatsuemon prized by Toyotomi Hideyoshi.

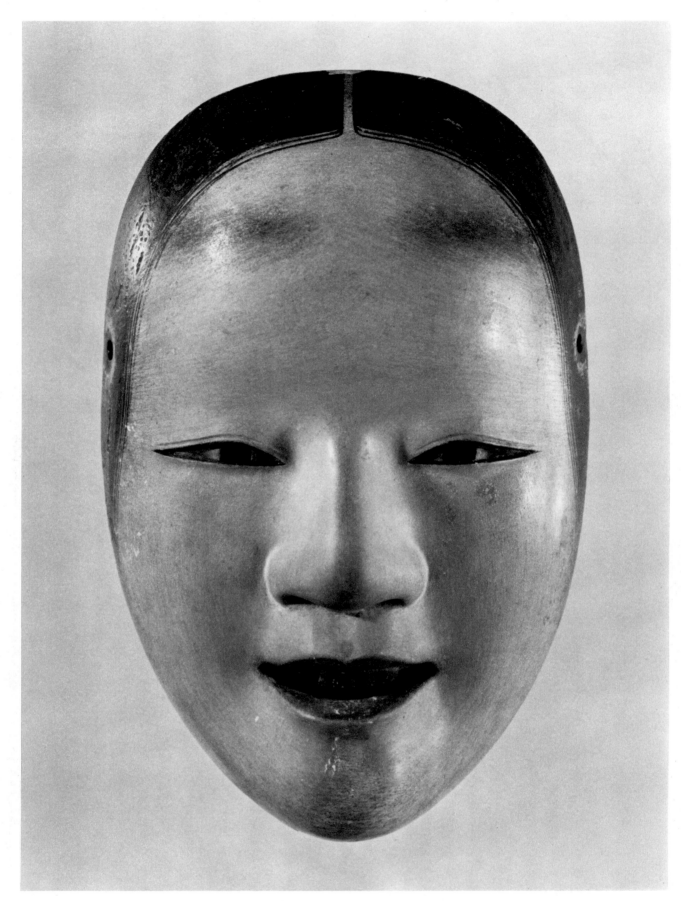

199. *Waka-onna* by Kawachi. Kanze Collection. 8¼″ × 5¼″.
Waka-onna means literally "young woman." This is the standard variety of young woman's mask used by the Kanze school in plays of the third category. Its expression lies between that of the *ko-omote* and the more mature *zō-onna*, being somewhat thinner and more worldly-looking than the *ko-omote*, yet still youthful.

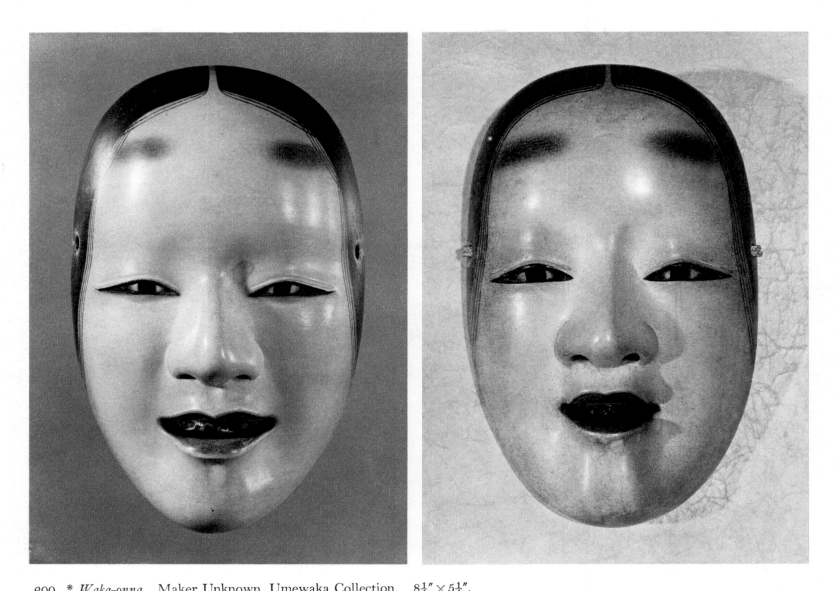

200. * *Waka-onna*   Maker Unknown. Umewaka Collection. $8\frac{1}{4}'' \times 5\frac{1}{4}''$.
201. *Magojirō*   by Kongōtayū Kageyori.   Kongō Collection. $8\frac{3}{8}'' \times 5\frac{3}{8}''$.
This mask of a young woman derives its name from the creator, Kongō Magojirō. Magojirō (1538–1564) is said to have been the second son of the sixth-generation head of the Kongō school, and to have made this mask to represent the features of his wife, who had died young. The *magojirō* mask, the standard one for the roles of young women as performed by the Kongō school, is a particularly elegant and beautiful variety. A shadow lurks behind its beauty, perhaps a reflection of the tragic fate of the original model.

187

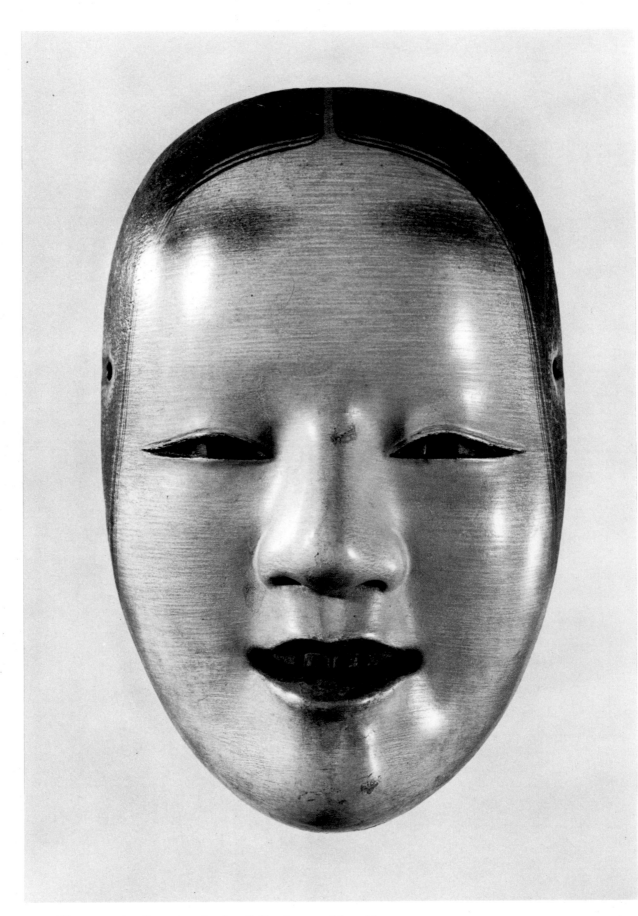

202. †*Zō-onna* by Zōami. Hōshō Collection. $8\frac{1}{4}'' \times 5\frac{1}{4}''$.
The *zō-onna* mask takes its name from its creator, Zōami. The Hōshō school uses this mask for the roles of young women, but it possesses such great dignity that the other schools tend to use it for angels or goddesses. This particular mask is called the *fushiki* (knotted wood) *zō* because knots are visible in the wood, especially on the left side, near the base of the nose. Seepage from the knots has somewhat discolored the mask.

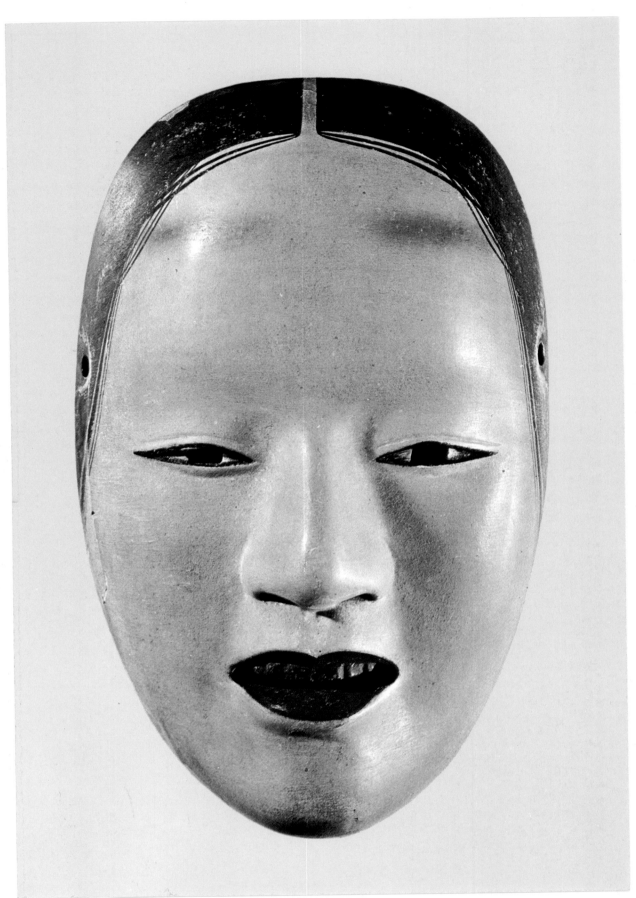

COLOR PLATE 6.
* *Zō-onna* by Zōami. Kanze Collection. $8\frac{1}{4}'' \times 5\frac{1}{4}''$.
The features of this *zō-onna* mask have a classical perfection and dignity that
make the mask particularly well suited for use in the roles of celestial beings, as
in *Hagoromo* or *Miwa*.

189

203. * *Ōmi Onna*   by Echi.   Kanze Collection. $8\frac{1}{4}'' \times 5\frac{1}{4}''$.
This mask depicts a woman probably slightly older than the women represented
by the *waka-onna* or *zō-onna*. The face has been described as that of a mature
woman who still harbors romantic feelings. The mask is suited for such roles as
the *shite* in the first part of *Dōjōji*, a victim of uncontrollable love. The name
seems to have originated in the use of the mask in the *sarugaku* of Ōmi.

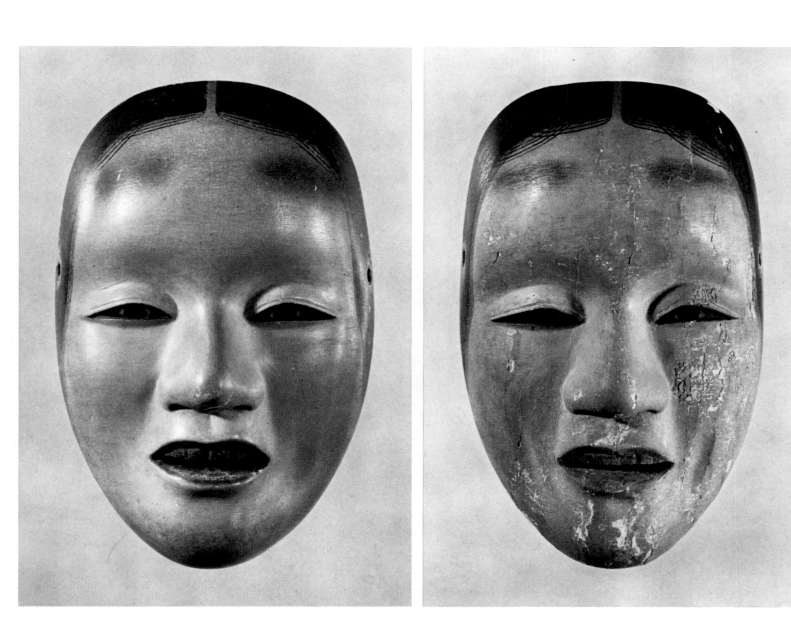

204. * *Fukai* by Tokuwaka. Umewaka Collection. $7\frac{7}{8}'' \times 5\frac{1}{2}''$.
Fukai is the mask of a woman in her thirties. Generally used for the roles of mothers, the expression is considered to embody maternal love. The eyes are set deeper than in the masks of young women, and the cheeks droop somewhat, giving the impression of a woman lost in thought. The origin of the name *fukai*, meaning "deep," is not clear, but perhaps means not only "deep" in age, but in feeling and experience. The *fukai* mask is used only by the Kanze school; other schools use *shakumi*.
205. * *Fukai* by Echi. Kanze Collection. $8\frac{1}{16}'' \times 5\frac{1}{4}''$.

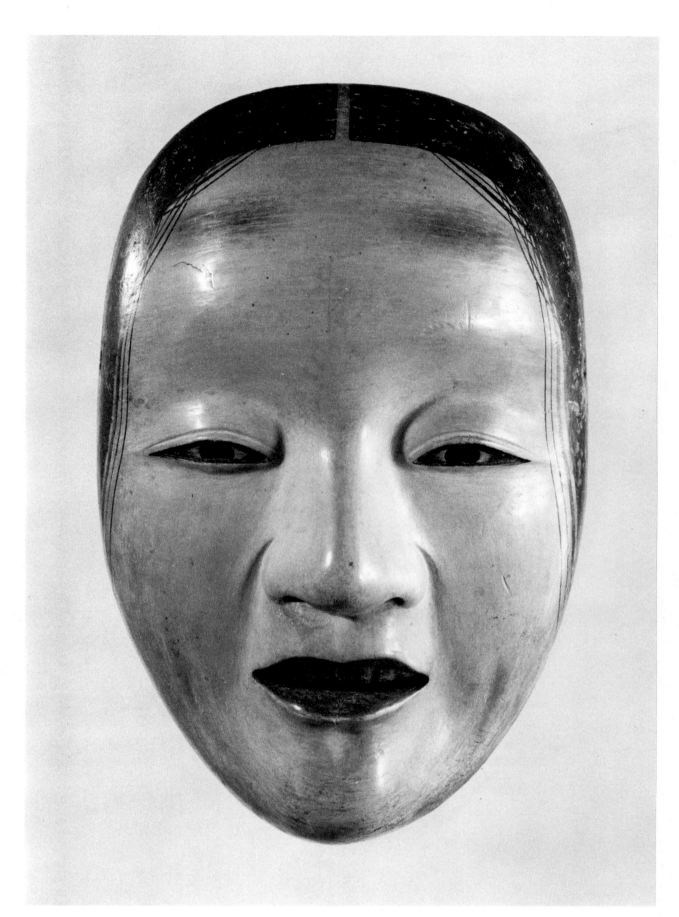

206. *Shakumi* by Kawachi. Hōshō Collection. $8\frac{1}{4}'' \times 5\frac{1}{2}''$.
This mask of a woman in her thirties derives its name from *shakumu*, meaning
to be sunken in the middle, a reference to the prominent forehead and jaw. Its
expression, like that of *fukai*, is maternal, and it is used for the roles of mothers
in all schools except Kanze. Its features seem to express deeper feelings of
anxiety than those of *fukai*.

192

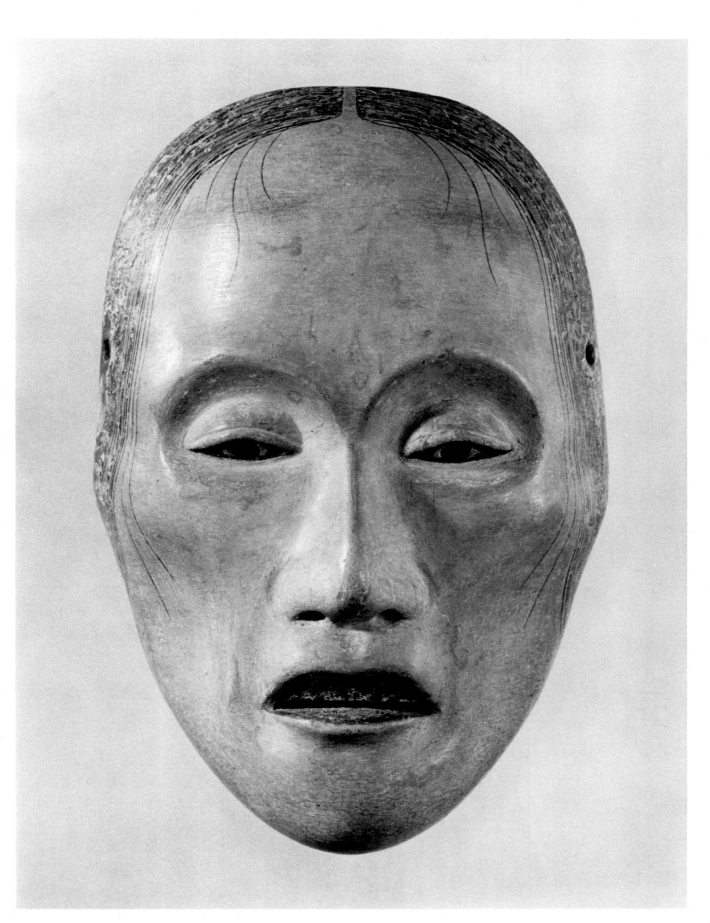

207. * *Rōjo* by Himi. Umewaka Collection. 8″ × 5¾″.
Rōjo is the mask of an old woman who once had been beautiful. It is especially
suited for the role of Komachi, a supremely beautiful woman reduced to misery
in her old age. The face reveals the character's age, but there are no wrinkles,
a lingering reminder of her former loveliness. The *rōjo* mask is worn in *Sekidera
Komachi* and *Sotoba Komachi*.

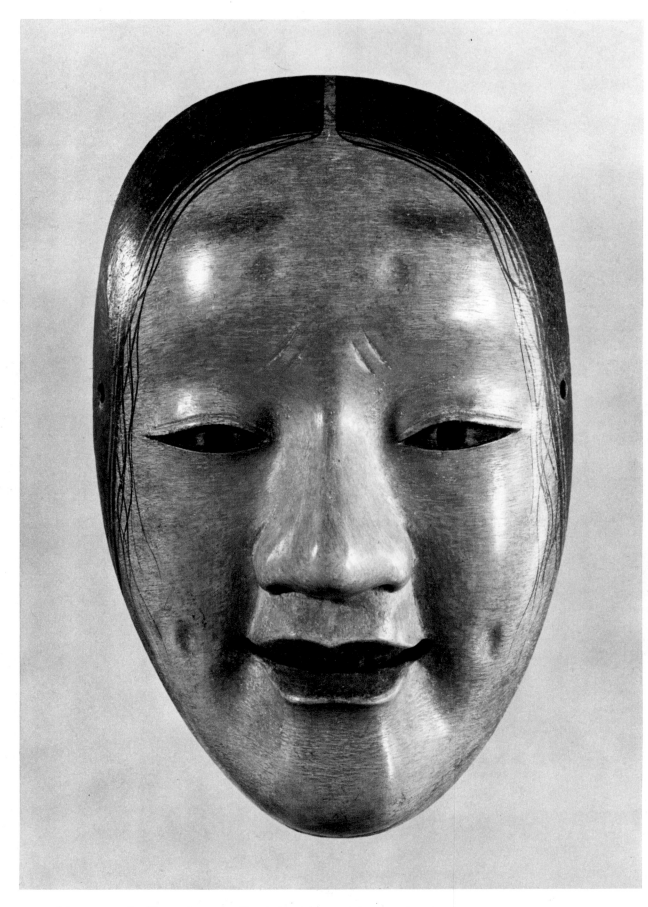

208. *Masugami* by Kawachi. Hōshō Collection. 8″ × 5¼″.
The mask depicts a deranged young woman. The wrinkles between the eyes
and the slight dents above them are the special marks of this mask. The dimples,
the slightly disheveled hair and the eyes also contribute to the air of distraction.
The features are those of a woman out of contact with this world who yet
preserves her dignity. The mask is worn by Sakagami in *Semimaru*.

194

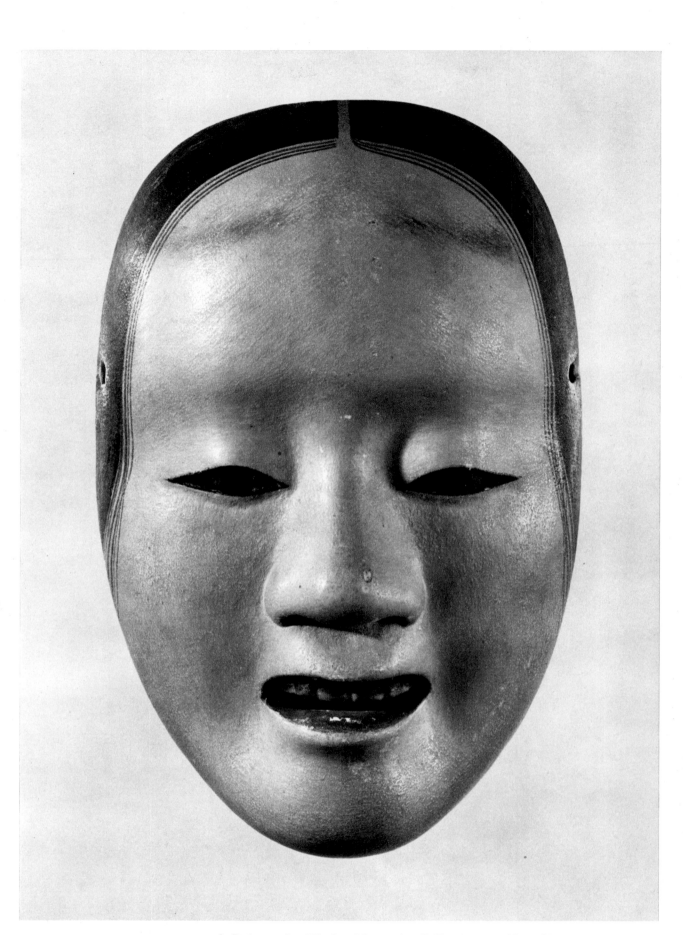

209. * *Deigan*   by Himi.   Umewaka Collection.   8¼″×5¼″.
The mask is used mainly for women sworn to exact revenge as spirits, or for dead women suffering torments in hell. The name *deigan* refers to the gold dust applied to color the eyes. The eyes were originally intended to suggest a celestial being, but the mask is now used for tormented ghosts in such plays as *Aoi no Ue* and *Kinuta*.

195

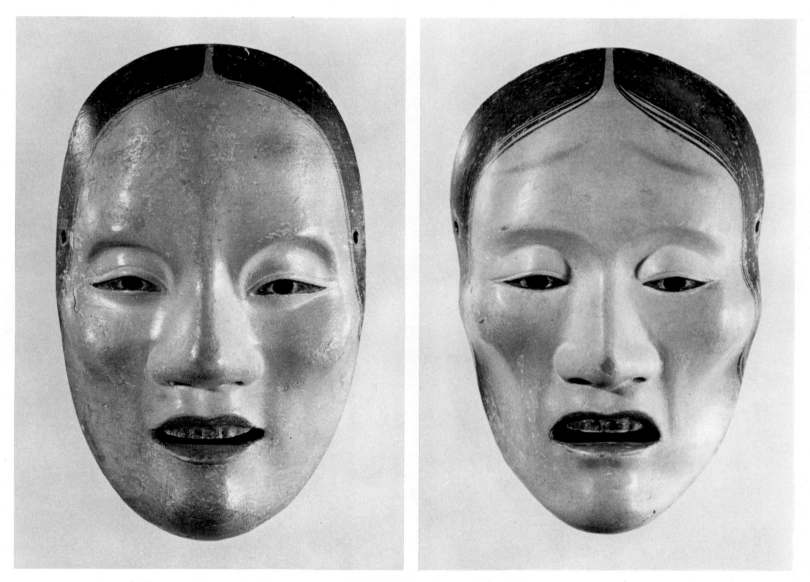

210. * *Kanawa Onna*   by Tatsuemon.   Hōshō Collection. $8\frac{1}{4}'' \times 7\frac{1}{2}''$.
The name is derived from its use in the first part of *Kanawa*, the story of a woman led by extreme jealousy to haunt a man. The *deigan* mask has similar traits, but also a beauty and dignity lacking in this mask. The *kanawa onna* mask depicts not a supernatural woman but an ordinary one, and her jealousy is unrelieved by nobler sentiments.
211. * *Ryō no Onna*   by Himi.   Kanze Collection. $7\frac{7}{8}'' \times 5\frac{1}{4}''$.
This mask, the effigy of a dead woman, depicts a woman who has died because of an infatuation which still tortures her. Suffering has made her features haggard, but they still possess something of her former beauty. The eyebrows painted on the upper forehead confirm this impression. The mask is used for the ghost in the second part of such plays as *Motomezuka* or *Kinuta*.

196

COLOR PLATE 7.
* *Hannya*   by Yasha.   Kanze Collection.   8″×6¾″.
This mask of a female ghost embodies her jealousy and hatred. Horns rise from
the head, and metal is inserted in the eyes and teeth. Only the eyebrows, faintly
visible high on the forehead, and the hair suggest that this is a woman. The
name *hannya* apparently derives from that of the creator, the mask-maker Hannyabō. It is worn in such plays as *Aoi no Ue* and *Dōjōji*.

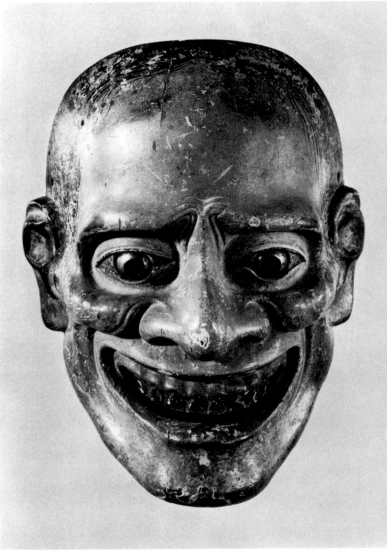

212. * *Shinja* by Tokuwaka. Umewaka Collection. $9\frac{3}{8}'' \times 6\frac{3}{4}''$.

This vengeful female ghost expresses its evil intentions even more forcefully than *hannya*, with an expression that carries jealousy to an absolute extreme. The horns are straighter and farther apart than in the *hannya* mask, and the lower jaw juts forward more prominently. It is worn in special performances of *Dōjōji*.

213. † *Yamauba* by Shakuzuru. Umewaka Collection. $8\frac{7}{8}'' \times 6\frac{7}{8}''$.

Yamauba is a witch who lives in the mountains. Though old and seemingly decrepit, she possesses evil powers of magic. This example, a modification of the normal *yamauba* mask, has ears.

214. *Shishiguchi* by Shakuzuru. Hōshō Collection. 8¼″×6¾″
215. *Kojishi* by Shakuzuru. Hōshō Collection. 8″×6¼″.
These special masks are used for *shishi* roles only. The *shishi* (usually translated as "lion") is not a wild beast but a frolicsome creature who enjoys disporting himself with peonies. The entire mask is colored gold, providing a striking contrast with the red mouth. It is used only in *Shakkyō*. In special performances of this play requiring more than one *shishi*, the *kojishi* mask is worn by the *tsure*.

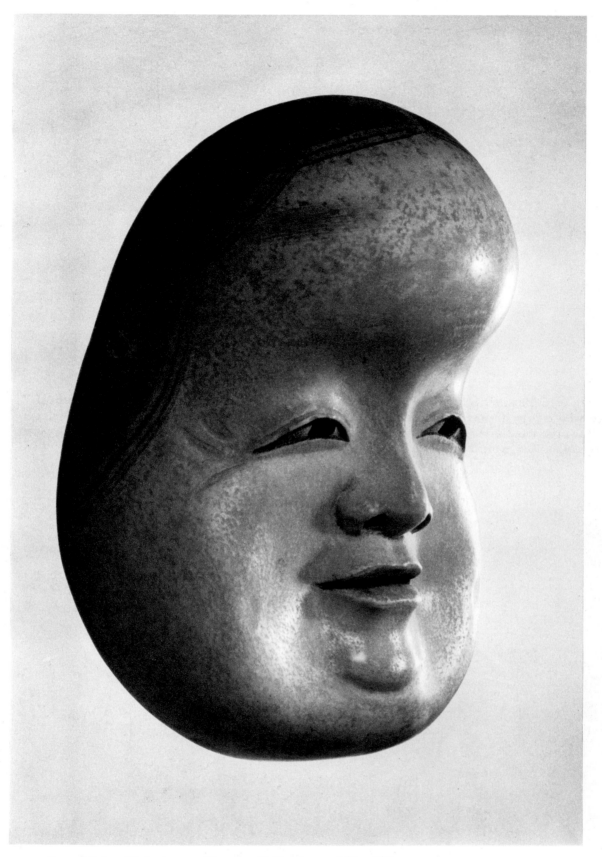

216. *Oto*   Maker Unknown.   Nomura Collection. $7\frac{1}{2}'' \times 5\frac{1}{2}''$.
Kyōgen actors usually do no more than tie a towel around their heads to indicate
they are taking the roles of women, but when they are obliged to look unusually
ugly, especially in plays about a man unlucky in his bride, they wear the *oto*
mask. The protruding forehead and chin, the flat nose and broad cheeks are
classically ugly features. Eighteenth century.

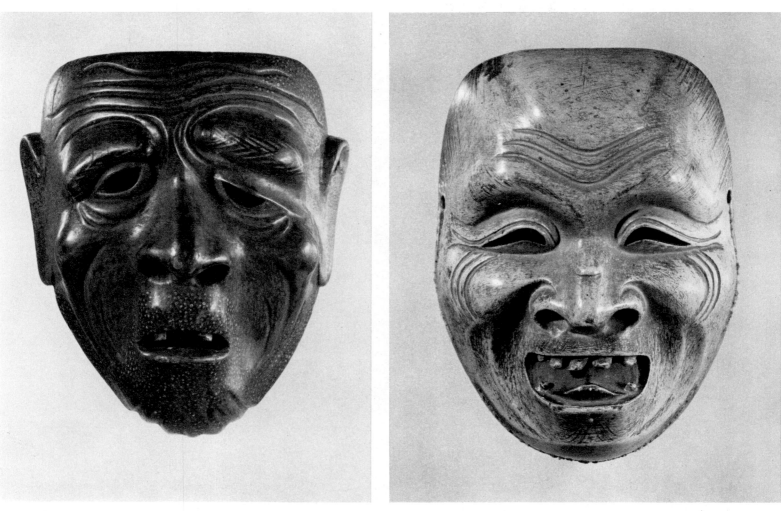

217. *Ōji* Maker Unknown. Nomura Collection. $6\frac{5}{8}'' \times 5\frac{1}{2}''$.
The *ōji* mask is often used for the roles of lecherous old men. The face utterly lacks the dignity of the Nō masks of old men: the two halves are asymmetrical, one eye drooping lower than the other; two decayed teeth protrude from the gaping mouth; the beard is untrimmed; the wrinkles form grotesque patterns. All in all, a comically repulsive character. Seventeenth century.
218. *Hanabiki* by Deme Tōhaku. Nomura Collection. $7\frac{7}{8}'' \times 5\frac{1}{2}''$.
This mask apparently owes its name to the low-bridged nose *(hana)*. The face, though undignified, is somehow appealing. It is used mainly in plays about cheerful ghosts. Eighteenth century.

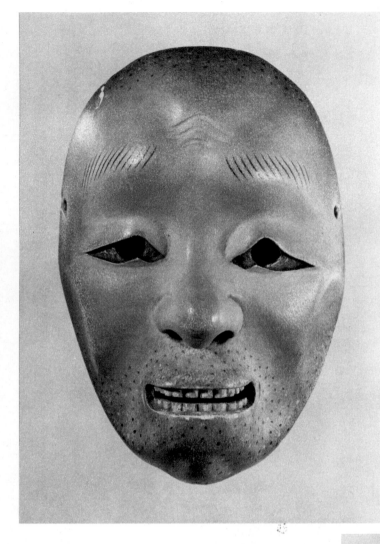

219. *Hakuzōsu* Maker Unknown. Nomura Collection. 8″ × 5½″.
This is the disguise in which the fox appears in *Tsurigitsune*, as the uncle of the fox-trapper. The eyes, teeth and eyebrows, however, are indicative of his true nature. Eighteenth century.

220. *Kitsune* by Izeki Bitchū-no-kami. Shigeyama Collection.
7⅞″ × 6¼″ × 5⅛″.
The fox mask is used in *Tsurigitsune*, a Kyōgen about a fox who assumes human form in order to induce a man to give up his fox traps. Later, when the smell of fried mice becomes too much for the fox to resist, he falls into the trap and reveals his true appearance. Seventeenth century.

221. *Usobuki* Maker Unknown. Nomura Collection. $6\frac{5}{8}'' \times 5\frac{5}{8}''$.
The name of the mask originally seems to have meant a whistler, referring to
the puckered mouth and the popping eyes. The *usobuki* mask is now used, however, for non-human beings—the spirit of a mosquito in *Kazumō*, of an octopus
in *Tako*, and of pinesap in *Matsuyani*. Fourteenth century.

222. *Kentoku*   Maker Unknown.   Shigeyama Collection. $6\frac{5}{8}'' \times 4\frac{3}{4}''$.
The origin of the name *kentoku* is much debated. The mask may have been intended to represent a horse in highly stylized (or humanized) form. It is used for this purpose in *Shidō Hōgaku*, but in other works also for an ox, a dog, and even a crab. Eighteenth century.

223. *Ebisu* Maker Unknown. Nomura Collection. 7" × 5½".

Ebisu is one of the seven gods of good fortune, usually depicted with his fishing tackle and catch. In Kyōgen he is known both for his fondness for saké and for the blessings he bestows on those whose piety has pleased him. The *ebisu* mask is worn in such plays as *Ebisu Bishamon*. Eighteenth century.

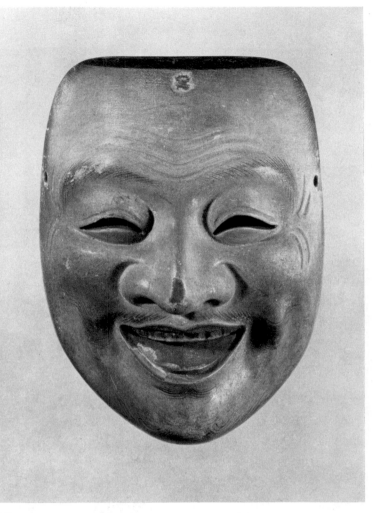

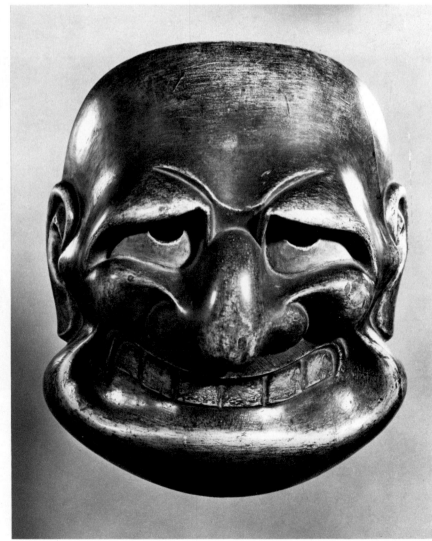

224. *Buaku* by Zekan. Shigeyama Collection. 8⅝" × 6¼".

The *buaku* mask is the Kyōgen version of the Nō mask *ōbeshimi*. The faint comical quality of the latter is here exaggerated in the sheepish grin of an ineffectual monster from hell. Devils in Kyōgen are represented usually as braggarts who are quickly vanquished by ordinary mortals. The name of this mask derives from that of the hero of *Buaku*, but the mask is used for many other roles. Seventeenth century.

205

225. The mask-maker Kitazawa Kōun begins chipping at a block of *hinoki* (Japanese cypress) wood.

226. The first stage in carving a mask is to split the block in quarters. The sides closer to the center of the original block become the surfaces of the mask. In this way any natural seepage of resin from the center outwards will appear only on the back of the mask. An *okina* mask is being carved here.

227. The familiar features of the *okina* mask, including the split jaw *(kiriago)*, are blocked out by the maker.

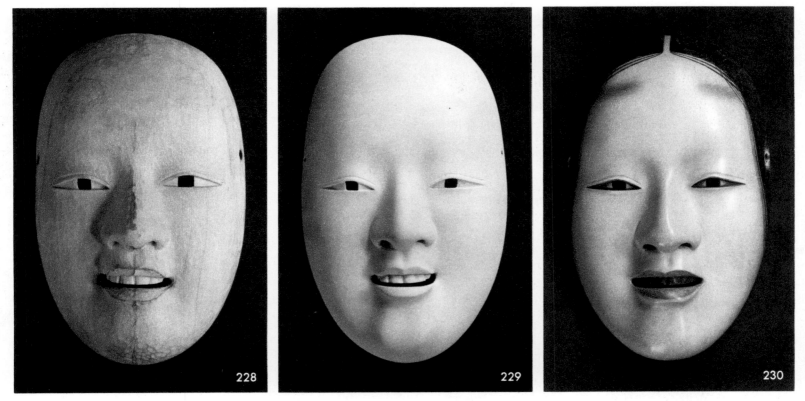

228. A *magojirō* mask when fully carved.
229. The mask after several dozen coatings of Chinese white have been applied.
230. The features are painted to complete the mask.

231. Kitazawa Kōun painting the *magojirō* mask.

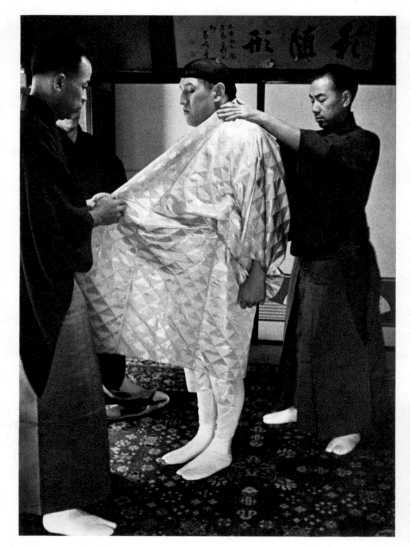

232. The *shite* (Kongō Iwao) attires himself for his role in *Dōjōji* by first putting on gauzy underclothes to absorb perspiration, stockings, and white *tabi*. Next come two layers of padding, intended to give his figure the desired bulk, especially when performing as a demon. Next, a collar piece, then (as in this picture) a *surihaku* kimono. The *uroko* (fish-scale) pattern is traditional for *Dōjōji*.

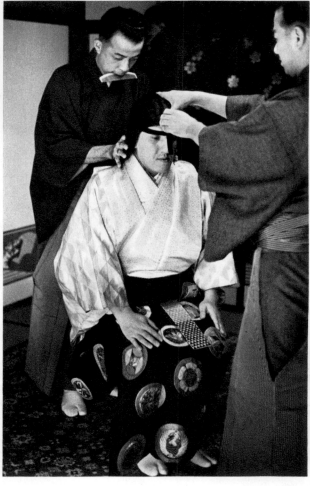

233. A *nuihaku* robe is placed over the *surihaku*. It is folded down at the waist. The pattern of the robe, consisting of many crests on a black background, is also traditional for the part. A sash is tied around the waist. Next, the assistants fit a wig on the actor's head.

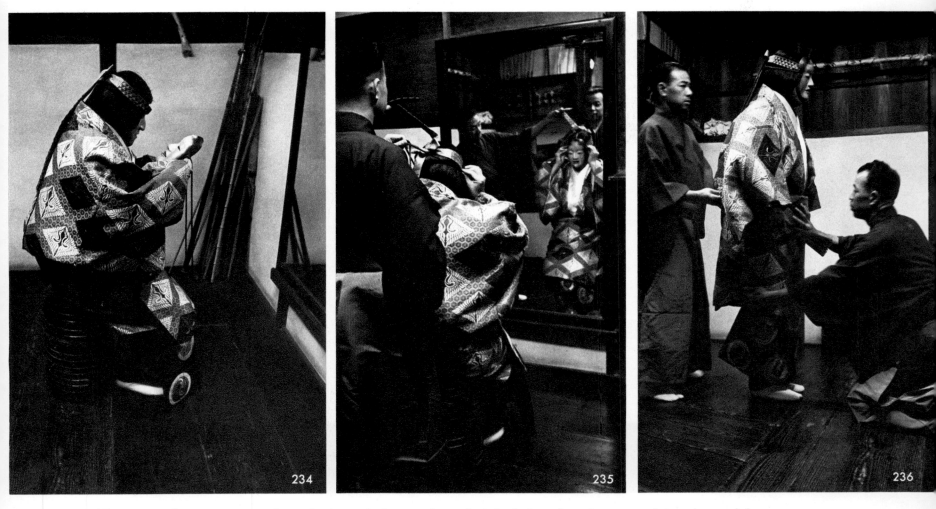

234. The actor, who now wears a *karaori* robe tucked up at the waist, sits before the mirror examining the mask he will wear.
235. The assistants help him to put on the mask, carefully tightening the strings with equal pressure on each side.
236. The assistants make a final check as they smooth out the costume of the fully attired actor.

COLOR PLATE 8.
Karaori. The literal meaning of *karaori* is "Chinese weave." Though originally the name of a kind of brocade imported from China, it came to designate an elaborately embroidered robe with short sleeves, generally worn in the Nō plays by female characters. This example has a design of hemp-spools *(odamaki)* and weeping-cherry blossoms *(shidarezakura)*. It has traditionally been used by the Kanze school for the leading role in *Dōjōji*. The use of red in the fabric *(iroiri)* indicates this *karaori* is worn by a young woman. Eighteenth century. Kanze Collection.

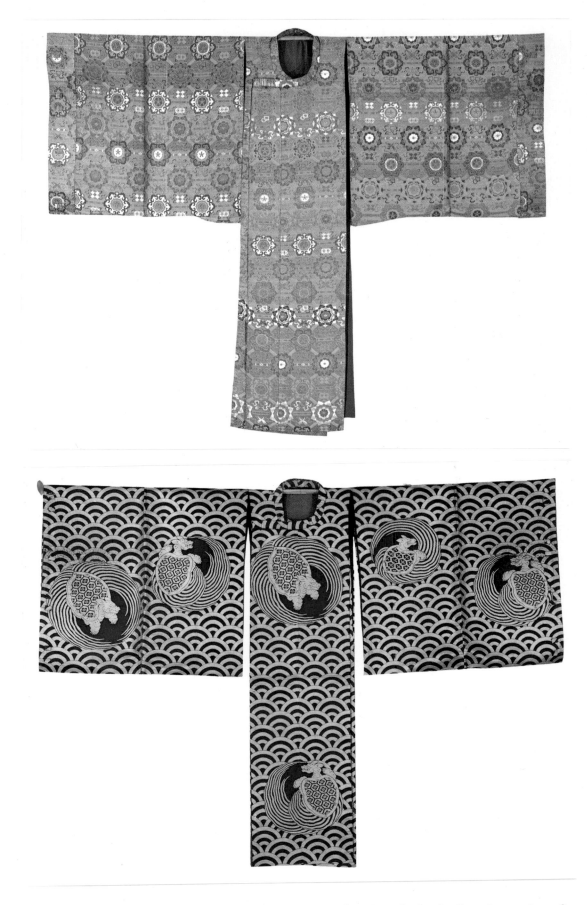

COLOR PLATE 9.
Okina kariginu. The *kariginu,* an outer robe worn by noblemen, originated as a hunting cloak, the literal meaning of the Japanese word. The garment is unusual in that the collar is round, and the front and back hang loose. This example, used exclusively for the role of Okina, was made into a Nō robe from a military cloak given the Kanze school by the Shogun Tokugawa Ieyasu. The pattern of the brocade is known as *shokkō,* consisting of hexagonal shapes. Early seventeenth century. Kanze Collection.

COLOR PLATE 10.
Kariginu. This garment, a present from Tokugawa Hidetada, the second shogun of his line, has a pattern of tortoises (a symbol of longevity) surrounded by waves. Brocade woven with this wave pattern is known as *seigaiha* from the *bugaku* piece of the same name, for which it was first used. A lined *kariginu* is generally worn on the Nō stage by courtiers. Early seventeenth century. Kanze Collection.

211

COLOR PLATE 11.

Karaori. The pattern is of cherry blossoms on flowing water. The *karaori* displays a lavish use of gold and silver thread on a heavy silk brocade. It may be worn in *kinagashi* style as an outer robe over an upper garment with printed patterns *(surihaku)*; or with the right sleeve slipped from the shoulder *(nugikake)* for the roles of deranged women; or tucked up *(tsubo-ori)* under a sash and worn with *ōkuchi* trousers; or with a *nuihaku* under-robe which has been folded down at the waist *(koshimaki)*. Early eighteenth century. Kongō Collection.

COLOR PLATE 12.

Nuihaku. The name *nuihaku* means "embroidery and gold leaf" a description of the ornamentation applied to the silk. Generally worn as an under-robe, the *nuihaku* is often folded down at the waist *(koshimaki)*. It is worn chiefly by women, but also by courtiers, youths and children. This example has a design of square and oblong cards used for poems or paintings. A willow pattern runs through the patches of different colors, imparting unity. The colors lack red, indicating the robe is normally worn by a middle-aged woman. Eighteenth century. Umewaka Collection.

212

COLOR PLATE 13.
Nuihaku. The design shows butterflies and pampas grass *(susuki)* against a silver background. This garment may have been presented by the Shogun Hidetada to the Kanze school. Late sixteenth century. Umewaka Collection.

COLOR PLATE 14.

Happi. An upper garment with wide sleeves. Front and back are stitched together only at the bottom, two inches at the hems. This example is unlined; it was meant to be worn by a nobleman in battle attire. Probably it was originally a garment worn by the Shogun Ashikaga Yoshimasa, who presented it to the head of the Kanze school after a performance. The design shows dragonflies framed in lozenges. The only touches of contrasting color to the dark green background are the red, blue, yellow and green of the eyes. Fifteenth century. Kanze Collection.

COLOR PLATE 15.

Happi. The bold design of this *happi* is of swallows, as stylized in the crest of Shibata Katsuie (1522–83). It is used for the younger "lion" *(shishi)* in *Shakkyō.* Seventeenth century. Kongō Collection.

214

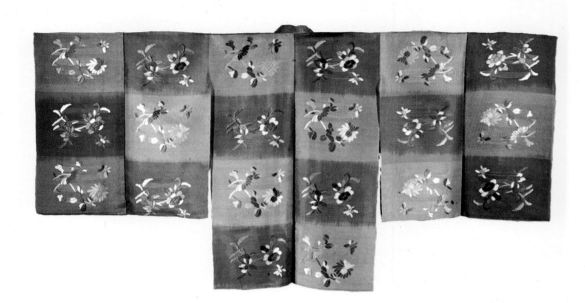

Chōken. The name means literally "long silk," referring to the length of the sleeves. The garment is tied in front by cords hanging from the neckline. Ornamental cords also hang from the ends of the sleeves. The *chōken* is an outer jacket worn by women and nobles. This example, a modern reproduction of one originally presented to the Kongō school by Ashikaga Yoshimasa, captures perfectly in its muted greens and browns the autumnal quality of a play like *Ochiba.* Kongō Collection.

Chōken. An unusual design of *torii* and pines. It is used for such roles as the poetess Izumi Shikibu in *Tōboku.* Eighteenth century. Hōshō Collection.

215

COLOR PLATE 18.
Atsuita. The name means literally "thick board," an appropriate description of the stiff silk. It is normally worn by male characters. This example, with its design of *shishi* ("lions") cavorting amidst peonies, is used for the parent *shishi* in *Shakkyō*. Early eighteenth century. Kongō Collection.

COLOR PLATE 19.
Kataginu. Another characteristic element of the Kyōgen costume is this sleeveless jacket worn over the *noshime*. It is woven of hemp and the design is likely to be of a humble or deliberately inelegant motif such as the roof tiles shown here. Nomura Collection.

216

COLOR PLATE 20.

Kazuraobi. The designs here are: pine, bamboo and plum (without red, for the roles of old women). Chinese fans against willows (with red, for young women); flowers and *noshi*, a strip of seaweed pasted on gifts (with red); arabesque design (*karakusa*, without red); and silk spools (*itomaki*, with red). Nineteenth century. Kongō Collection.

COLOR PLATE 21.

Kazuraobi. Even the bands used to tie the wig in place are beautifully woven, though scarcely visible to the audience. The designs, from left to right, are: orange blossoms; leaves and flowers; butterflies with uplifted wings; and the seven famous plants of autumn. The designs lack red, an indication that these bands are worn for the roles of middle-aged women. Nineteenth century. Kongō Collection.

COLOR PLATE 22.

Koshiobi. The patterns of these sashes, from left to right, are: kerria roses *(yamabuki)*, worn by an old woman; Genji wheels *(genjiguruma)* and pine sprigs, also worn by an old woman; flowers in circles, a pattern worn by a young woman of high birth; and fish scales *(uroko)*, worn by the *shite* in *Dōjōji*. Nineteenth century. Kongō Collection.

COLOR PLATE 23.

Koshiobi. These are sashes worn around *kariginu, happi* and other outer garments. They are tied in front with the ends hanging down. These examples were woven to designs by the great artist Ogata Kōrin (1658–1716), himself the son of a Kyoto silk merchant. The designs from left to right are: daffodils among clouds, camellia and plum blossoms, and maple leaves on flowing water. All have red in the design and are used with *karaori* worn by young women. The white part of the sash indicates the wearer is a woman of high birth. Kongō Collection.

217

COLOR PLATE 24.
Three symbols of longevity—pine, crane, and tortoise—are illustrated on this fan. It is used by the *shite* in *Okina*.
COLOR PLATE 25.
Waves and the setting sun are depicted on this fan, which is used by the *shite* in warrior plays about defeated heroes.
COLOR PLATE 26.
Court ladies are illustrated on this fan, which is used only by the *shite* in woman plays.
COLOR PLATE 27.
Autumn plants are depicted on this fan (without red). It is used by the *shite* (middle-aged woman) in mad-woman plays such as *Sumidagawa, Miidera*, etc.
COLOR PLATE
This fan has circular flower designs and is used by the *shite*, both male and female, in plays such as *Aoi no Ue, Tamura*, and *Tōru*.
COLOR PLATE 28.
The chrysanthemum and flowing water design is depicted on this fan, which is used by the *shite* in *Shōjō*.

218

THE GESTURES OF NŌ

The movements of a Nō actor are stylized throughout. Even when he employs some representational gesture—the warrior's brandishing of a sword or a blind man's tottering on his staff—it accords with prescribed patterns. Most gestures in Nō have no specific meaning of their own, but acquire a meaning when combined with other movements or when associated with a particular section of a text. The larger patterns of gesture, known as *kata* in Japanese, make up the dances of Nō. Each school has its own traditions, and countless varieties of *kata* are employed, but these of the Kanze school, performed by Kanze Hisao, are typical.

237. *Shita-i.* The actor kneels with one knee raised. Kanze and Hōshō school actors raise the left knee, but *shite* actors of the Komparu, Kongō and Kita schools raise the right knee. This *kata* indicates that the person is sitting.

238. *Tatsu.* The standing posture is considered exceedingly important. The actor's chest is forward, his chin pulled back, and his head held erect; in addition, his feet are aligned and his hands kept at his sides. The farther apart the feet, the stronger the personage represented. When a woman is portrayed, the toes and heels of both feet touch.

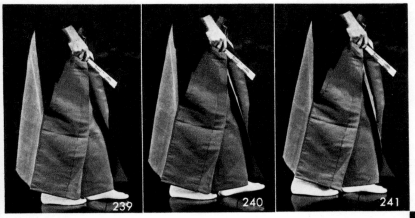

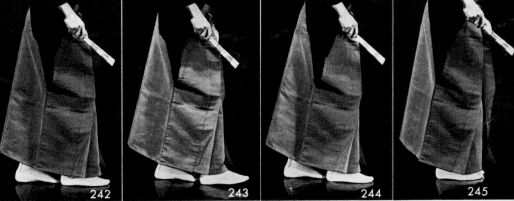

239–245. *Umpo* or *hakobi.* This is the *kata* of walking. (240) The actor glides on his heels, curving back the toes, (241) and only then resting the whole foot on the floor. The walk is strikingly similar to that of Zen priests.

246–247. *Agehaōgi.* (246) In this *kata* the opened fan is held before the face, (247) lifted over the head as the actor takes three steps backwards, then lowered to the right. The gesture has no intrinsic meaning, but may indicate, according to the text, such varied actions as looking off into the distance or removing a cloak.

219

248–249. *Sayū*. This *kata* follows the *agehaōgi*. The actor takes a step to the left with his left arm outstretched. Then, with a stamp of the left foot, he extends his right arm and takes a step to the right. This *kata*, a dance movement, generally serves to conclude a section.

252–253. *Kasumi no ōgi*. The opened fan is slowly lowered and turned over to parallel the floor. The name of this *kata*, "mist fan," indicates it is used to suggest mist, when it occurs in the text; it is also used for waterfalls, winds blowing down mountains, etc.

250–251. *Sashikomi* and *hiraki*. The *kata* of *sashikomi* involves lifting and thrusting forward the closed fan. It is followed by *hiraki*, a spreading open of the arms. These gestures generally are meaningless dance movements, but on occasion denote authority or dignity.

254. *Kumo no ōgi*. In performing the *kata* of the "cloud fan," the actor holds his left hand forward, and his right over the fan. He then draws his hands apart, looking upwards at the same time. The *kata* is intended to represent gazing at clouds, the sky or mountains.

255. *Tsuki no ōgi*. The "moon fan" is performed by touching the left shoulder with the opened fan while looking upwards and diagonally to the right. This *kata* generally signifies looking at the moon.

220

256. *Tsumami ōgi.* The actor grasps the opened fan by the first rib and, keeping it erect, extends the fan forward. This rather unusual *kata* is used in *Futari Shizuka* to suggest falling blossoms, in *Akogi* for the lowering of fishing nets, and in *Izutsu* for children measuring their heights against a well-curb.

257. *Makura no ōgi.* This *kata*, the "pillow fan," is used to represent taking a nap. The opened fan is held in the left hand over the face, concealing it.

258–259. *Maneki ōgi.* As the name "inviting fan" indicates, the *kata* is used for beckoning, but it also serves as a sign of affection. (258) The opened fan is lifted above the shoulder, (259) then turned over in a fanning motion. The gesture is usually repeated.

260. *Yūken ōgi.* Usually expresses joy, but sometimes it is purely decorative. The opened fan is held to the chest, then lifted to the right, generally twice.

261. *Shiori.* A familiar *kata*, suggesting grief. The left or right hand is lifted to the face, the palm held a short distance from the eyes. The head is lowered somewhat. The *kata* may indicate weeping, or holding back tears, or hiding a tear-stained face. The fan is held closed.

262–263. *Sorikaeri.* The actor, his hands held before him, shifts his weight to his left leg, then spins round to the left, twisting his body slightly forward. He lowers his right foot on completing the turn. This *kata* is used to suggest great pain or such actions as leaping into the sea.

264. In this *kata*, the fan is used to represent a shield, generally in some martial scene.

265. Here the fan represents a broadsword, held over the head.

266–267. The halberd *(naginata)* is used in scenes of combat, as in *Funa Benkei*. (266) The actor holds it in readiness or (267) brandishes it.

268. In some plays, notably *Yoroboshi*, a blind man leans on a stick in this *kata*.

269. *Munazue.* The actor leans his chest on a stick, gazing into the distance, suggesting age or weariness, as in *Kinuta*.

270. *Tsuki no ōgi.* This *kata* is used in Kyōgen dance movements. The actor crosses his legs, moves the opened fan in his right hand to his left shoulder, and looks up toward the sky on his right. The attitude is one of looking at and conveying the presence of the moon or some other beautiful scene in the direction faced.

271. *Ame no ōgi.* The "rain fan" *kata* is also used in Kyōgen dance movements. The actor is in a half-stooped position with both hands raised, the right hand and fan forming a mountain shape with the left hand. This gesture indicates rain falling, or a person walking in the rain or standing in the rain with an umbrella over his head.

272. This is the gesture of rowing a boat. It involves movements of bending forward and thrusting both arms out and then pulling the oar back as shown here.
273. The gesture is that of aiming an arrow. The closed fan is used as the bow.

274. The gesture of *nozoki-mi* or "peeping" is made with an opened fan. The fan at once suggests the object behind which the actor is concealing himself and the opening through which he is peeping.
275. The gesture is of opening a sliding door. The opened fan, held in the right hand, is the door. The actor, with left hand extended, makes a semi-circular movement to the left to indicate the door being opened.

276–279. *Nemuru kata*. The four main *kata* of "sleeping" in Kyōgen.
276. This is the most common pose used in Kyōgen to represent sleep. The actor closes his eyes, leans slightly to the right with the closed fan held vertically on his right knee.
277. The fan, held in both hands, covers the face, again indicating that the actor is sleeping.
278. The opened fan, raised with the left hand, conceals the face and indicates a standing sleeping pose.
279. The actor lies on his side, using his folded arm as a pillow. This pose is often used to indicate sleep under the influence of alcohol. (performed by Nomura Mannojō)

280. *Annai*. This kata shows a person seeking admission to a house. The actor on the right, with an opened fan in his right hand, is seeking entrance, and the actor on the left is the master of the house. When the actor partly conceals his face with the fan, it means that he does not wish to be immediately identified by the master.

281. *Soriuchi*. The actor on the right, a person of high rank or position, is shown in a rage or in the act of intimidating the character on the left, a subordinate or a servant. The position of the hands of the actor on the right indicates the unsheathing of his sword.
282. *Shaku no kata*. This tableau indicates a drinking scene. The actor on the right, holding his opened fan by its edge before his face, is pouring saké for the actor on the left, who spreads out his fan to receive the drink. One fan serves as a saké bottle, the other a cup. The actor serving the saké slowly moves his fan downwards to indicate pouring.

224

283. *Tachigiki*. This is the gesture of eavesdropping. The actor on the right is saying something to himself and the actor on the left quietly listens in.

284–285. *Oikomi*. This *kata* provides a typical conclusion to a Kyōgen. The master or man of high rank, on the right, is enraged at his servant, on the left, for some blunder. (284) The master tries to punish the servant, who apologizes and tries to escape the blows. (285) Finally, the servant runs to the *hashigakari* and off the stage with his master following.

286–287. *Oni*. These movements are expressions of an enraged *oni* (demon), or an *oni* attempting to intimidate someone. The *oni* always carries a staff, walks with his knees brought up high, and often spreads his arms to express anger. (performed by Nomura Mannojō and Nomura Mansaku)

225

288–290. Gestures of the blind man in *Kawakamı*.
288. The ordinary gestures of a blind man feeling his way.
289. The blind man, having bumped into an obstacle, is trying to determine what it is.
290. The blind man measures the height of some steps with his cane.

291–293. Gestures of the thief in *Uri Nusubito* ("The Melon Thief").
291. The thief, using his fan as a saw, cuts an opening in the fence.
292. He breaks the fence to make his entrance.
293. Dismayed by the noise he has made breaking the fence, he covers his ears. (performed by Nomura Manzō)

226

294. A front view of the entire Nō stage. The *hashigakari* is seen extending to the left and the performing stage on the right.

PLAN OF NŌ STAGE

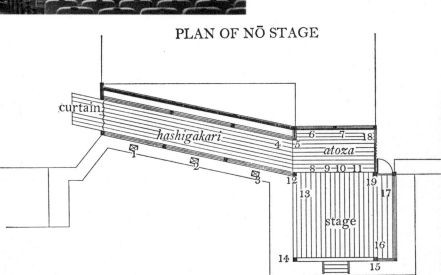

1. third pine
2. second pine
3. first pine
4. Kyōgen performer's seat
5. Kyōgen pillar
6. *kōken*'s seat
7. *kagami ita*
8. *taiko* player's seat
9. *ōkawa* player's seat
10. *kozutsumi* player's seat
11. flutist's seat
12. *shite* pillar
13. *shite* performer's seat
14. "eye-fixing" pillar
15. *waki* pillar
16. *waki* performer's seat
17. seats for the chorus
18. *kirido*
19. flute pillar

295. The Kongō Nō Theatre in Kyoto was built in 1879. The ground floor is divided into boxes which seat four or five spectators. The audience sits on cushions placed on the straw-matted floor. Tea is served, and hibachis provide warmth in winter.

296. Large jars under the stage, tilted towards the center, increase the resonance of the actor's footfalls.

297. The bell used in *Dōjōji* is carried along the *hashigakari* to the stage. The hanging of the bell, the largest prop used in Nō, is accompanied by amusing dialogue of the Kyōgen actors when presented by the Kongō school, as here.
298. The bell is suspended from a ring in the ceiling and braced by a rope fastened at the side of the stage, both of which are used exclusively for this prop.

299. The *torii* used in *Nonomiya* is brought onstage by an assistant (*kōken*).

300. Assistants remove the cloth which has concealed the interior of the "hut" where the one-horned demon of *Ikkaku Sennin* dwells.
301. When the cloth is lowered the audience sees the grinning demon within the simple bamboo structure that represents the demon's lair.

302. The part of an emperor is normally taken by a child, presumably to avoid any suggestion of sacrilege. The prop being held over the boy's head in this scene from *Kuzu* represents the palanquin in which he is being carried.

303. A more dignified, but hardly more elaborate, structure is this prop representing the palace of *Yōkihi*.
304. The den of the monstrous spider in *Tsuchigumo* is indicated by this prop with its cobwebbed door and growth of trees on top. The "spider" sits inside.

305. The carriage in which Yuya rides to Kiyomizu is represented by this prop, intended to suggest the festive gaiety of the occasion.

306. The boy and his mother in *Torioi-bune* are forced to scare away birds from the rice seedlings. They sit in this prop, which is furnished with noisemakers to frighten the birds.

307. Entrance of musicians and chorus. The musicians travel over the *hashigakari* to the stage, led by the flute player (about to sit); the chorus enters through the low door at stage left.

308. During a passage which is declaimed rather than sung, the musicians and chorus rest. The musicians place their instruments on the stage, the members of the chorus the fans which will be picked up when they begin to sing.

309. The musicians ready for a performance: the *taiko* drummer seated on the stage, the *ōkawa* player and *kotsuzumi* player on stools, and the flutist on the stage.

310. The *taiko* drummer (Kanze Motonobu) raises his stick to beat the drum on its tilted stand.

311. The *ōkawa* (or *ōtsuzumi*) player (Yasufuku Haruo) balances his instrument on his left knee, and strikes the surface with a sharp blow from the right. His lips are formed to make one of the cries *(kakegoe)* with which he stresses the points of rhythmic tension.

312. The *kotsuzumi* player (Kō Yoshimitsu) holds his instrument on the right shoulder and strikes it from below with fainter, almost hesitant, beats. He too utters *kakegoe* to accentuate his beat.

313. The flutist (Fujita Daigorō) sits in Japanese style on the stage. The flute is heard most often at the beginnings of scenes and at climactic moments in the story.

314. *Uchito-mōde*   Kongō School
This festive play describes a "visit to the Inner and Outer shrines at Ise" by a courtier, at the
Emperor's command. He encounters a Shinto priest *(shite)* and a *miko* priestess *(tsure)*. At the
courtier's request the *miko* performs a *kagura* dance and the priest a "lion dance" *(shishimai)*. The
night of festivities ended, the rising sun sparkling over the two shrines is an auspicious sign for
the New Year. Normally a red wig is worn in this role; the art of performing in a white wig is a
tradition secretly transmitted within the school, and performances are exceedingly rare. The
actor is Kongō Iwao. A "god" play.

315. *Yashima*   Kita School

A priest and his attendants arrive at Yashima. They are lodged in the hut of a fisherman who describes the battle of Yashima so vividly that the priest asks his name. The fisherman indicates that he is actually the ghost of Yoshitsune. In the second part of the play, as the priest sleeps, the *shite* reappears, this time in his true guise, as a young warrior. He describes his exploits, then fades away with the dawn. The *shite* (Kita Sadayo) appears in the splendid robes of Yoshitsune, the great warrior. He wears a *heita* mask. A "warrior" play.

316. *Hagoromo*
Kanze School
In this scene from the play analyzed on pages 117–121, the angel begs the fisherman to return the robe, without which she cannot return to heaven. The *shite* (Katayama Hiro-tarō) wears the *zō-onna* mask, used for celestial beings.

317. *Yoshino Tenjin*   Kanze School
A gentleman from the capital visits Yoshino when the cherry trees are in blossom and encounters an aristocratic-looking woman*(shite)*. While admiring the blossoms together she confesses that she is a heavenly being *(tenjin)* and promises to dance for him that night. The *shite* (Kanze Moto-masa), wearing a *zo-onna* mask and a crown, makes a gesture with her right sleeve which means "playing with the blossoms." A "woman" play.

318–319. *Izutsu*
　　　　Kanze School

A priest visits the Ariwara Temple where, many years earlier, the famous lover Narihira had lived with the daughter of Ki no Aritsune. As he prays, a young woman *(shite)* appears. She speaks of the past, especially of how she and Narihira as children had compared heights when standing by a well-curb *(izutsu)*. She disappears, only to come back, this time wearing the hat and cloak Narihira gave her. She vanishes again when dawn comes and the priest awakens. A "woman" play.

318. The *shite* (Kanze Hisao) visits the abandoned old temple and looks at a grave mound covered by weeds. She carries a Buddhist rosary in her right hand. The mask is the *zō-onna*.

319. Wearing Narihira's court cap and *chōken*, the *shite* stands before the well-curb. She pushes aside the bush of flowering *susuki* to peer into the depths and sees his reflection, not her own.

320–321. *Tōboku*   Kita School

A priest visiting the capital for the first time notices a beautiful plum tree in flower. A woman *(shite)* appears and tells him its history, particularly its connection with Lady Izumi. She hints, before vanishing into the shadows of the tree, that she is herself a ghost. When she reappears it is in the splendid robes of the court lady, Izumi Shikibu. She describes how, by virtue of her poetry, she became a bodhisattva of music and dance. A "woman" play.

320. The *shite* (Kita Nagayo) appears while the priest and his attendants are admiring the plum tree. She wears the *ko-omote* mask.

321. In the second part, as Izumi Shikibu, the *shite* wears a *chōken* and scarlet divided skirts. As she dances before the priest and his two attendants, she recalls days when she was a slave to her passions.

322. *Matsukaze*　　Kongō School

Matsukaze *(shite)* and Murasame *(tsure)* are sisters living by the shore at Suma. They dip salt
water from the sea to eke out a living, but their lives are colored by rememberances of Yukihira,
a nobleman who had loved them both. A traveling priest asks for lodging. He gradually discovers they are ghosts who are unable to give up their attachment to the scene of their happiness.
They ask the priest to pray for them, then fade away with the dawn. A "woman" play.

Matsukaze (Kongō Iwao) dips water from the sea. The pail and the cart for carrying pails are
mere toys, and a fan serves as a ladle. Murasame (Taneda Michio) stands behind her sister.
Matsukaze wears the *magojirō* mask, Murasame the *ko-omote* mask.

323. *Genji Kuyō*   Kongō School

Some priests visiting the Ishiyama Temple by the shores of Lake Biwa are addressed by a woman *(shite)* who asks them to say a memorial service *(kuyō)* for Prince Genji. She declares that her failure to include a service in her novel has deprived her of salvation. The priest asks if she is Lady Murasaki, the author of *The Tale of Genji*, but she disappears without answering. In the second part, she confesses she is Murasaki. The priest promises to pray for Genji, and in return asks that she dance for him. At the end we discover she is actually the bodhisattva Kannon. A "woman" play.

The *shite* (Teshima Yazaemon) joins her hands in gratitude when the priest agrees to pray for Genji. She wears a court cap, a *chōken*, and a *magojirō* mask.

240

324. *Nonomiya*   Kita School

A priest worshiping at the Shrine in the Fields *(nonomiya)* meets a girl who tells him how Prince Genji once came here to visit the Lady Rokujō. She describes the autumnal beauty of the season so vividly that the priest realizes she must be the ghost of Rokujō. In the second part she appears in the robes of a court lady, and tells how she and Genji's wife, Aoi, first became enemies. But she realizes that the events she describes happened long ago, the people are all dead, and the Shrine in the Fields itself deserted. She utters a final prayer that she may escape "the burning house" of worldly attachment. A "woman" play.

Rokujō (Kita Minoru) stands under the *torii*, which seems to her a boundary between life and death. She puts forward her foot in a gesture of renunciation of worldly attachments, only to withdraw it, unable to give up her love for Genji. Passing under the *torii* is her gesture of renunciation of worldly attachments. The actor uses shadows to darken the *ko-omote* mask, intensifying the poignancy of the moment.

241

325. *Yōkihi*   Kita School

Yōkihi is the Japanese rendering of Yang Kuei-fei, the name of a celebrated Chinese beauty. A sorcerer is commanded by the Emperor to seek out the spirit of Yōkihi *(shite)*, who has died. He finds her on the Island of Everlasting Youth. She speaks of her longing for the Emperor and dances for the sorcerer before disappearing, a prey to grief over a past she can never recapture. A "woman" play.

Yōkihi (Awaya Shintarō) dances as the chorus describes her past happiness with the Emperor. She wears the *ko-omote* mask, an elaborate headdress, and a *karaori* robe.

326. *Futari Shizuka*   Kanze School

A priest of a Shinto shrine at Yoshino sends a girl *(tsure)* to gather herbs for the spring festival.
When she reaches the riverside she is addressed by a young woman *(shite)* who asks her to
transmit a request that sutras be copied on her behalf. The woman warns that if questions are
asked, her spirit will take possession of the girl. When the girl reports what has happened, the
priest insists on knowing the woman's name. The *shite*, speaking through the *tsure*, identifies
herself as Shizuka. The priest asks her to dance. The *tsure* puts on the Shizuka hat and *chōken*.
The *shite* appears in identical costume and they dance together, then disappear. A "woman" play.
The *shite* (Umewaka Rokurō) and *tsure* (Umewaka Manzaburō) in their final dance. Both wear
waka-onna masks.

243

327–328. *Yuya*   Kita School

Yuya *(shite)*, the favorite of the nobleman Munemori, learns that her mother is seriously ill. She asks permission to return home, but Munemori insists that she accompany him to Kiyomizu, to enjoy the cherry blossoms. Yuya has no choice but to go. Later, however, she composes a poem which describes her feelings so poignantly that Munemori permits her to leave. A "woman" play.

327. Yuya (Awaya Kikuo) reads to Munemori the letter in which her mother describes her illness. She wears the *ko-omote* mask.

328. Yuya stands inside the prop representing the carriage in which she rides on her way to Kiyomizu.

244

329–330. *Sōshi Arai*   Hōshō School

The poet Ōtomo no Kuronushi announces that the Emperor has commanded that a poetry contest be held the next day. Kuronushi's opponent will be Ono no Komachi *(shite)*. Knowing that he cannot win by fair means, Kuronushi secretly goes to her house and eavesdrops as she is composing her poem for the contest. The next day, in the presence of the Emperor, Kuronushi accuses Komachi of having plagiarized her poem, and offers as proof a page from the anthology *Manyōshū* with the poem. But Komachi, noticing that the ink is not dry, washes the manuscript *(sōshi arai)*, and the interpolated poem disappears. She is exonerated from the charge of plagiarism and wins the contest. A "woman" play.

329. Komachi (Hōshō Kurō) stands before the desk where she will place the poem she has composed for the contest. The actor wears the celebrated *fushiki zō* mask.

330. Komachi mimes the gesture of pouring water over the manuscript, thereby washing away the forged poem.

246

331–332. *Sotoba Komachi*
Hōshō School
Some priests on their way to the capital encounter an old woman *(shite)*. They reprimand her for sitting on a holy stupa *(sotoba)*, but she gets the better of them in a theological dispute. She reveals that she is Komachi, and tells of her former beauty, contrasting it with her present wretchedness. As she speaks, the spirit of Fukakusa no Shō-shō, the man she treated cruelly, possesses her, and she speaks in his voice, describing his agony. At the end, as she describes his death, she hopes she may yet gain salvation. Fourth category.
331. Komachi (Kondō Kenzō) weeps as she identifies herself. The actor wears a new mask created for the role.
332. Changing to her lover's ➡ cap and cloak, she dances as she recalls in his voice the ninety-nine nights he visited her fruitlessly before he died.

333–334. *Kayoi Komachi*   Kita School

An unknown young woman *(tsure)* appears each day to offer fruits and firewood to a priest. He asks her name, but after hinting that she is Ono no Komachi, the poet, she disappears. Later, the priest offers prayers for the woman's salvation and she returns, asking that he administer to her the Buddhist ordination. But a voice calls out forbidding this. Komachi pleads to be given the chance of salvation, but the ghost of her rejected lover Fukakusa *(shite)* seeks to prevent Komachi from deserting him in hell. In the end, his wrath is appeased and both attain the way of the Buddha. Fourth category.

Komachi (Tomoeda Kikuo), wearing a *ko-omote* mask, turns at the appearance of the *shite* (Kita Minoru), who lifts the cloak in which he has hidden himself. He wears the *yase-otoko* mask.

251

335–336. *Kagekiyo*   Kanze School

Kagekiyo *(shite)*, a defeated Heike warrior, is living in exile in distant Hyūga. His daughter visits him, but he is too proud to let her see him in his wretchedness. He turns her away, denying he is Kagekiyo. However, a villager informs the daughter that the old man is in fact her father. She returns, and this time he admits his identity. He describes his last battle, then sends her away. Fourth category.

335. Kagekiyo (Kanze Tetsunojō) stands in his hut and clutches the pillar, listening to the waves. "I hear the waves breaking on the rough shore," he cries. He wears the *kagekiyo* mask.

336. Kagekiyo mimes the actions of his struggle with a Genji warrior. He opens his arms in the gesture of grappling for the neck-piece of the enemy's helmet.

253

337–338. *Hanjo*   Kanze School

Hanago *(shite)*, a courtesan, falls in love with Yoshida, an officer who has spent the night with her in an inn. As pledges of love they exchange fans, but he must go away. He promises to return, and Hanago waits for him, too much in love to entertain any other guests. She is accordingly driven from the inn and goes off in search of Yoshida. He returns shortly after her departure, and cannot find her. Hanago wanders, crazed by her grief. By chance an attendant of Yoshida sees her, and mocks her for clutching her fan like the Chinese court lady Hanjo, who likened herself to a fan discarded after a summer's use. This encounter leads to Yoshida's finding Hanago and to their reunion.

337. Hanago (Umewaka Rokurō), ordered to leave the inn, laments her fate. In this variation *(kogaki)*, she carries *sasa* bamboo, comparing the number of her griefs to the knots in the bamboo. Her *karaori* robe is bared from one shoulder to indicate her distracted mind.

338. The *shite* appears in the second part. She stands by the first pine on the *hashigakari* and describes her wanderings in search of her lover.

254

339–340. *Sumidagawa*   Kanze School

A woman *(shite)* whose child has been kidnapped wanders in search of him, almost out of her mind with grief. When she reaches the Sumida River, the boatman *(waki)* tells her about the death of a child a year before. Services are being conducted that day on the opposite shore. The woman prays before the child's grave and for a moment her son appears before her, only to vanish again. Fourth category.

339. The woman (Kanze Tetsunojō) steps forward in the gesture of boarding the boat. She wears a *fukai* mask.
340. The *waki* (Matsumoto Kenzō), poling the boat, relates the story of the death of the woman's son. She weeps in the *shiori* gesture. The other passenger is a traveler from the capital.

341–342. *Fujito*   Komparu School
Moritsuna *(waki)*, the general victorious at Fujito, issues a proclamation that
anyone with complaints should present
himself. An old woman *(shite)* appears
and accuses Moritsuna of having killed
her son, a fisherman. He admits the
deed, but claims it was unavoidable. The
woman, throwing herself before him,
asks that he kill her too, but he refuses.
In the second part, while Moritsuna is
offering prayers for the fisherman, the
dead man's ghost appears. At first filled
with hatred, he is gradually appeased by
Moritsuna's prayers and senses that he
will be saved. Fourth category.
341. The fisherman's mother (Honda
Hideo) makes her entrance, pausing on
the *hashigakari* to sing:
    "I cross the waves of old age—
    Would that the days and nights at
        Fujito
    Could return to the springs of the
        past."
The *shite* wears the *shakumi* mask.
342. As the fisherman, the *shite* wears
a *yase-otoko* mask and humble garb. He
describes how he was killed.

258

343. *Nishikigı*   Kanze School

The play is based on the legend of a suitor setting up "brocade trees" *(nishikigi)* before the house of the woman he loves. If she takes them in, it signifies she will marry him; if not, he may persist for three years, until the woman at last is persuaded. In the play, a traveling priest encounters a man *(shite)* and woman *(tsure)* with local products to sell. He asks what they are and discovers the man carries a "brocade tree" and the woman some cloth. The man and woman disappear, to re-emerge as ghosts and tell of unrequited love. Fourth category.

In the second part of the play the ghost of the man (Kanze Shizuo) holds the "brocade tree," a branch covered with red satin, in his left hand as he recounts the legend. The *tsure* (Oku Zensuke) emerges from the prop, which represents a grave mound. The *shite* wears the *yase-otoko* mask, the *tsure* a *ko-omote* mask.

260

344. *Tōsen*   Kanze School

A local ruler in Kyushu, having captured in battle a Chinese ship *(tōsen)*, forces a Chinese aboard to be his servant. For thirteen years the Chinese, Sokei Kanjin by name, has lived in Japan, when his two Chinese children arrive, bearing rich presents for the ruler in return for their father's freedom. But Sokei Kanjin *(shite)* also has two Japanese children, and they are brokenhearted at the thought of parting. The father is about to commit suicide in despair, but the ruler permits the Japanese children to accompany him to China. The father and his four sons joyfully board the ship. Fourth category.

Sokei Kanjin (Umewaka Manzaburō) stands in the prow of the boat, waving a Chinese fan as it sets sail. He wears the *akobujō* mask. The boat, unlike the simple frames used in most plays, has a large damask sail.

261

345. *Aoi no Ue*
        Hōshō School
Aoi, the wife of Prince Genji,
lies mysteriously ill. A sorceress
summons up the spirit which is
afflicting her, and Lady Rokujō
(*shite*) appears. Though at first
ladylike in manners, the spirit
is driven eventually by fierce
jealousy to attack Aoi, her rival
for Genji's love. A holy man is
sent for, and now Rokujō reveals herself as a terrible demon.
She furiously combats the
priest, but in the end his
prayers overcome her. Fourth
category.
The *shite* (Hōshō Fusao) assumes an attitude of defiance as
the monk prays. She wears a
hannya mask and carries a
demon's rod.

346. *Kinuta* Kanze School

A woman, consumed by jealousy over her husband's long absence, calls for a fulling-block (*kinuta*) and declares that she will beat out her emotions so loudly that her husband will hear. The woman (*shite*) dies, and when her spirit is summoned up by her husband, she vents her bitter resentment. Eventually, however, she is saved by the force of prayer. Fourth category. The ghost of the wife (Matsuyama Nagaaki) returns from the world of the dead, and she describes the torments she suffers. She wears the *fukai* mask and leans on a stick in the *kata* known as *munazue*.

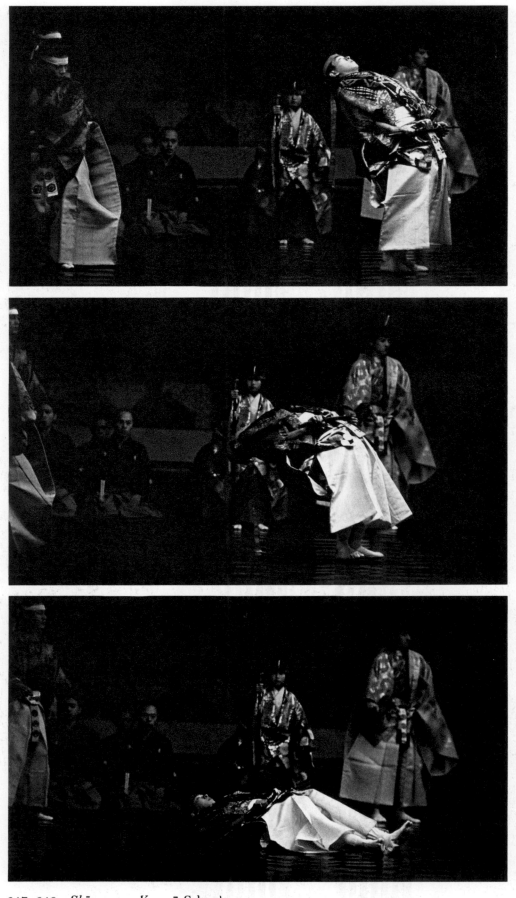

347–349. *Shōzon*   Kongō School
The treacherous Tosabō Shōzon plots to kill Yoshitsune, at the behest of Yoshitsune's brother Yoritomo. Benkei, Yoshitsune's retainer, learns that Shōzon and
his henchmen are preparing to attack. He kills the henchmen and makes Shōzon
his prisoner. This highly dramatic work is closer to Kabuki than to Nō. Fourth
category.
A henchman of Shōzon (Hirota Taizō) is felled by one of Yoshitsune's men.
The actor falls backwards in a seemingly perpendicular fashion, a specialty of the
Kongō school. The camera has caught the stages of the fall before the crack of
his back against the wooden floor.

350–351. *Youchi Soga*

Kanze School

Youchi Soga ("The Soga Attack by Night") is a realistic play *(genzaimono)* performed without masks. It deals with the vengeance exacted by the two Soga brothers on their father's enemy. The older brother Sukenari *(tsure)* is killed, and the younger brother Tokimune *(shite)* is tricked into being captured. Fourth category.

350. Tokimune (to left, Kanze Motoaki) and Sukenari (Kanze Motomasa) arrive at the hunting preserve below Mount Fuji where they will attack their enemy. Two retainers accompany them. Sukenari carries a letter in the fold of his kimono, Tokimune a memento of his mother in a bag around his neck.

351. Tokimune fights with Gosho no Gorōmaru. The latter, disguising himself as a woman, has tricked Tokimune into letting him pass. Here he grapples with Tokimune, who has dropped his sword.

265

352–353. *Ikkaku Sennin*   Komparu School

The curious plot, reminiscent of a fairy tale, tells of an immortal *(shite)* distinguished by a single horn *(ikkaku)* on his forehead. He quarrels with the Dragon God of the Sea and shuts him up inside a cave. This stops the rain from falling, to the great unhappiness of the people. A statesman sends the beautiful Lady Senda *(tsure)* to tempt the immortal and induce him to release the Dragon God. She succeeds. The immortal loses his magic powers and the Dragon God escapes, bringing rain. A "demon" play.

352. Entrance of *tsure* (Sakurama Tatsuma). The attendants carry a prop that indicates the lady is riding in a palanquin. The *tsure* wears the *zō-onna* mask. The men sing a description of their journey.

353. The immortal (Komparu Nobutaka) carries a fan shaped like an oak leaf, unique to this role. He wears the rarely used *shinkaku* mask and a golden horn on his head. Here he dances before the prop representing his dwelling.

266

354–355. *Kurama Tengu*   Hōshō School

Tengu, fabulous creatures dwelling in the mountains, figure both as good and evil beings in various plays. "The Tengu of Kurama" tells of Ushiwaka, the boy later known as Yoshitsune, who is taught the military arts by the demons while living at Kurama Temple. A "demon" play.

354. In this variation *(kogaki)* of the standard version, the chief *tengu (shite)* wears a white wig and white costume, and is accompanied by seven *tengu*, six of whom appear here. Only a rich school like Hōshō has the costumes and *tengu* fans needed to stage this variant.

355. The *shite* (Hōshō Fusao) wears the *beshimi akujō* mask and carries a special stick known as *kasezue*, both marks of a performance of great "dignity."

356. *Tsuchigumo*   Kongō School

The warrior Raikō is afflicted by a mysterious illness. A priest *(shite)* comes and tells Raikō that his illness is caused by a great spider *(tsuchigumo)*. Raikō sees through the priest's disguise and recognizes that he is the spider. They fight, and the wounded spider flees. In the second part a retainer of Raikō tracks the spider to its lair and kills it. A "demon" play.

The spider (Hirota Norikazu), fighting with the retainer, attempts to enmesh him in its web. This spectacular bit of stage business, for long a special tradition of the Kongō school, is now used by other schools too. The prop represents the spider's lair. The *shite* wears the *shishiguchi* mask.

269

357. *Kuruma Zō*   Kanze School

A certain priest is renowned because he travels about in a broken carriage *(kuruma)* not pulled by any beast. A *tengu* disguised as a *yamabushi* (mountain ascete) confronts the priest and attempts to outwit him in a theological dispute, but he is defeated. In the second part the *tengu (shite)*, in his true guise, tests his magic powers against the priest's and again is defeated. A "demon" play.

The *tengu* (Kanze Yoshiyuki) proposes that he and the priest test their respective powers. He wears the *ōbeshimi* mask and carries the feather fan characteristic of *tengu*.

270

358. *Funa Benkei*   Kita School
This play is analyzed in detail on pages 136–141. Here the *shite* (Gotō Tokuzō) dances as Shizuka in the first scene. He wears the *magojirō* mask.

271

359–360. *Kokaji*   Kanze School

An envoy brings word to Kokaji Munechika, the famous swordsmith, of the Emperor's desire for a new sword. Munechika is perplexed because he has no suitable partner at the anvil. He prays at the Inari Shrine for divine assistance. A mysterious youth *(shite)* appears to encourage Munechika with stories of famous swords. He promises to help forge the new sword, then disappears. Munechika sets up an anvil, whereupon the Inari god himself joins him as his partner. A "demon" play.

359. The youth (Kanze Motoaki) dances as he describes famous swords of antiquity, urging Munechika to forge one which will be their equal. He wears the *kasshiki* mask.

360. The god appears as Munechika prepares the anvil. His *deitobide* mask is a variant of the *ōtobide*.

272

361-362. *Tōru*   Kanze School

A traveling priest visiting the capital stops to examine the ruins of the Rokujō Palace. An old man *(shite)* appears carrying buckets of water slung from a carrying-pole. He tells of former days, when the courtier Tōru built a replica in the capital of Shiogama Beach on the northern coast, exact even to having saltwater pools. The old man goes off to dip more water. That night Tōru himself appears in the priest's dream and describes the beauty of the moon over Shiogama and over his own garden. A "demon" play.

361. The old man (Umewaka Rokurō) lifts the buckets as he starts off to dip more brine. He wears the *sankōjō* mask.

362. The *shite* appears in the second part as Tōru, wearing the *chūjō* mask. He dances a *hayamai* as the chorus recites of the moon.

363. *Matsuyani*   Ōkura School

A gentleman decides to hold a New Year celebration in a pine forest with his friends. As they are singing about the healing properties of *matsuyani* (pine sap), a strangely dressed figure appears, and reveals himself as the "spirit of pine sap." Later, in response to the men's request, the spirit fills two containers with pine-sap medicine, performing an energetic dance. The actor (Zenchiku Keigorō) wears the *usobuki* mask.

364–365 *Suehirogari*   Ōkura School
A rich gentleman sends his servant Tarōkaja (Yamamoto Norinao) to the capital to buy a
suehirogari. He describes how it opens out, the importance of choosing one with strong ribs and
a good design on the paper, but fails to tell the servant that *suehirogari* is the auspicious name
for a fan. The servant is tricked by a city merchant into taking an umbrella instead, which tallies
exactly in description with a *suehirogari*.(364) Tarōkaja offers the master the *suehirogari*. The
master is enraged at the servant's stupidity, but when Tarōkaja sings an infectious tune, also
learned in the capital, (365) the master (Yamamoto Norihisa) joins him in dancing, and for-
gives his error.

366–367. *Imamairı* Ōkura School
Tarōkaja (Zenchiku Keigorō) recruits
a new servant (Zenchiku Kōshirō). He
informs him that the best way to get
into the master's good graces is to show
skill at punning, and teaches the new
man a few examples. At first, the strat-
agem works, but the new man makes a
bad pun, displeasing the master. (366)
Tarōkaja (center) tries to restore good
relations between the servant (left) and
the master (Ōkura Yatarō). The servant follows the master with his eyes.
He finally confesses that he can really
compose good puns only to a tune. The
master is intrigued, and after testing
the new man in several rounds of puns,
(367) joins with him in a final dance.

368–369. *Mikazuki*   Ōkura School

A certain man is so preoccupied with composing linked-verse that he neglects his household. His exasperated wife demands a divorce. He at length consents, giving her a winnow to carry on her head as she leaves the house, a sign that they are divorced. But as she starts to leave, the husband composes a *hokku* on the sight, to which the wife responds with so clever a verse that he decides he cannot let her go. He promises henceforth to devote greater attention to the household. (368) The husband (Zenchiku Yagorō) offers the wife (Ōkura Yatarō) some saké as a pledge of their reconciliation. The fan serves to represent a container of saké. The winnow lies on the floor by the wife. (369) In a final dance the husband celebrates his long-lasting union with his wife.

370–371. *Nakiama* ("The Weeping Nun") Izumi School
A priest (Izumi Yasuyuki), lacking confidence in the efficacy of his sermons, takes along a nun (Miyake Tōkurō) who always weeps at his preaching. (370) But no sooner does he begin his sermon than the nun dozes off. He angrily rebukes her, "Anyone who falls asleep in these holy precincts must be a terrible evil-doer. Ahem! Ahem!" (371) After the sermon, through which she has dozed instead of wept, the nun demands a share of the fee. When refused, she bursts into a tantrum and pursues the priest.

280

372–374. *Kombu Uri* ("The Seaweed Peddler")   Izumi School
A daimyo on his way to the capital overtakes a man selling edible seaweed. He forces the man to carry his sword, but (372) when next he gives the man an arrogant order, the peddler (Nomura Manzō) brandishes the sword to threaten the terrified daimyo (Nomura Mannojō). (373) and (374) The peddler demands that as a price for returning the sword the daimyo sing in different styles the chant used by seaweed peddlers. The daimyo sings and the peddler prances to his tune.

281

375–377. *Kirokuda* ("Six Loads of Lumber")   Izumi School

Tarōkaja (Nomura Manzō), having been sent out in the snow with oxen loaded with lumber for his master's uncle, looks up at the sky. (375) "It's starting to fall—look how black the sky is! Yes, that's snow falling, all right. It'd be bad enough to get through this heavy snow myself, but I've got to drive twelve oxen with me." He stops at a teahouse on the way and drinks some of the saké with which he has been entrusted. In high spirits, he performs a quail-catching dance. (376) "Look at that! Fifty thousand quail all coming down for me!" (377) Having drunk all the saké, Tarōkaja sadly shakes the cask and realizes from the sound that it must be empty.

378–379. *Shūron* ("The Theological Dispute")
Izumi School
A priest of the Nichiren sect (Miyake Tōkurō) on a pilgrimage meets with a priest of the Amida sect (Nomura Manzō). (378) The two stage a theological dispute during which the Amida priest tries to force a rosary of his sect on the other priest. (379) Later, the Amida priest, having pursued his opponent to a wayside inn, prays beside him, uttering mainly nonsense syllables. At the end the two men so confuse each other that each is happily proclaiming the virtues of the other's sect.

380–381. *Kagyū*　　Izumi School

Tarōkaja (Nomura Manzō) is ordered by his master to go into the woods and find a snail. The master uses *kagyū*, a difficult word for "snail," describing it as having a black head, a shell at its waist, and sometimes putting out horns. (380) Tarōkaja bumps into a *yamabushi* (Nomura Mansaku), a mountain ascete, sleeping in the woods. (381) He decides that the description of the *kagyū* fits the costume of the *yamabushi* exactly. The ascete, discovering Tarōkaja's error, is much amused.

382–383. *Negi Yamabushi*   Izumi School

A *negi* (Shinto priest), resting at a teahouse, is overtaken by a *yamabushi* (mountain ascete) who abuses him. (382)
The *yamabushi* (Nomura Manzō) insists that the *negi* (Nomura Mansaku) shoulder his pack. The teahouse owner
(Izumi Yasuyuki) attempts to restrain him. (383) The owner brings in the god Daikokuten (Nomura Kōsuke), and
asks both men to pray for his favors. The one chosen by the god is entitled to have the other carry his pack. Both
pray fervently, with victory going to the *negi*.

285

384–388. *Tōzumō* ("Chinese Wrestling")   Ōkura School

All available actors are mustered to perform this work, the only Kyōgen with a Chinese setting. The actors, except for the Japanese wrestler (Shigeyama Sennojō) wear Chinese clothes, old and valuable costumes used exclusively in this play. This performance was staged in a modern theatre adapted for use by Nō and Kyōgen actors.

(384) The members of the Chinese court line up along the *hashigakari* and across the stage, bowing before the Emperor (Shigeyama Sensaku), who sits on his dais to the right. (385) A Japanese wrestler, long domiciled at the Chinese court, announces his intention of returning home. He offers to take on the entire court in a farewell series of bouts. Here he engages the interpreter (Shigeyama Sengorō). (386) Two officials stage a combined attack on the Japanese, but he throws them both, and sets them standing on their heads. (387) After all his officials have been defeated, the Emperor himself takes on the Japanese. In order to prevent himself from being polluted by the foreigner, he wraps himself in matting, dancing the while to the beat of drums. (388) The Emperor is also defeated, but the courtiers, acting as if nothing had happened, leave singing a "Chinese" refrain: *kon ken kon chon non chon chin kon ken pon.*

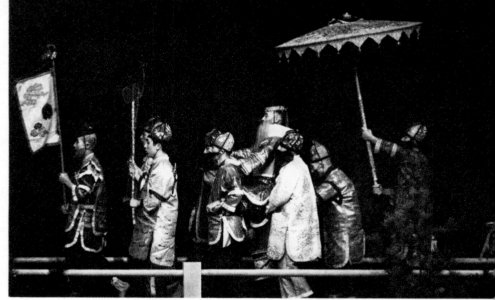

389–390. *Kaminari* ("Lightning")
Ōkura School

(389) The god of lightning (Zenchiku Chūichirō), having fallen in a field and injured his back, summons a doctor (Zenchiku Genzaburō). The doctor, afraid of being struck by lightning, gingerly tenders his needle, but the god, no less frightened, shrinks back. (390) Thanks to the doctor's treatment, the god of lightning recovers and announces he is ready to return to heaven. He fingers the drum at his waist with which he makes the thunder. But the doctor insists on a fee for his services. The god wears a *buaku* mask.

LIST OF NŌ PLAYS CURRENTLY PERFORMED

Unless otherwise stated, plays are performed by all schools.

OKINA (翁) (first play)
Author unknown

ADACHIGAHARA (安達原) (demon play)
Author unknown
Referred to as *Kurozuka* by schools other than Kanze

AIZOMEGAWA (藍染川) (miscellaneous play)
Author unknown
Performed by Kanze and Komparu schools only

AKOGI (阿漕) (miscellaneous play)
Attributed to Zeami, but Zeami probably reworked text of an earlier play

AMA (海土) (demon play)
Author unknown, but work antedates Zeami

AOI NO UE (葵上) (miscellaneous play)
Adapted by Zeami from an Ōmi *sarugaku* play

ARASHIYAMA (嵐山) (god play)
by Komparu Zempō

ARIDŌSHI (蟻通) (miscellaneous play)
by Zeami

ASHIKARI (芦刈) (miscellaneous play)
Adapted by Zeami

ASUKAGAWA (飛鳥川) (miscellaneous play)
Attributed to Zeami
Performed by Kongō and Kita schools only

ATAGO KŪYA (愛宕空也) (demon play)
by Kanze Kojirō Nobumitsu
Performed by Kita school only

ATAKA (安宅) (miscellaneous play)
by Kanze Kojirō Nobumitsu

ATSUMORI (敦盛) (warrior play)
by Zeami

AWAJI (淡路) (god play)
by Kannami
Performed by Kanze, Komparu and Kita schools

AYA NO TSUZUMI (綾鼓) (miscellaneous play)
by Zeami
Performed by Hōshō, Kongō and Kita schools

BASHŌ (芭蕉) (woman play)
by Komparu Zenchiku

CHIKUBU SHIMA (竹生島) (god play)
Author unknown

CHŌBUKU SOGA (調伏曾我) (miscellaneous or demon play)

by Miyamasu
Performed by Hōshō, Kongō and Kita schools

CHŌRYŌ (張良) (demon play)
by Kanze Kojirō Nobumitsu

DAIBUTSU KUYŌ (大仏供養) (miscellaneous play)
Author unknown

DAIE (大会) (demon play)
Author unknown

DAIROKUTEN (第六天) (demon play)
Author unknown
Performed by Kanze school only

DAMPŪ (壇風) (miscellaneous or demon play)
Author unknown, but attributed to Zeami
Performed by Hōshō, Kongō and Kita schools

DŌJŌJI (道成寺) (miscellaneous play)
by Kanze Kojirō Nobumitsu

DŌMYŌJI (道明寺) (god play)
Attributed to Zeami
Performed by Kanze, Kongō and Kita schools

EBIRA (箙) (warrior play)
Attributed to Zeami

EBOSHI ORI (烏帽子折) (miscellaneous play)
by Miyamasu
Performed by all schools except Komparu

EGUCHI (江口) (woman play)
by Kannami

EMA (絵馬) (god play)
Author unknown
Performed by all schools except Komparu

ENOSHIMA (江島) (god play)
by Kanze Yajirō Nagatoshi
Performed by Kanze school only

FUE NO MAKI (笛之巻) (miscellaneous play)
Author unknown
Performed by Kanze school only

FUJI (藤) (woman play)
by Hiyoshi Saami (?)
Performed by Kanze, Hōshō, and Kongō schools

FUJISAN (富士山) (god play)
Probably by Zeami
Performed by Kongō and Komparu schools

FUJI TAIKO (富士太鼓) (miscellaneous play)
Attributed to Zeami

FUJITO (藤戸) (miscellaneous play)

Author unknown, but generally attributed to Zeami

FUNABASHI (船橋) (miscellaneous play)
Adapted by Zeami from a *dengaku* Nō

FUNA BENKEI (船弁慶) (demon play)
by Kanze Kojirō Nobumitsu

FUTARI SHIZUKA (二人静) (woman play)
Author unknown
Performed by all schools except Hōshō

GEMBUKU SOGA (元服曾我) (warrior or miscellaneous play)
by Miyamasu
Performed by Kita school only

GENDAYŪ (源太夫) (god play)
Probably by Kiami
Performed by Komparu and Kita schools

GENJŌ (玄象) (demon play)
Author unknown

GENJI KUYŌ (源氏供養) (woman play)
Attributed to Zeami

GENZAI NUE (現在鵺) (miscellaneous or demon play)
Author unknown
Performed by Komparu and Kita schools

GENZAI SHICHIMEN (現在七面) (miscellaneous play)
Author unknown
Performed by Kanze and Kongō schools

GENZAI TADANORI (現在忠度) (warrior or miscellaneous play)
Author unknown
Performed by Kongō school only

GIŌ (祇王) (woman play)
Attributed to Zeami
Performed by Hōshō, Kongō and Kita schools

HACHINOKI (鉢木) (miscellaneous play)
Author unknown

HAGOROMO (羽衣) (woman play)
Author unknown

HAJITOMI (半蔀) (woman play)
by Naitō Tōzaemon

HAKURAKUTEN (白楽天) (god play)
Author unknown, but usually attributed to Zeami
Performed by all schools except Hōshō

HANAGATAMI (花筐) (miscellaneous play)
by Zeami

HANJO (班女) (miscellaneous play)
by Zeami

HASHI BENKEI (橋弁慶) (miscellaneous play)
Author unknown

HATSUYUKI (初雪) (woman play)
by Komparu Zempō
Performed by Komparu school only

HIBARIYAMA (雲雀山) (miscellaneous play)
Attributed to Zeami

HIGAKI (桧垣) (woman play)
by Zeami
Performed by all schools except Komparu

HIMURO (氷室) (god play)
by Miyamasu

HIUN (飛雲) (demon play)
Author unknown
Performed by all schools except Komparu

HŌJŌGAWA (放生川) (god play)
by Zeami

HŌKAZŌ (放下僧) (miscellaneous play)
Author unknown, but probably by Miyamasu

HŌSO (彭祖) (miscellaneous play)

Performed by Kongō school only

HOTOKENOHARA (仏原) (woman play)
Attributed to Zeami
Performed by Kanze, Kongō and Kita schools

HYAKUMAN (百万) (miscellaneous or demon play)
by Komparu Zempō
Performed by all schools except Hōshō

IKKAKU SENNIN (一角仙人) (miscellaneous or demon play)
by Komparu Zempō
Performed by all schools except Hōshō

IKARIZUKI (碇潜) (warrior or miscellaneous play)
Author unknown
Performed by Kanze and Kongō schools

IKUTA ATSUMORI (生田敦盛) (warrior play)
by Komparu Zempō
Performed by all schools except Kita

IWAFUNE (岩船) (demon play)
Author unknown

IZUTSU (井筒) (woman play)
by Zeami

JINEN KOJI (自然居士) (miscellaneous play)
by Kannami

KAGEKIYO (景清) (miscellaneous play)
Author unknown, but usually attributed to Zeami

KAGETSU (花月) (miscellaneous play)
Author unknown, but probably by Zeami

KAKITSUBATA (杜若) (woman play)
Probably by Zeami

KAMO (賀茂) (god play)
Author unknown, but attributed to Komparu Zenchiku

KAMO MONOGURUI (加茂物狂) (miscellaneous play)
by Komparu Zenchiku
Performed by Hōshō, Kongō and Kita schools

KANAWA (鉄輪) (miscellaneous play)
Author unknown

KANEHIRA (兼平) (warrior play)
Attributed to Zeami

KANTAN (邯鄲) (miscellaneous play)
Author uncertain, but probably by Zeami

KANYŌKYŪ (咸陽宮) (miscellaneous play)
Author unknown
Performed by all schools except Komparu

KAPPO (合浦) (demon play)
Author unknown
Performed by Kanze school only

KASHIWAZAKI (柏崎) (miscellaneous play)
by Enami Saemon Gorō
Adapted by Zeami
Performed by all schools except Kita

KASUGA RYŪJIN (春日竜神) (demon play)
Attributed to Zeami
Performed by all schools except Kita

KAYOI KOMACHI (通小町) (miscellaneous play)
by Kannami

KAZURAGI (葛城) (woman or miscellaneous play)
Author unknown, but attributed to Zeami

KAZURAGI TENGU (葛城天狗) (demon play)
by Kongō Nagatoshi
Performed by Kita school only

KIKUJIDŌ (菊慈童) (miscellaneous play)
Author unknown
Referred to as *Makurajidō* by schools other than

Kanze

KINSATSU (金札) (demon play)
    by Kannami

KINUTA (砧) (miscellaneous play)
    by Zeami

KISO (木曾) (miscellaneous play)
    Author unknown
    Performed by Kanze school only

KIYOTSUNE (清経) (warrior play)
    by Zeami

KOCHŌ (胡蝶) (woman play)
    by Kanze Kojirō Nobumitsu
    Performed by all schools except Kita

KOGŌ (小督) (miscellaneous play)
    Attributed to Zeami

KOI NO OMONI (恋重荷) (miscellaneous play)
    by Zeami
    Performed by Kanze and Komparu schools only

KOKAJI (小鍛冶) (demon play)
    Author unknown

KŌTEI (皇帝) (demon play)
    by Kanze Kojirō Nobumitsu
    Performed by all schools except Komparu

KOSODE SOGA (小袖曾我) (miscellaneous play)
    Author unknown, but attributed to Miyamasu

KŌU (項羽) (miscellaneous or demon play)
    Attributed to Zeami

KŌYA MONOGURUI (高野物狂) (miscellaneous play)
    Author unknown
    Performed by all schools except Komparu

KUMASAKA (熊坂) (demon play)
    Author unknown

KURAMA TENGU (鞍馬天拘) (demon play)
    by Miyamasu

KUREHA (呉服) (god play)
    Attributed to Zeami

KUROZUKA (黒塚) (demon play)
    Author unknown

KURUMAZO (車僧) (demon play)
    Attributed to Zeami

KUSANAGI (草薙) (miscellaneous or demon play)
    Author unknown
    Performed by Hōshō school only

KUSENOTO (九世戸) (god play)
    by Kanze Kojirō Nobumitsu
    Performed by Kanze school only

KUSU NO TSUYU (楠露) (miscellaneous play)
    Author unknown
    Performed by Kanze school only

KUZU (国栖) (demon play)
    Author unknown

MAKIGINU (巻絹) (miscellaneous play)
    Author unknown
    Performed by all schools except Komparu

MAKURAJIDŌ (枕慈童) (miscellaneous play)
    Author unknown
    Referred to as *Kikujidō* by schools other than Kanze

MANJŪ (満仲) (miscellaneous play)
    Author unknown

MATSUKAZE (松風) (woman play)
    by Kannami, adapted by Zeami

MATSUMUSHI (松虫) (miscellaneous play)
    Author unknown

MATSUNO-O (松尾) (god play)

    Author unknown, but possibly by Zeami
    Performed by Hōshō school only

MATSUYAMA KAGAMI (松山鏡) (demon play)
    Author unknown, but possibly by Zeami
    Performed by Kanze, Kongō and Kita schools

MATSUYAMA TENGU (松山天拘) (demon play)
    Author unknown
    Performed by Kongō school only

MEKARI (和布刈) (god play)
    Author unknown
    Performed by all schools except Komparu

MICHIMORI (通盛) (warrior play)
    Text by Iami, revised by Zeami

MIIDERA (三井寺) (miscellaneous play)
    Author unknown

MIMOSUSO (御裳濯) (god play)
    Probably by Zeami
    Performed by Komparu and Kita schools

MINASE (水無瀬) (miscellaneous play)
    Author unknown
    Performed by Kita school only

MINAZUKIBARAI (水無月祓) (miscellaneous play)
    by Zeami
    Performed by Kanze school only

MINOBU (身延) (woman play)
    Author unknown
    Performed by Kanze school only

MITSUYAMA (三山) (miscellaneous play)
    Attributed to Zeami
    Performed by Hōshō and Kongō schools

MIWA (三輪) (woman or miscellaneous play)
    Author unknown

MOCHIZUKI (望月) (warrior or miscellaneous play)
    Author unknown

MOMIJIGARI (紅葉狩) (demon play)
    by Kanze Kojirō Nobumitsu

MORIHISA (盛久) (miscellaneous play)
    by Kanze Jūrō Motomasa

MOTOMEZUKA (求塚) (miscellaneous play)
    by Kannami
    Performed by all schools except Komparu

MUROGIMI (室君) (miscellaneous play)
    Author unknown
    Performed by Kanze and Komparu schools

MUTSURA (六浦) (woman play)
    Author unknown

NAKAMITSU (仲光) (miscellaneous play)
    Author unknown
    Performed by all schools except Komparu. Referred to as *Manjū* by schools other than Kanze

NANIWA (難波) (god play)
    by Zeami

NEZAME (寝覚) (god play)
    Author unknown
    Performed by Kanze school only

NISHIKIGI (錦木) (miscellaneous play)
    by Zeami

NISHIKIDO (錦戸) (miscellaneous play)
    by Miyamasu
    Performed by Kanze and Hōshō schools

NONOMIYA (野宮) (woman play)
    Author not certain, but generally ascribed to Zeami

NOMORI (野守) (demon play)
    by Zeami

NUE (鵼) (demon play)

by Zeami

OBASUTE (姨捨) (woman play)
by Zeami
Performed by all schools except Komparu

OCHIBA (落葉) (woman play)
Attributed to Zeami
Performed by Kongō and Kita schools

OJIO (小塩) (miscellaneous play)
by Komparu Zenchiku

OHARA GOKŌ (小原御幸) (woman play)
Author unknown, but sometimes attributed to Zeami

OIMATSU (老松) (god play)
by Zeami

OMINAESHI (女郎花) (miscellaneous play)
Author unknown

ŌEYAMA (大江山) (demon play)
by Miyamasu

ŌMU KOMACHI (鸚鵡小町) (woman play)
Attributed to Zeami
Performed by all schools except Komparu

ŌYASHIRO (大社) (god play)
by Kanze Yajirō Nagatoshi
Performed by Kanze, Kongō and Kita schools

OROCHI (大蛇) (miscellaneous or demon play)
by Kanze Kojirō Nobumitsu
Performed by Hōshō, Kongō and Kita schools

RAIDEN (雷電) (demon play)
Author unknown
Performed by all schools except Komparu

RASHŌMON (羅生門) (miscellaneous or demon play)
by Kanze Kojirō Nobumitsu
Performed by all schools except Komparu

RINZŌ (輪蔵) (god or demon play)
by Kanze Yajirō Nagatoshi
Performed by Kanze and Kita schools

RŌDAIKO (籠太鼓)
Attributed to Zeami

RŌGIŌ (籠祇王) (miscellaneous play)
Author unknown
Performed by Kita school only

RYŌKO (竜虎) (demon play)
by Kanze Kojiro Nobumitsu
Performed by Kanze and Kita schools

SAGI (鷺) (woman or miscellaneous play)
Author unknown
Performed by all schools except Komparu

SAIGYŌZAKURA (西行桜) (woman and miscellaneous play)
by Zeami

SAKAHOKO (逆矛) (god play)
Author unknown
Performed by Kanze school only

SAKURAGAWA (桜川) (miscellaneous play)
by Zeami

SANEMORI (実盛) (warrior play)
by Zeami

SANSHŌ (三笑) (miscellaneous play)
Author unknown
Performed by all schools except Komparu

SAOYAMA (佐保山) (god play)
Attributed to Zeami
Performed by Komparu school only

SEIGANJI (誓願寺) (woman play)
Attributed to Zeami

SEIŌBO (西王母) (god play)
Attributed to Zeami

SEKIDERA KOMACHI (関寺小町) (woman or miscellaneous play)
Author uncertain, but probably by Zeami

SEKIHARA YOICHI (関原与一) (warrior or miscellaneous play)
Author unknown
Performed by Kita school only

SEMIMARU (蟬丸) (miscellaneous play)
by Zeami

SENJU (千手) (woman play)
Often attributed to Komparu Zenchiku, but probably by Zeami

SESSHŌSEKI (殺生石) (miscellaneous or demon play)
Author unknown, but possibly by Saami

SETTAI (摂待) (miscellaneous play)
Author unknown
Performed by all schools except Komparu

SHAKKYŌ (石橋) (demon play)
Author unknown

SHARI (舎利) (demon play)
Attributed to Zeami

SHICHIKIOCHI (七騎落) (miscellaneous play)
Author unknown

SHIGA (志賀) (god play)
Attributed to Zeami
Performed by all schools except Komparu

SHIGEMORI (重盛) (miscellaneous play)
Author unknown
Performed by Kita school only

SHIRAHIGE (白髭) (god play)
Attributed to Kannami
Performed by Kanze, Komparu and Kita schools

SHIRONUSHI (代主) (god play)
Author unknown, but possibly by Zeami
Performed by Kanze school only

SHŌJŌ (猩々) (demon play)
Author unknown

SHŌKI (鐘馗) (demon play)
Author unknown

SHŌKUN (昭君) (demon play)
Author unknown, but text may antedate Zeami

SHŌZON (正尊) (miscellaneous play)
by Kanze Yajirō Nagatoshi

SHUNKAN (俊寛) (miscellaneous play)
Author unknown

SHUNNEI (春栄) (miscellaneous play)
by Zeami

SHUNZEI TADANORI (俊成忠度) (warrior play)
by Naitō Kawachi-no-kami
Performed by all schools except Komparu

SŌSHI ARAI KOMACHI (草子洗小町) (woman play)
Author unknown

SOTOBA KOMACHI (卒都婆小町) (miscellaneous play)
by Kannami

SUMA GENJI (須磨源氏) (demon play)
Adapted by Zeami
Performed by all schools except Komparu

SUMIDAGAWA (隅田川) (miscellaneous play)
by Kanze Jūrō Motomasa

SUMIYOSHI-MŌDE (住吉詣) (woman or miscellaneous play)
Author unknown
Performed by Kanze, Kongō and Kita schools

SUMIZOME SAKURA (墨染桜) (woman play)
Author unknown
Performed by Kongō school only
TADANOBU (忠信) (miscellaneous play)
by Komparu Zenchiku
Performed by Kanze and Hōshō schools
TADANORI (忠度) (warrior play)
by Zeami
Performed by Kanze, Kongō and Kita schools
TAEMA (当麻) (demon play)
by Zeami
TAIHEI SHŌJŌ (大瓶猩々) (demon play)
Author unknown
Performed by Kanze school only
TAIZAN BUKUN (泰山府君) (miscellaneous and demon play)
by Zeami
Performed by Kongō school only
TAKASAGO (高砂) (god play)
by Zeami
TAKENOYUKI (竹雪) (miscellaneous play)
Attributed to Zeami
Performed by Hōshō and Kita schools
TAMAKAZURA (玉葛) (miscellaneous play)
by Komparu Zenchiku
TAMANOI (玉井) (god play)
by Kanze Kojirō Nobumitsu
Performed by Kanze, Kongō and Kita schools
TAMURA (田村) (warrior play)
Attributed to Zeami
TANIKŌ (谷行) (miscellaneous or demon play)
by Komparu Zenchiku
TATSUTA (竜田) (woman or miscellaneous play)
Author unknown, but probably by Zeami
Performed by Kanze school only
TEIKA (定家) (woman play)
Probably by Komparu Zenchiku
TENKO (天鼓) (miscellaneous play)
Author unknown
TŌBOKU (東北) (woman play)
Probably by Zeami
TŌBŌSAKU (東方朔) (god play)
by Komparu Zempō
Performed by Kanze, Komparu and Kita schools
TŌEI (藤栄) (warrior or miscellaneous play)
Author unknown
Performed by all schools except Kanze
TŌGAN KOJI (東岸居士) (miscellaneous play)
by Zeami
Performed by all schools except Komparu
TOKUSA (木賊) (woman and miscellaneous play)
Probably by Zeami
Performed by all schools except Komparu
TOMOAKIRA (知章) (warrior play)
Probably by Zeami
Performed by all schools except Hōshō
TOMOE (巴) (warrior play)
Author unknown
TOMONAGA (朝長) (warrior play)
Probably by Zeami
TORIOIBUNE (鳥追舟) (miscellaneous play)
Author unknown
TŌRU (融) (demon play)
by Zeami
TŌSEN (唐船) (miscellaneous play)

by Toyama Matagorō Yoshihiro
TSUCHIGUMO (土蜘蛛) (demon play)
Author unknown
TSUCHIGURUMA (土車) (miscellaneous play)
by Zeami
Performed by Kanze and Kita schools
TSUNEMASA (経政) (warrior play)
Author unknown
TSURUKAME (鶴亀) (god play)
Author unknown
UCHITO-MŌDE (内外詣) (god play)
by Kongō Matabei Nagayori
Performed by Kongō school only
UGETSU (雨月) (miscellaneous play)
by Komparu Zenchiku
UKAI (鵜飼) (demon play)
by Enami Saemon Gorō; adapted by Zeami
UKIFUNE (浮舟) (miscellaneous play)
Text by Yokoo Motohisa; music by Zeami
Performed by all schools except Hōshō
UKON (右近) (god play)
by Zeami (minor adaptation by Kanze Kojirō)
Performed by Kanze, Hōshō and Kongō schools
UME (梅) (woman play)
by Kamo no Mabuchi (?)
Performed by Kanze school only
UMEGAE (梅枝) (miscellaneous play)
Attributed to Zeami
UNEME (采女) (woman play)
by Zeami
UNOMATSURI (鵜祭) (god play)
Author unknown
Performed by Komparu school only
UNRININ (雲林院) (miscellaneous play)
Author unknown. Text in Zeami's hand survives
Performed by all schools except Komparu
UROKOGATA (鱗形) (god play)
Author unknown
Performed by Kongō and Kita schools
UTAURA (歌占) (miscellaneous play)
by Kanze Jūrō Motomasa
UTŌ (善知鳥) (miscellaneous play)
Author unknown
YAMAHIME (山姫) (woman play)
Author unknown
Performed by Kita school
YAMAUBA (山姥) (demon play)
Author uncertain, but probably by Zeami
YASHIMA (八島) (warrior play)
Author uncertain, but probably by Zeami
YORIMASA (頼政) (warrior play)
by Zeami
YOROBOSHI (弱法師) (miscellaneous play)
by Kanze Jūrō Motomasa
YŌRŌ (養老) (god play)
by Zeami
YOSHINO SHIZUKA (吉野静) (woman or miscellaneous play)
by Kannami
YOSHINO TENJIN (吉野天人) (woman play)
by Kanze Kojirō Nobumitsu
Performed by Kanze school only
YOUCHI SOGA (夜討曾我) (miscellaneous play)
by Miyamasu
YŌKIHI (楊貴妃) (woman play)

by Komparu Zenchiku
Yūgao (夕顔) (woman play)
by Zeami
Performed by Kanze, Kongō and Kita schools
Yugyō yanagi (遊行柳) (woman or miscellaneous play)
by Kanze Kojirō Nobumitsu
Yuki (雪) (woman play)
Author unknown
Performed by Kongō school only
Yumi yawata (弓八幡) (god play)
by Zeami

Yuya (熊野) (woman play)
Author unknown, but generally attributed to Zeami
Zegai (善界) (demon play)
by Takeda Hōin Munemori
Zenji soga (禅師曾我) (miscellaneous play)
Author unknown
Performed by Kanze, Hōshō and Kita schools

Note. The authorship of the plays has yet to be established firmly. The above attributions reflect current scholarship in Japan.

BIBLIOGRAPHY

Note: With two exceptions, the following list is confined to books.

Translations and Studies in Western Languages

Araki, James T. *The Ballad-Drama of Medieval Japan.* Berkeley, 1964.

Fenollosa, Ernest, and Pound, Ezra. *The Classic Noh Theatre of Japan.*, New York, 1959.

Komiya, Toyotaka. *Japanese Music and Drama in the Meiji Era*, Tokyo, 1956.

Murakami, Upton. *A Spectator's Handbook of Noh.* Tokyo, 1963.

Nippon Gakujutsu Shinkōkai. *Japanese Noh Drama.* 3 vols. Tokyo, 1955–60.

O'Neill, P.G. *Early Nō Drama*, London, 1958.

Peri, Noël. *Le Nô.* Tokio, 1944.

Renondeau, Gaston. *Nô*, Tokio, 1954.

Sakanishi, Shio. *Kyōgen: Comic Interludes of Japan*, Boston, 1938. (Reprinted as *The Ink-Smeared Lady and Other Kyōgen*, Tokyo, 1960).

Sieffert, René. *La Tradition Secrète du Nô*, Paris, 1960. (A translation of critical writings by Zeami, and of a program of Nō and Kyōgen plays.)

Ueda, Makoto. *The Old Pine Tree and Other Noh Plays*, Lincoln, 1962.

Waley, Arthur. *The Nō Plays of Japan.* London, 1921.

Texts of Nō and Kyōgen

Koyama, Hiroshi 小山弘志. *Kyōgen Shū* 狂言集. *Nihon Koten Bungaku Taikei* series. 2 vols. 1960–61. Texts of the Ōkura school in modern orthography. The notes consist mainly of quotations from the 1603 Japanese-Portuguese dictionary.

Nonomura, Kaizō 野々村戒三 and Furukawa Hisashi 古川久. *Kyōgen Shū. Nihon Koten Zensho* series. 3 vols. 1953–56. An excellent edition of texts of the now defunct Sagi school of Kyōgen.

Nonomura, Kaizō. *Yōkyoku Sambyakugojūban Shū. Nihon Meicho Zenshū* series. 1928. Valuable for the texts of plays no longer in the repertory.

Ōwada, Tateki 大和田建樹 *Yōkyoku Hyōshaku.* 1907. Outdated in most respects, this volume is still useful for texts not easily found elsewhere.

Sanari, Kentarō 佐成謙太郎. *Yōkyoku Taikan* 謡曲大観. 7 vols. 2nd ed. 1954. An indispensable work. Gives texts with modern language translations.

Sasano, Ken 笹野堅. *Nō Kyōgen.* 3 vols. *Iwanami Bunko* series. 2nd ed., 1956. Texts of the Ōkura school. A lengthy introduction but no notes.

Tanaka, Mitsuru 田中充. *Bangai Yōkyoku. Koten Bunko* series. 1950. Texts of plays not in current repertory. No notes.

Tanaka, Mitsuru. *Yōkyoku Shū. Nihon Koten Zensho* series. 3 vols. 1949–57. Notes, exceedingly scarce in the first volume, are generous by the third. Gives Kurumaya texts, the basic ones of Komparu school.

Yokomichi, Mario 横道萬里雄 and Omote, Akira 表章. *Yōkyoku Shū. Nihon Koten Bungaku Taikei* series. 1963. Excellent annotated texts, but a rigid criterion of authorship results in some masterpieces by unidentified writers being omitted or given far less attention than poor works by identified writers.

General Works

Engeki Hyakka Daijiten 演劇百科大辞典. 6 vols. 1961. An invaluable encyclopedia of the theatre.

Furukawa, Hisashi. *Nō no Sekai.* 1960. An unpretentious but excellent introduction.

Hayashiya, Tatsusaburō 林屋辰三郎. *Kabuki Izen.* 1954. A study of Japanese theatre and its social background before the rise of Kabuki.

Kobayashi, Shizuo 小林静雄. *Nōgakushi Kenkyū.* 1945. A scholarly and well-documented study of the history of Nō, especially during the Muromachi period.

Kongō, Iwao 金剛巌. *Nō.* 1948. Much of the material is elementary, but the book is dotted with observations worthy of a master actor.

Maruoka, Akira 丸岡明. *Nihon no Nō.* 1957. Interesting descriptions of performances since the war.

Miyake, Noboru 三宅襄. *Nō.* 1948. Excellent general study.

Nishio, Minoru 西尾実 and others. *Yōkyoku Kyōgen.* 1961. Extremely valuable for its surveys of studies in different aspects of Nō and Kyōgen, and for its reproduction of various important historical and critical texts.

Nogami, Toyoichirō 野上豊一郎. *Nō: Kenkyū to Hakken.* 1930. A pioneer work of scholarship, containing stimulating essays.

Nogami, Toyoichirō (ed.) *Nōgaku Zensho*. 6 vols. 1942–44. Indispensable collection of essays on all aspects of Nō and Kyōgen. The 1952–58 revision in five volumes is inferior.

Nose, Asaji 能勢朝次. *Nōgaku Genryū Kō*. 1938. The basic study of the development of Nō. A masterpiece.

Nose, Asaji. *Nōgaku Kenkyū*. 1940. Excellent essays on various topics.

Yokoi, Haruno 横井春野. *Nōgaku Zenshi*. 1917. Extremely detailed for Tokugawa period. Not to be consulted lightly.

Yokomichi, Mario and Masuda, Shōzō 増田正造. *Nō to Kyōgen*. 1959. Basic information on Nō and Kyōgen.

Ikeuchi, Nobuyoshi 池内信嘉. *Nōgaku Seisuiki*. 2 vols. 1925–6. A massive compilation of materials on Nō during the Tokugawa and Meiji eras.

Biographical

Kobayashi, Shizuo. *Zeami* 世阿弥. 1958. A brilliant study of Zeami's life, art, plays, and critical works.

Kobayashi, Shizuo. *Yōkyoku Sakusha no Kenkyū*. 1941. Biographies of the principal Nō dramatists. A careful study.

Kōzai, Tsutomu 香西精. *Zeami Shinkō*. 1962. Important essays on Zeami's life, religious beliefs, and style.

Nogami, Toyoichirō. *Kannami Kiyotugu* 観阿弥清次. 1949. Stretches out to 155 pages a meagre number of facts.

Nogami, Toyoichirō. *Zeami Motokiyo*. 1938. A useful study of Zeami and his art.

Usui, Nobuyoshi 臼井信義. *Ashikaga Yoshimitsu* 足利義満. *Jimbutsu Sōsho* series. 1960. A useful biography of Zeami's great patron.

Nō Criticism

Kawase, Kazuma 川瀬一馬. *Gendaigoyaku Kadensho*. 1962. A translation into modern Japanese of Zeami's most famous work.

Konishi, Jinichi 小西甚一. *Nōgakuron Kenkyū*. 1961. Brilliant essays on the theories of Zeami and later dramatists.

Konishi, Jinichi. *Zeami Jūrokubu Shū*. 1954. A translation into modern Japanese of important treatises by Zeami.

Nishio, Minoru (ed.). *Karon Shū; Nōgakuron Shū*. *Nihon Koten Bungaku Taikei* series. 1961. Excellent edition with ample notes of Zeami's writings.

Nose, Asaji. *Zeami Jūrokubu Shū Hyōshaku*. 2 vols. 1944. Indispensable translation of and commentary on Zeami's writings.

Omote, Akira (ed.) *Bushō Goma* 舞正語磨. 1958. Text of the seventeenth-century attack on the Kita school, with an introduction.

Masks

Gotō, Hajime 後藤淑. *Nōmenshi Kenkyū Josetsu*. 1964. An important study of masks preserved at various remote shrines and temples. Provides a means of understanding the later masks.

Kaneko, Ryōun 金子良運. *Kamen no Bi*. 1961. A well-illustrated introduction to all varieties of masks in Japan, with helpful pointers for identifying them.

Kongō, Iwao. *Nō to Nōmen*. 1951. A great actor's personal view of the beauty of the masks.

Nogami, Toyoichirō. *Nōmen Ronkō*. 1944. A comprehensive treatment of the masks.

Noma, Seiroku 野間清六. *Nihon Kamen Shi*. 1943. Good especially for pre-Nō masks.

Shirasu, Masako 白洲正子. *Nōmen*. 1964. Fine photographs and a sensitive appreciation of the masks.

Costumes

Fujishiro, Tsugio 藤城継夫. *Shashin de Miru Nō no Funsō*. 1962. A most useful guide to Nō costumes.

Noma, Seiroku. *Kosode to Nō Ishō*. 1965. Lovely reproductions of Nō and Kyōgen robes, but the text is insufficiently informative.

The Actors

Nogami, Toyoichirō. (ed.) *Yōkyoku Geijutsu*. 1936. In addition to the general discussion by the editor, the book contains accounts by outstanding actors of their interpretations of different genres of Nō.

Sakurama, Kyūsen 桜間弓川. *Sakurama Geiwa*. 1948. A small volume of recollections and observations by a great actor.

Shigeyama, Sensaku 茂山千作. *Kyōgen Hachijūnen*. 1951. Reminiscences of the famous Kyōgen actor.

Shirasu, Masako. *Umewaka Minoru Kikigaki* 梅若実聞書. 1951. The story, in a transcription of his own words, of the son of the great Meiji actor, a self-effacing artist who never achieved the highest fame.

Yanagizawa, Hideki 柳沢英樹. *Hōshō Kurō Den* 宝生九郎傳. 1944. Ostensibly a biography of the great actor of the Meiji era, it hardly attempts to penetrate surface facts; valuable instead for its account of Nō during a critical period.

Regional Entertainments

Honda, Yasuji 本田安次. *Minzoku Geinō* 民族芸能. 1962. Brief descriptions with photographs of many regional entertainments.

Honda, Yasuji. *Nō oyobi Kyōgen Kō*. 1943. Miscellaneous essays in which the author attempts to discover early forms of Nō and Kyōgen in surviving rural theatricals.

Honda, Yasuji. *Okina sono hoka*. 1958. Intended as a continuation of the preceding title, it describes in addition to *Okina* various old forms of Nō and Kyōgen surviving today, including Mibu Kyōgen.

Ikeda, Yasaburō 池田弥三郎. *Nihon Geinō Denshō Ron*. 1962. Essays on the folkloristic and social background of the Japanese arts and their transmission. Popularly written.

Takeuchi, Katsutarō 竹内勝太郎. *Geijutsu Minzokugaku Kenkyū*. 1949. Includes essays on the beginnings of Nō and on Mibu Kyōgen.

Toita, Michizō 戸井田道三. *Nō: Kami to Kojiki no Geijutsu*. 1964. An interesting approach to Nō from a folkloristic and anthropological viewpoint.

Performance of Nō and Kyōgen

Araki, Yoshio 荒木良雄 and Shigeyama Sennojō 茂山千之丞. *Kyōgen*. 1956. The historical appreciation of Kyōgen by Araki is followed by Shigeyama's elucidation of the techniques of performance.

Kobayashi, Shizuo. *Yōkyoku no Kanshō*. 1939. Though intended primarily for high-school students, the book is important because of its discussion of how the plays considered are performed.

Miyake, Noboru. *Nō Enshutsu no Kenkyū*. 1948. The most detailed explanations of the *kogaki* and other aspects of performance.

Suda, Atsuo 須田敦夫. *Nihon Gekijō Shi no Kenkyū*. 1957. Devoted in part to a study of the Nō stage.

Music

Kikkawa, Eiji 吉川英史. *Nihon Ongaku no Rekishi*. 1965. An impressive study of all aspects of Japanese music.

Minagawa, Tatsuo 皆川達夫. "Japanese Noh Music" in *Journal of the American Musicological Society*, Vol. X, No. 3, 1957.

Yokomichi, Mario. "Nō no Ongaku" in booklet accompanying records of Nō produced in 1963 for the six hundredth anniversary of Zeami's birth.

ROLES AND THEIR COSTUMES

1. Man dressed for working
mizugoromo (cloak) worn
over kimono

2. Man dressed for working
mizugoromo (cloak); *ōkuchi*
(divided skirts)

3. Ordinary male attire
suō (upper and lower garment)

4. Man in traveling clothes
suō (cloak); *ōkuchi* (skirt)

5. Ordinary samurai attire
hitatare (cloak); *ōkuchi* (divided skirts)

6. Samurai official
nashiuchi eboshi (hat); *hitatare* (upper and lower garment)

7. Samurai guard
happi (cloak); *ōkuchi* (divided skirts)

8. Samurai dressed for war
nashiuchi eboshi (hat); *sobatsugi* (upper garment); *ōkuchi* (divided skirts)

9. Samurai dressed for combat
hachimaki (head band); *sobatsugi* (upper garment); *ōkuchi* (divided skirts)

10. Soldier dressed for combat
atsuita (kimono); *ōkuchi* (divided skirts)

11. Nobleman
kazaori eboshi (hat); *chōken* (cloak); *ōkuchi* (divided skirts)

12. Nobleman
kazaori eboshi (hat); *kariginu* (cloak); *ōkuchi* (divided skirts)

13. Minister (*waki* in god play)
daijin eboshi (hat); *kariginu* (cloak); *ōkuchi* (divided skirts)

14. Court official
hora eboshi (hat); *kariginu* (cloak); *ōkuchi* (divided skirts)

15. Nobleman of ancient times
or of China
tōkammuri (hat); *kariginu* (cloak); *ōkuchi* (divided skirts)

 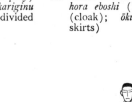  

16. Chinese
sobatsugi (upper garment);
ōkuchi (divided skirts)

17. Emperor or nobleman
uikammuri (hat); *kariginu* (cloak); *ōkuchi* (divided skirts)

18. Palanquin bearer
atsuita (kimono); *ōkuchi* (divided skirts)

19. Prisoner
kara (surplice); *atsuita* (kimono); *ōkuchi* (divided skirts)

20. Lay priest
kara (surplice); *atsuita* (kimono); *nagabakama* (long trousers)

21. Shinto priest
okina eboshi (hat); *kariginu* (cloak); *ōkuchi* (divided skirts)

22. Ordinary priest
sumbōshi (hat); *mizugoromo* (cloak)

23. Priest of rank
sumbōshi (hat); *mizugoromo* (cloak); *ōkuchi* (divided skirts)

24. High-ranking priest
shamon bōshi (hat); *mizugoromo* (cloak); *ōkuchi* (divided skirts)

25. Mountain ascetics (*yamabushi*)
tokin (hat); *suzukake* (surplice); *mizugoromo* (cloak); *ōkuchi* (divided skirts)

MALE ATTIRE (Parts without Masks) (1—21)
MEN IN RELIGIOUS ORDERS (22—28)

26. Priest-warrior
shamon bōshi (hat); *happi* (upper garment); *ōkuchi* (divided skirts)

27. Priest-warrior
zukin (hood); *happi* (upper garment); *hangiri* (skirt)

28. Novice priest (boy)
mizugoromo (cloak); *ōkuchi* (divided skirts); *kasshiki* mask

29. Ordinary old man
mizugoromo (cloak); *sankōjō, asakurajō* or *koujijō* mask

30. Old man dressed for working
mizugoromo (cloak); *sankōjō* or *waraijō* mask

31. Old Chinese man
tō bōshi (hat); *mizugoromo* (cloak); *koujijō* or *akobujō* mask

32. Dignified old man
mizugoromo (cloak); *ōkuchi* (divided skirts); *koujijō* mask

33. Shinto priest
okina eboshi (hat); *kariginu* (cloak); *ōkuchi* (divided skirts); *koujijō* mask

34. Plant spirit
kazaori eboshi (hat); *kariginu* (cloak); *ōkuchi* (divided skirts); *shiwajō, maijō* or *ishiōjō* mask

35. Aged god
uikammuri (hat); *kariginu* (cloak); *ōkuchi* (divided skirts); *shiwajō, maijō* or *ishiōjō* mask

36. Spirit of Chinese priest
tō bōshi (hat); *kariginu* (cloak); *hangiri* (divided skirts); *shiwajō, maijō* or *ishiōjō* mask

37. Majestic aged god
tori kabuto (hat); *kariginu* (cloak); *hangiri* (divided skirts); *akujō* mask

38. Vengeful ghost of old man
happi (outer garment); *hangiri* (divided skirts); *akujō* mask

39. Ordinary dress for woman, irrespective of status
karaori (kimono); ordinary female mask

40. Mad woman or woman dressed for working
karaori (kimono); ordinary female mask

41. Chinese woman
sobatsugi (outer garment); ordinary female mask

42. Attire for woman performing work or traveling
mizugoromo (cloak); ordinary female mask

43. Court lady's outdoor attire
karaori (kimono) tucked up at waist; ordinary female mask (rarely, *deigan* or *rōjo* mask)

44. Woman in male attire
kazaori eboshi (hat); *chōken* (cloak); ordinary female mask

45. Woman in male attire
uikammuri (hat); *chōken* (cloak); ordinary female mask

46. Female entertainer
tate eboshi (hat); *chōken* (cloak); ordinary female mask

47. Dancer *(shirabyōshi)* formal attire
tate eboshi (hat); *chōken* (cloak); *ōkuchi* (divided skirts); ordinary female mask

48. Court lady in formal attire
chōken (cloak); *ōkuchi* (divided skirts); ordinary female mask (rarely, *rōjo* or *yase-onna* mask)

49. Court lady in semi-formal attire
karaori (kimono) tucked up at waist; *ōkuchi* (divided skirts); ordinary female mask

50. Princess
tenkan (crown); *karaori* (kimono) tucked up at waist; *ōkuchi* (divided skirts); ordinary female mask

OLD MEN (29—38)
FEMALE ATTIRE (39—59)

51. Celestial lady or goddess
tenkan (crown); *chōken* (cloak); *ōkuchi* (divided skirts); *zō-onna* or *ko-omote* mask

52. Dragon woman (demonic being living in the sea)
ryūtai (crown); *maiginu* (cloak); *ōkuchi* (divided skirts); *deigan* or *hashihime* mask

53. Celestial being
tenkan (crown); *chōken* (cloak); *zō-onna* or *ko-omote* mask

54. Female demon
urokohaku (upper kimono); *nuihaku* (lower kimono); *hannya* mask

55. Woman suffering in hell
shiroaya (cloak) tucked up at waist; *ōkuchi* (divided skirts); *yase-onna* or *deigan* mask

56. Old woman
mizugoromo (cloak); *uba* (mask)

57. Shrine priestess
mizugoromo (cloak); ordinary female mask

58. Nun
hana no bōshi (hood); *kosode* (kimono); *uba* or ordinary female mask

59. Nun
hana no bōshi (hood); *mizugoromo* (cloak); ordinary female mask

60. Warrior ghost
nashiuchi eboshi (hat); *happi* (cloak); *hangiri* (divided skirts); *heita* mask

61. Ghosts of the Genji and Heike warriors
nashiuchi eboshi (hat); *chōken* or *happi* (cloak); *ōkuchi* (divided skirts); *chūjō* or *imawaka* mask

62. Spirit of an emperor or nobleman
uikammuri (hat); *kariginu* (cloak); *sashinuki* (divided skirts); *chūjō* or similar mask

63. Elegant god
kazaori eboshi (hat); *kariginu* (cloak); *ōkuchi* (divided skirts); *kantan otoko* mask

64. Brave young god
suikammuri (hat); *kariginu* (cloak); *ōkuchi* (divided skirts); *kantan otoko* or *mikazuki* mask

65. Violent god
suikammuri (hat); *happi* (cloak); *hangiri* (divided skirts); *mikazuki* mask

66. God who conquers evil demons
rinkan (hat); *sobatsugi* (outer garment); *ōkuchi* (divided skirts); *tenjin* mask

67. Man punished in hell
mizugoromo (cloak); *ōkuchi* (divided skirts); *yase-otoko* mask

68. A transformed being
mizugoromo (cloak); *ayakashi* mask

69. Vengeful ghost of a warrior
happi (outer garment); *hangiri* (divided skirts); *ayakashi* mask, horns on head

70. A transformed animal spirit
happi (outer garment); *hangiri* (divided skirts); *kotobide* mask

71. Powerful god
tōkammuri (hat); *kariginu* (cloak); *hangiri* (divided skirts); *ōtobide* mask

72. Dragon god
ryūtai (crown); *happi* (cloak); *hangiri* (divided skirts); *kurohige* mask

73. Aged dragon god
ryūtai (crown); *kariginu* (cloak); *hangiri* (divided skirts); *akujō* mask

74. Malicious demon
happi (outer garment); *hangiri* (divided skirts); *shikami* mask

75. Benevolent demon or spirit of a brave warrior
tōkammuri (hat); *happi* (cloak); *hangiri* (divided skirts); *kobeshimi* mask

MARTIAL GHOSTS (60—61)
CELESTIAL BEINGS (62—66)
TRANSFORMED BEINGS, GHOSTS AND DEMONS (67—76)

76. *Tengu* (Goblin)
ōtokin (hat); *kariginu* (cloak); *hangiri* (divided skirts); *ōbeshimi* mask

77. Chinese child
happi (outer garment); *hangiri* (divided skirts); *jidō* or *dōji* mask

78. Youth with divine attributes
mizugoromo (cloak) worn over kimono; *jidō* or *dōji* mask

79. Boy dressed for working
kimono folded down to waist over underkimono

80. Ordinary boy
nuihaku (kimono); *chigo bakama* (long divided skirts)

81. Samurai boy in active part
nuihaku (kimon); *ōkuchi* (divided skirts)

82. Acolyte
chōken (cloak); *ōkuchi* (divided skirts)

83. Girl
karaori (kimono) with trailing sleeves

84. Ordinary man or servant
kataginu (outer garment); *hambakama* (short divided skirts)

85. Ordinary man or servant in active part
kataginu (outer garment); *kukuribakama* (breeches with leggings)

  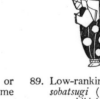  

86. Messenger
kataginu (outer garment); *kukuribakama* (breeches with leggings)

87. Townsman
nagakamishimo (hempen upper and lower garment) over kimono

88. Low-ranking official or townsman in formal costume
suō (cloak) over kimono; *kukuribakama* (breeches with leggings)

89. Low-ranking Chinese official
sobatsugi (outer garment); *momohiki* (trousers)

90. Temple servant
mizugoromo (cloak); *kukuribakama* (breeches with leggings)

91. Porter
atsuita (kimono); *kukuribakama* (breeches with leggings)

92. Woman
binankazura; nuihaku (kimono)

93. God of a minor shrine
mizugoromo (outer garment); *kukuribakama* (breeches with leggings); *noborihige* or similar mask

94. Sprite
mizugoromo (cloak); *kukuribakama* (breeches with leggings); *kentoku, usobuki* or similar mask

95. Subordinate of a *tengu*
mizugoromo (cloak); *kukuribakama* (breeches with leggings); *tobi* or *kentoku* mask

CHILDREN (77—83)
AI-KYŌGEN ROLES (84—95)

INDEX

chorus, 25, 26, 27, 46, 75, 76, 230
Chōryō, 44
chūbeshimi mask, 104
chūjō mask, 69, 110, 179, 275
chūkei fan, 87, 218
chūnomai (Nō dance), 80, 81
chū-nori rhythm, 76
Chūsonji, Nō and *ennen* performances at, 159
climax, see *kyū*
color in costumes, 73–74
comedy, see Kyōgen
comic origins of Nō, 19–20
commedia dell'arte, 32
"companion," see *tsure*
Confucian ethics of Tokugawa shogunate, 46
Confucius, 42
congratulatory play, 62, 142–45; see also *Okina*
contemporary events as Nō themes, 45–46; see also *genzaimono*
"contemporary plays," see *genzaimono*
"Conversations on *Sarugaku*," see *Sarugaku Dangi*
"correctness" as element in acting, 30, 31
costumes, 20, 26, 47, 73–74, 208–17
"crudity and coarseness" as elements in acting, 30
curtain, 25, 26, 227

Daichifumi, 157
daijin eboshi (courtier's hat), 99
daimyo: as patrons and performers of Nō, 32, 38, 39, 45, 47; as subjects of Kyōgen, 32, 48, 63
Dainembutsu, 161
"Damask Drum, The," see *Aya no Tsuzumi*
dance as element of Nō, 23, 24–25, 27, 35, 36–37, 60, 79–81
dance forms, 80–81
Date Masamune, 47
deigan mask, 71, 195
deitobide mask, 272
Deme Tōhaku (mask-maker), 201
demon plays (*kiri* Nō), 27, 28, 43, 60–61, 136–41, 266–70; in Kyōgen, 32
dengaku, 37, 41, 84, 148, 158
development section of Nō play, see *ha*
"dignity" (*kurai*), 24, 69–70, 75, 76, 77, 79, 268
display scenes, 61
Dōami (Inuō), 38, 40
dōji mask, 184
Dōjōji, 2, 43, 50–51, 60, 67, 72, 74, 79, 81, 86, 190, 197, 198, 208–9, 211, 217, 228
Dragon God of the Sea (Ryūjin), 173; in *Ikkaku Sennin*, 266
drums, 21, 26, 78, 230–31

Ebisu, 205; in *Ebisu Bishamon*, 104–7
Ebisu Bishamon, 104–7, 205
Ebisu mask, 205
eboshi (hat), 99, 106, 110, 127, 136
Echi (mask-maker), 72, 190–91
Edinburgh, Duke of, 50
Edo, Nō performances in, 46–47
Edo period, see Tokugawa period
Eguchi (*Eguchi*), 29
Eguchi, 39, 44, 52, 54, 71

Eishō, Empress Dowager, 50, 51
Emai *sarugaku* troupe, 37
emmeikaja mask, 104
emotional appeal of Nō, 16, 21
engo ("related words"), 54
ennen, 37, 148, 158–59
European drama, see Western drama
expression in masks, 70, 71
eye-fixing pillar, 227

"faint patterns" as element in acting, 30, 31
"Fallen Leaves," see *Ochiba*
fans, 86–87; gestures with, 219–21, 222, 223–24, 226
farce, see Kyōgen
farces, European, 32, 33, 63
"Feather Cloak, The," see *Hagoromo*
fifth-category plays, see demon plays
financial support of Nō, 51, 52
first-category plays, see god plays
flower arrangement, 14
"flower" mask, 72
"flower" metaphor for Nō, 14, 29–31, 40, 43
flute, 25–26, 77, 231
flute pillar, 84, 227
fourth-category plays, see *genzaimono*
Fuji, see Mount Fuji
Fujita Daigorō, 231
Fujito, 69, 176, 177, 258
Fujiwara Michinori, 147
Fujiwara no Shunzei, 28
fukai mask, 73, 191, 257, 263
Fukakusa: in *Kayoi Komachi*, 255; in *Sotoba Komachi*, 248
Fukurai (mask-maker), 167, 169, 175
Funa Benkei ("Benkei in the Boat"), 22, 26, 27, 31, 52, 60–61, 81, 84, 136–41, 174, 175, 222, 271
Fūshi Kaden ("The Transmission of the Flower of the Art"), 13, 14
fushiki zō mask, 188, 246
Futari Shizuka, 67–68, 221, 243

gaku (Nō dance), 80
Garbo, Greta, 30
gembuku ceremony, 69
Gen'e, 33
Genji, Prince, 21, 58–59, 240, 241, 262
Genji Kuyō, 240
genjōraku form of *bugaku*, 147
genzaimono ("contemporary plays"), 27, 28, 60, 70, 248–65
gestures, see *kata*
Gien, 41; see also Ashikaga Yoshinori
gigaku, 36, 71, 147, 168
gigaku masks, 71, 147, 168
Gion Festival, 39
Girlhoods of Shakespeare's Heroines, The, 24
Gluck, C. W., 26, 77
god Kyōgen, see *waki* Kyōgen
god plays (*waki* Nō), 19, 27, 28, 32, 35, 45, 55–57, 93–103, 232
Go-Komatsu, Emperor, 40
Gosho no Gorōmaru (*Youchi Soga*), 265
Gotō Hajime, 70
Gotō Tokuzō, 271

Go-Yōzei, Emperor, 45
Grant, Ulysses S., 51
Great Shrine of Ise, 38, 232
Greek drama, 27

ha (development section of Nō play), 27, 36, 55–56, 80
Hachinoki, 54, 60, 61, 86
Hagoromo ("The Feather Cloak"), 24, 52, 60, 61, 71, 79, 81, 117–21, 189, 234
hakama trousers, 127
hakobi, gesture of, 219
Hakuga no Sammi *(Semimaru)*, 127–28
Hakuryō *(Hagoromo)*, 117–18
Hakusan Shrine, Nō performances at, 160
hakushikijō mask, 95, 162
hakuzōsu mask, 202
hanabiki mask, 200
Hanago, see *Hanjo*
Hanago (Kyōgen play), 122–26
Hana Nusubito, 161
Hanaori, 158
hand drum, see *ōkawa*
hangiri trousers, 140
Hanjo *(Hanjo)*, 54, 254
Hanjo, 53–54, 62, 81, 91, 254
Hannyabō (mask-maker), 72, 197
hannya mask, 72, 197, 262
happi cloak, 73, 110, 140, 214
hashigakari (passageway to stage), 25, 26, 77, 83, 84, 85, 227–28, 230
Hashimoto Chikanobu, 153
hatachi amari mask, 177
hataraki (Nō dance), 80, 81, 141
Hatsuyuki, 44, 61
hayamai (Nō dance), 275
headgear, 73, 74; see also *eboshi, kammuri*
Heike (Taira), 57, 58, 60, 87
heita, 178, 233
hie ("chill"), 32
Himi (mask-maker), 72, 176, 177, 193, 195, 196
hinoki wood, 25, 71, 206
hiraki, gesture of, 97, 111, 120
hira-nori rhythm, 76
Hirota Norikazu, 269
Hirota Taizō, 258
Hōjō, 45
Hōjō Takatoki, 37
Honda Hideo, 258
Honnami Kōetsu, 152
Hōrakuwari, 161
Hōshō Fusao, 142, 262, 268
Hōshō Kurō (former), 23, 49–50, 51, 65, 66, 67, 69–70, 75, 85, 153; (present), 246
Hōshō school of Nō, 37, 44, 46, 49, 51, 67, 68, 77, 87; scenes from performances by, 142–45, 152, 246, 248, 262, 268
Hōshō Yagorō, 49
Hōshō Yaichi, 127, 136

Ichijō Kaneyoshi, 43
Ichinotani, battle of, 57
iemoto system, 66–67
Ieyasu, see Tokugawa Ieyasu

Igui, 151
ikebana, see flower arrangement
Ikeda Eisen, 152
Ikkaku Sennin, 228, 266
Ikkyū, 43
Ikuta Atsumori, 180
Imakumano Shrine, Nō performances at, 38, 39, 149
imawaka mask, 180
"imitation of things," see *monomane*
"Imperial Warship," see *Miikusabune*
Inari *(Kokaji)*, 272
India, dances of, 31; music of, 36
Inland Sea, 25, 38, 84
innovations in modern Nō theatre, 85
inori (Nō dance), 81
Inoue Reisuke, 99
interlude, see *ai*
interpretation of roles, 21, 22
introduction of Nō play, see *jo*
Inuō, see Dōami
"Iris, The," see *Kakitsubata*
iro, see color in costumes
iroe (Nō dance), 81
Ise Monogatari, 24
Ise Shrine, see Great Shrine of Ise
Ishigami, 63
Ishihara Hajime, 132
Ishikawa Tatsuemon (mask-maker), 72, 181, 183, 184, 185, 196
issei (entrance song), 55, 76, 117
Itsukushima Shrine, Nō performances at, 156; Nō stage at, 25, 84–85
Iwakura Tomomi, 50, 51, 66
Iwasaki Yanosuke, 85
Izeki Bitchū-no-kami (mask-maker), 202
Izumi school of Kyōgen, 48, 62, 68, 87; scenes from performances by, 104–7, 122–26, 280–85
Izumi Shikibu *(Tōboku)*, 214, 238
Izumi Yasuyuki, 280, 285
Izutsu, 29, 59, 86, 221, 236

Jakujo ("The Young Woman), 159
jars under Nō stage, 25, 85, 227
Jidō mask, 183
Jinen Koji *(Jinen Koji)*, 60
Jinen Koji, 39, 60, 181
jo (introduction of Nō play), 27, 36, 55, 80
Jones, Stanleigh H., 58
jonomai (Nō dance), 81, 120

Kabuki, 28, 44, 46, 50, 51, 60, 67, 264
Kaburagi Mineo, 117
Kadensho ("The Book of the Transmission of the Flower"), 40
kagami-ita ("mirror boards"), 19, 227
Kagamiotoko, 154
Kagekiyo *(Kagekiyo)*, 77, 86, 253
Kagekiyo, 61, 77, 86, 253
Kagekiyo mask, 253
Kageyori (mask-maker), 187
Kagura (Shinto dances), 20
kagura (Nō dance), 80
Kagyū, 284

EXCERPTS FROM *FUNA BENKEI*

(KOMPARU SCHOOL)

shite: (First part) Shizuka; (second part) the ghost of Tomomori (Nishikawa Michio)
waki: Benkei (Hōshō Yaichi)
waki tsure: A retainer (Hōshō Kan)
kokata: Yoshitsune (Moriya Yasutoshi)
ai: A boatman (Nomura Manzō)

(First part)
Journey from Kyoto to Amagasaki
(Minamoto no Yoshitsune appears on stage with his retainers, including Musashibō Benkei. Yoshitsune faces his followers at the center of the stage.)
Benkei and Retainers:

Kyō omoitatsu tabigoromo	Today, we set out on our journey
kyō omoitatsu tabigoromo	Today, we set out on our journey
kiraku wo itsu to sadamen	When shall we return to the capital?

Chorus:

kyō omoitatsu tabigoromo	Today, we set out on our journey
kiraku wo itsu to sadamen.	When shall we return to the capital?

(Benkei, facing the audience, introduces himself.)
Benkei:

Kore wa Saitō no Musashibō Benkei nite sōrō. Sate mo wagakimi Hōgan-dono wa Saikoku no kata e on-gekō sōrō aida konnichi yo wo kome Tsu-no-kuni Amagasaki Daimotsu no Ura ni on-tsukite sōrō.	I am Musashibō Benkei of the Western Pagoda. My master, the Hōgan, is fleeing to the west, and we are therefore hurrying today towards Daimotsu Bay at Amagasaki in the Province of Tsu, traveling day and night.

(Acting to show that the journey is over, the entourage faces the audience.)
Benkei:

Onnisogi sōrō hodo ni Tsu-no-kuni Amagasaki Daimotsu no Ura ni on-tsukite sōrō.	Because we have hurried, we have reached Daimotsu Bay at Amagasaki, in the Province of Tsu.

(Yoshitsune proceeds to the *waki* pillar and sits. His retainers also sit by his side. Benkei goes to the *shite* pillar.)
Yoshitsune's quarters at Amagasaki
(The "prelude" for the dance continues.)
Chorus:

Tada tanome	Have but faith

(Shizuka gracefully performs the *chūnomai* dance in rhythm with the music. She finishes dancing.)
Shizuka:

tada tanome	Have but faith
Shimeji-ga-hara no sashimogusa	Though you are helpless as the weeds of Shimeji Plain,

Chorus:

ware yo-no-naka ni aran kagiri wa.	so long as I exist in this world.

(Second part)
Aboard Yoshitsune's boat on the Inland Sea
Benkei:

Ara shōshi ya, kaze ga kawatte sōrō. Ano Mukoyama oroshi, Yuzuriha-ga-take yori fuki orosu arashi ni kono	Alas! The wind has changed. A gale blowing down from Mount Muko and a storm wind from

on-pune no rokuji ni tsuku beki yō zo naki. Mina, mina, shinjū ni go-kinen sōrae.

Retainer:

Ikani Musashi-dono ni mōsu beki koto no sōrō.

Benkei:

Nanigoto nite sōrō-zo.

Retainer:

Kono on-pune ni wa ayakashi ga tsukite sōrō.

Benkei:

Aa shibaraku, senchū nite sayō no kotoba mōsanu koto nite sōrō. Nanigoto mo Musashi to sendō ni onmakase sōrae.

Boatman:

Aa, koko na hito no iidashita koto wa saki ni kara nani yara sashi deta sō na kuchimoto ja to omōta. Doko ni ka senchū de sono yōna koto wo yū to yū koto ga aru mono de oryaru ka.

Benkei:

Iya, iya, senchū buannai no koto nite sōrō aida nanigoto mo Musashi ni menzerare sōrae.

Boatman:

Kashikomatte gozaru. Kasanete osharu-na. Iei, iei. Ya, mata mukō kara makkuro ni natte nami ga mairu wa. A-rya, a-rya, a-rya, a-rya, a-rya, a-rya, a-rya. Nami yo, nami yo, nami ya, nami yo, nami yo, nami yo, nami yo, nami yo, nami yo. Shi-i.

(Benkei looks out over the sea.)

Benkei:

Ara fushigi ya, kaijō mireba
saikoku nite horobishi Heike no kindachi

ono ono ukami idetaru zo ya
kakaru jisetto wo ukagaite

Urami wo nasu mo kotowari nari.

Yoshitsune:

Ikani Benkei.

Benkei:

On-mae nite sōrō.

Yoshitsune:

Tatoi akuryō urami wo nasu tomo
nanihodo no koto no aru beki zo
akugyaku mudō no sono tsumori
shimmei butsuda no myōkan ni somuki
temmei ni shizumi shi Heike no ichirui

Chorus:

Ichimon no gekkei unka no gotoku
nami ni ukamite mietaru zo ya.

(Tomomori, his hair disheveled, a halberd under his arm, rushes out to the stage.)

Tomomori:

Somo somo kore wa
Kammu Tenno kudai no kōin
Taira no Tomomori no yūrei nari.

(He makes this declaration and looks into the boat)

Ara mezurashi ya, ikani Yoshitsune
omoi mo yoranu uranami no

Chorus:

koe wo shirubeni
idebune no.

Yuzuriha peak leave no hope that our boat will reach shore. Everyone, pray with all your hearts!

Musashi, sir, I have something to say.

What is it?

This boat is possessed by an evil spirit.

Ah, wait a moment. You should not say such things aboard a boat. Leave everything to me and the boatman.

(somewhat annoyed) I have been expecting him to say something of the sort. I could see it on his face. How could anyone aboard a boat say such a thing?

(trying to calm the boatman) Don't take it amiss. It's simply because he doesn't know about boats. Please forgive him for my sake.

Very well, sirs. (turning to the retainer) Don't talk that way. Iei! Iei! (the music becomes louder) Ah! a great big black wave is coming from yonder again! A-rya, a-rya, a-rya, a-rya, a-rya, a-rya, a-rya. Look at those waves, those waves, those waves. Calm down, calm, calm . . . (the waves subside)

A strange and wondrous sight!
I can see across the waves the Heike nobles who perished in the West,
each of them rising from the sea.
Small wonder they have awaited just such a moment
to wreak their vengeance!

(firmly) Come here, Benkei.

(kneeling) At your service, my lord.

Whatever harm the evil spirit may intend,
there is nothing to fear.
Their many evil, wicked deeds,
defying the gods and buddhas,
Have caused the entire Heike clan to drown by the will of Heaven.

The lords of the clan like clouds or mist
rising over the waves emerge into sight.

I am the ghost of Taira no Tomomori, the ninth generation descendant of the Emperor Kammu.

An unexpected pleasure, Yoshitsune!
I never thought I would meet you at sea.

Guided by the sounds of waves, I hurried to your boat.

(The phono-sheet enclosed contains excerpts from *Nō*, record SJ-3006, by Victor Company of Japan Ltd.)

雲居の、

刀てたるや　　　根本

天皇九代の流れ乃　　盛衰

まめなりしも

思ひも　　　浦波の

しほへみおろし

流れ　　三日槻

みやびに